AIR POWER AND THE FIGHT FOR KHE SANH

AIR POWER AND THE FIGHT FOR KHE SANH

Bernard C. Nalty

GOVERNMENT REPRINTS PRESS
Washington, D.C.

© Ross & Perry, Inc. 2001 All rights reserved.

No claim to U.S. government work contained throughout this book.

Protected under the Berne Convention. Published 2001

Printed in The United States of America
Ross & Perry, Inc. Publishers
717 Second St., N.E., Suite 200
Washington, D.C. 20002
Telephone (202) 675-8300
Facsimile (202) 675-8400
info@RossPerry.com

SAN 253-8555

Government Reprints Press Edition 2001

Government Reprints Press is an Imprint of Ross & Perry, Inc.

Library of Congress Control Number: 2001094490

http://www.GPOreprints.com

ISBN 1-931641-84-6

∞ The paper used in this publication meets the requirements for permanence established by the American National Standard for Information Sciences "Permanence of Paper for Printed Library Materials" (ANSI Z39.48-1984).

All rights reserved. No copyrighted part of this publication may be reproduced, stored in a retrieval system, or transmitted, in any form or by any means, electronic, photocopying, recording, or otherwise, without the prior written permission of the publisher.

FOREWORD

The 1968 fight for Khe Sanh pitted some 6,000 U.S. Marines and South Vietnamese Rangers against an enemy force roughly three times as large. For more than 70 days North Vietnamese troops maintained pressure on Khe Sanh's defenders, who had dug in around the base's airstrip. The original purpose for deploying the Marines and South Vietnamese into the northwest corner of South Vietnam was to block Communist troop movements along Highway 9 toward Quang Tri City and the heavily populated coastal areas. When U.S. intelligence detected large enemy forces assembling near Khe Sanh, the senior American commander in Vietnam, Gen. William C. Westmoreland, ordered the Marines to hold the base.

General Westmoreland suspected that North Vietnam's Defense Minister, Gen. Vo Nguyen Giap, might be tempted to mount a major attack against the base in hopes of achieving "a climactic victory, such as he had done in 1954 at Dien Bien Phu." If Giap did order such an attack, General Westmoreland believed it would provide U.S. air power "a singular opportunity" to destroy a massed enemy force in a relatively uninhabited, isolated region of South Vietnam. In late January 1968 General Westmoreland advised the Chairman of the Joint Chiefs of Staff in Washington, D.C., of his decision to defend Khe Sanh. The Chiefs backed him unanimously.

During the siege that followed, U.S. strike aircraft rained nearly 100,000 tons of munitions down upon the North Vietnamese while other planes—primarily U.S. Air Force transports—flew in essential supplies of food, ammunition, and other necessities to Khe Sanh's defenders. The Leathernecks also used their own aircraft to provision Marine outposts which denied the enemy the high ground overlooking the base. Other military elements participating in the battle included U.S. Army artillerymen dug in east of Khe Sanh, who fired deadly concentrations against the besieging forces. Marine howitzers and mortars added to the heavy U.S. fire, while Army engineers joined Navy Seabees in helping prepare airstrips which supported the allied defense effort. Finally, the relief of Khe Sanh—though spearheaded by Army troops—also involved American Marines and soldiers of the Army of the Republic of Vietnam.

In preparing this history, the author has attempted to describe the essential contributions of the Army, Navy, and Marines as well as the Air Force.

But primarily, he has concentrated upon the operations, activities, and accomplishments of the U.S. Air Force. He also has included in this narrative a discussion of several controversies and problem areas which arose during the battle—such as General Westmoreland's appointment of Gen. William W. Momyer, his deputy for air, as single manager for air operations.

For his review of this manuscript, the Office of Air Force History is especially indebted to General Momyer, who commanded the Seventh Air Force at the time of the battle. His comments on the siege and the additional information he provided concerning the events leading to his designation as single manager for air were most helpful. In addition, we are grateful to members of the Air Staff, especially those in the Office of the Deputy Chief of Staff, Plans and Operations, who commented on an early draft and contributed additional data on various aspects of the battle. Finally, we must express our thanks to Brig. Gen. James L. Collins, Jr., USA, Chief of Military History, Department of the Army; Vice Adm. Edwin B. Hooper, USN (Ret.), Director of Naval History and Curator for the Navy Department; and Brig. Gen. E. H. Simmons, USMC (Ret.), Director of Marine Corps History and Museums, whose knowledgeable staffs reviewed the narrative and generously shared with us the fruits of their own research.

BRIAN S. GUNDERSON, Brig. Gen., USAF
Chief, Office of Air Force History

AUTHOR'S ACKNOWLEDGMENT

Two individuals have played major roles in shaping this narrative. Maj. Gen. Robert N. Ginsburgh, USAF, who was Chief, Office of Air Force History, during the writing of the early drafts, generously shared the insights he had acquired while serving as senior staff member, National Security Council Staff, during the Khe Sanh action. Dr. Thomas G. Belden, Chief Historian, Office of Air Force History, selected Khe Sanh as a battle worth recording and shepherded the account to its completion.

Because of the complexity of the action, it was necessary to consult several collections of documents. Three members of the Office of Air Force History—Mrs. Mary Ann Cresswell, Mr. David Schoem, and SSgt. Francis Laignel, Jr.—helped obtain Air Force records from the Albert F. Simpson Historical Research Center at Maxwell AFB, Ala. Record copies of Seventh Air Force and Pacific Air Forces documents repose in the center as do the histories of Air Force tactical units that took part in the battle.

Other Air Force records were made available by Mrs. Rosalie H. Waldron, Directorate of Plans, Headquarters USAF, and by Mr. D. P. "Danny" O'Boyle and Miss Laura M. Lowe of the Executive Support Division, Office of the Secretary of the Air Force.

A number of pertinent papers of the Joint Chiefs of Staff (JCS) were on file in the Directorate of Plans. Additional items were studied at the JCS Historical Division through the cooperation of Mr. Wilber W. Hoare, Jr.

Navy records, dealing mainly with aviation and construction units, were provided by Dr. O. P. Fitzgerald, Operational Archives Branch, Naval History Division.

Mr. Harold Lane of the Washington National Records Center, Suitland, Md., served as guide to the documents retired by the U.S. Military Assistance Command, Vietnam (USMACV). Of greatest value was an extensive file assembled by uniformed historians assigned to MACV headquarters in Saigon.

Mr. Vincent H. Demma, Office of the Chief of Military History, made available the records of Army units involved in the Khe Sanh operation.

Mrs. Frances Rubright of the Documentation Unit, U.S. Marine Corps

Historical Division, opened an impressive collection of reports and chronologies prepared by both ground and air units. Also made available were the historical summaries submitted each month by Fleet Marine Force, Pacific.

Dr. R. A. Winnacker, the Historian, Office of the Secretary of Defense, granted access to a file of messages maintained for Secretary Robert S. McNamara and his successor, Mr. Clark M. Clifford.

Mr. Charles Cooke, while with the Department of Health, Education, and Welfare, discussed his experiences as an Air Force major in the Office of Assistant Secretary of Defense (International Security Affairs) during the Khe Sanh crisis.

Members of the Special Histories Branch, Office of Air Force History, advised the author and commented on the successive drafts that he prepared. Of special value were the suggestions of Col. Ray L. Bowers, USAF, and Miss Doris E. Krudener.

The task of typing the manuscript in its numerous revisions was shared by Mrs. Selma Shear, Mrs. Eleanor Patterson, and Mrs. Polly Jacobs.

Mr. Lawrence Paszek selected the photographs and prepared both layout and index.

NOTE

Illustrations used in this history were obtained from official government sources, except for the photo on p. 36, which was contributed by Lt. Col. W. R. Smith, USAF.

CONTENTS

FOREWORD	iii
Author's Acknowledgement	v
I. THE SIGNS OF WAR ADVANCE	3
The Battleground	4
Principal Commands and Commanders	9
The Enemy Masses	13
American Preparations	14
President Johnson Takes a Hand	16
II. THE PRECEDENT OF DIEN BIEN PHU	18
The French Prepare	18
Comparison with Khe Sanh	19
Why Khe Sanh?	21
III. ENCIRCLEMENT	23
The Battle is Joined	23
The Tet Offensive	28
February: The Critical Month	31
Press Reaction to the Continuing Siege	38
IV. AN AERIAL HIGHWAY	42
Landing Under Fire	43
Supply by Parachute	46
Cargo Extraction Systems	51
Airmen on the Ground at Khe Sanh	54
Supplying the Outposts	56
The Task Completed	58
V. TACTICAL TEAMWORK	60
Cooperation Among the Services	60
Escorting the Transports	62
The Falconers	64
Radar Control	66

VI.	APPOINTMENT OF A SINGLE MANAGER FOR AIR	68
	First Steps Towards Centralization	68
	To Reconcile the Irreconcilable	68
	The 22 January Agreement	72
	Air Force Dissatisfaction	74
	Appointment of a Single Manager	79
	A Look at the Results	74
VII.	"THE THING THAT BROKE THEIR BACKS"	82
	Increasing the Tempo	82
	Close Support	83
	Results	86
VIII.	BEYOND THE NEXT HILL	90
	Intelligence Preparations	90
	An Electronic Battlefield	90
	Planting the Sensors	91
	Using Sensor Data	92
	Gravel Munitions	94
	Summing Up the Sensor Operation	95
IX.	THE FIGHT IS WON	96
	Plans and Preparations	96
	The Attack Westward	98
	After the Siege	100
X.	AFTERMATH OF VICTORY	103
CHRONOLOGY		107
NOTES		110
GLOSSARY OF TERMS AND ABBREVIATIONS		119
BIBLIOGRAPHY		124
INDEX		127

LIST OF ILLUSTRATIONS

	Page
U.S. Marine Patrol Near the Rock Pile, November 1966	4
President Lyndon B. Johnson is Briefed at the White House on the Situation at Khe Sanh	9
Adm. U. S. Grant Sharp	10
Gen. John D. Ryan	10
Adm. John J. Hyland	11
Gen. Dwight E. Beach	11
Gen. William C. Westmoreland, Ambassador Ellsworth Bunker, and Gen. Earle G. Wheeler, Tan Son Nhut, South Vietnam, February 1968	12
Monitoring a Tactical Strike Aboard a C-130 Airborne Battlefield Command and Control Center, 1967, Generals Ryan and Momyer	13
President Johnson, Brig. Gen. Robert N. Ginsburgh, and Dr. Walt W. Rostow, Study a Terrain Model of the Khe Sanh Battlefield	16
Gen. Vo Nguyen Giap	19
USAF C-47's Delivered to Indochina in 1952 to Bolster the French Campaign Against Viet Minh Guerrillas	20
Victorious Viet Minh Troops Cross Doumer Bridge into Hanoi	21
Ho Chi Minh	22
Aerial View of the Khe Sanh Combat Base	24
A Fuel Dump is Hit by Enemy Mortar Fire	27
Vietnamese Refugees Are Evacuated from the Base	27
Can Tho, Victim of the Communist Tet Offensive, 1968	29
The Citadel of Hue	30
Lt. Col. H. M. Dallman	32
A Navy A-1 Skyraider is Positioned for Launch	35
Lt. Col. W. R. Smith in Front of Khe Sanh's Base Operations and Control Tower Building	36
A C-123 Burns After Being Hit By an Enemy Mortar	37
Air Force Medics Move a Casualty to a Waiting C-130	37
Khe Sanh, Seen from the Cockpit of a C-130 Arriving at the Base	39
News Headlines on the Siege	40
Maj. Gen. B. W. McLaughlin	43
Friendly Fighters Attack Enemy Positions While a C-130 Lands Under Enemy Fire	44
Aerial Resupply of the Marines at Khe Sanh	48
A Low Altitude Parachute Extraction Supply Drop	52

	Page
Supplies Delivered to Khe Sanh by a Ground Proximity Extraction System	53
An Airman at Khe Sanh Catches 40 Winks	55
Marine Helicopters on a Resupply Mission to Khe Sanh Outposts	57
Their Tours Over, Khe Sanh Marines Prepare to Board a C-130	58
A Supply Drop Over Khe Sanh	59
T-28 and Marine A-6 Aircraft	61
A Navy A-4 Skyhawk	63
An Air Force F-4	64
A Soviet 37-mm Antiaircraft Gun	65
An O-1E Observation Aircraft	66
A Combat Skyspot Site, South Vietnam	67
Lt. Gen. Robert E. Cushman, Jr.	69
B-52 Bomb Run	70
Interior View, Airborne Battlefield Command and Control Center	72
Maj. Gen. N. J. Anderson	73
General William W. Momyer	78
Khe Sanh Radar and Control Tower	81
Maj. Gen. Selmon W. Wells	83
Aerial View of B-52 Bomb Pattern Around Khe Sanh	84
B-52's Being Serviced on Guam; One Bomber Lifts Off	87
A B-52 Prepares for Refueling	89
A Stratofortress Drops Its Bombs	89
Helosid (Seismic) Sensor	92
A Helicopter Crewman Prepares to Launch a Seismic Sensor	94
A Sensor Drops From a CH-3 Helicopter	95
A Night-Flying AC-47 Attacks Communist Positions Around Khe Sanh	97
Maj. Gen. J. J. Tolson, III	98
Col. David E. Lownds, Chaplain J. W. McElroy, and Lt. Gen. V. H. Krulak, Commanding General, Marine Force, Pacific, Discuss Khe Sanh's Situation Before the Siege	99
1st Cavalry Division Troops Arrive at Khe Sanh to Relieve the Marines	100
1st Cavalry Troops Take Over Marine Trenches	101

LIST OF MAPS AND CHARTS

I Corps, South Vietnam	Frontispiece
Upper I Corps Below the Demilitarized Zone	6
Command Relationships for Khe Sanh	14
Khe Sanh and the Immediate Environs	24
Marine Corps Position on Command and Control	75
Unified Management of Tactical Strike Aircraft	76
Immediate Air Requests, Strike and Reconnaissance Support	79

AIR POWER

AND

THE FIGHT FOR KHE SANH

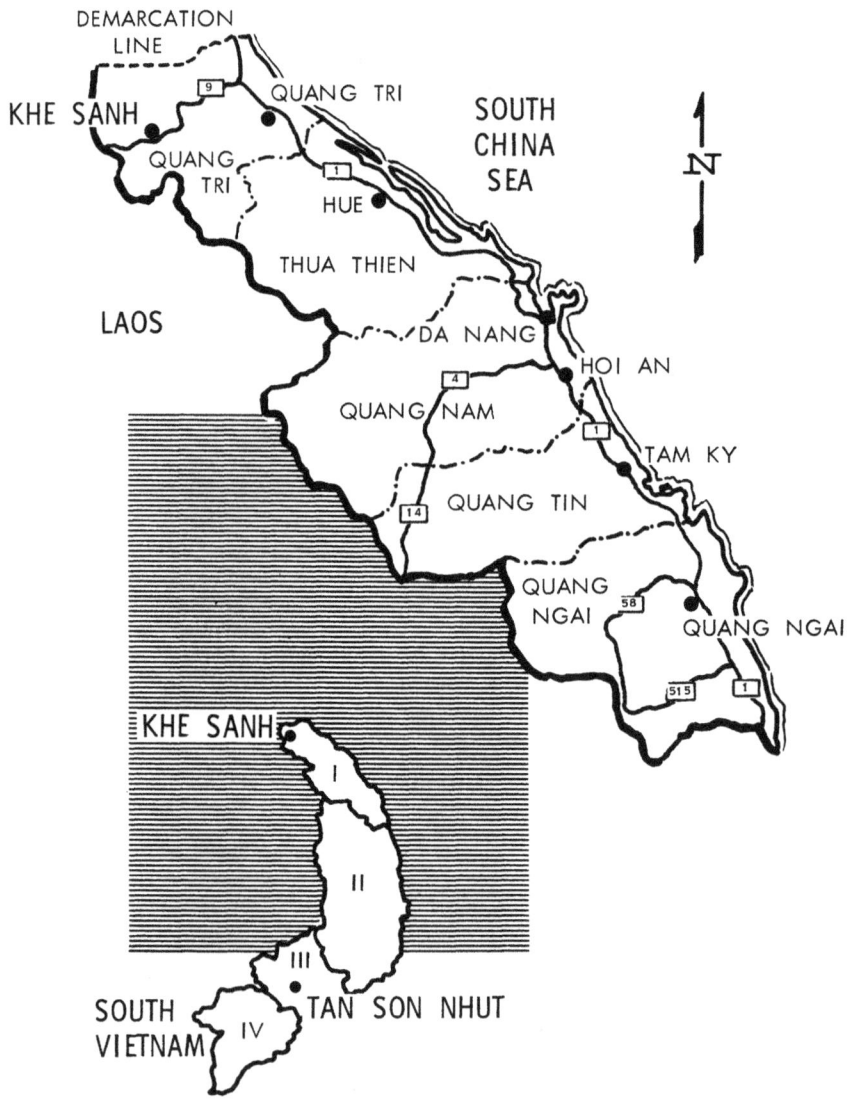

I. THE SIGNS OF WAR ADVANCE

As 1967 passed into history, the war in South Vietnam seemed to be entering a new phase, a transition from end of the beginning to beginning of the end. Gen. William C. Westmoreland, Commander, U.S. Military Assistance Command, Vietnam, on 21 November had reported to the American people that "whereas in 1965 the enemy was winning, today he is certainly losing." Elaborating upon the reversal of the enemy's fortunes, the general divided the war into four phases.

The first of these, from February 1965 to the summer of 1966, was the period when, he said, "we came to the aid of South Vietnam, prevented its collapse under the massive Communist threat, built up our bases, and began to deploy our forces." * During Phase II, lasting through 1967, the Allies had driven the enemy's divisions back to their sanctuaries or into hiding, entered enemy base areas and destroyed his supplies, and inflicted heavy casualties. It also was a period in which the United States had expanded its training of the South Vietnamese armed forces and moved to strengthen South Vietnam's economy.

Looking to the start of Phase III in 1968, Westmoreland foresaw continued military progress, further improvement in the Vietnamese army, which would take on an increasing share of the war effort, and economic and political gains in South Vietnam. Finally, in a fourth phase lasting "probably several years," he predicted the allies would achieve their basic military objectives, enabling U.S. forces to begin to phase down while the South Vietnamese took charge of "the final mopping up of the Vietcong." [1]

It appeared the North Vietnamese might pursue two possible courses of action, singly or in combination, during 1968. The likeliest enemy strategy would be to continue to fight a guerrilla war—trying to lure the allies into remote areas near his sanctuaries in Laos and Cambodia where he could attack swiftly, break off the action if forced to by American firepower, and vanish across the convenient border. However, as 1967 drew to a close, North Vietnamese combat units began appearing in increasing numbers within South Vietnam. Though these deployments did not rule out further hit-and-run tactics, they raised the possibility that the enemy might gamble upon a sustained attack designed to produce a spectacular victory damaging to American and South Vietnamese morale.

Whichever course the North Vietnamese high command selected for its regular formations—or however it combined the two strategies—the role of the Viet Cong would probably remain the same. While units from the North kept the Americans and South Vietnamese regulars occupied, "local and guerrilla forces" would "harass,

---

* President Lyndon B. Johnson ordered the launching of sustained air strikes against North Vietnam in February 1965. By July of that year he had set in motion a large-scale deployment of U.S. ground forces to South Vietnam.

3

and terrorize many areas of the countryside." The enemy also could mass troops, as he had in 1967 just south of the demilitarized zone, in numbers that were "formidable in a local sense." These concentrations were by no means decisive, and they offered opportunities for "careful exploitation of the enemy's vulnerability and application of our superior firepower and mobility." So declared the official Military Assistance Command year-end review of the war, which predicted that "our gains in 1967 in South Vietnam" ought to be increased many-fold in 1968." [2]

The Battleground

The North Vietnamese buildup detected by U.S. intelligence seemed directed at the Khe Sanh combat base located roughly halfway between the 16th and 17th parallels, north latitude, in northwestern South Vietnam. (See Map, p. 6). The base lay within striking distance of not one but two enemy sanctuaries—or partial sanctuaries since American bombs had fallen on both—Laos, just 16 kilometers* due west, and the demilitarized zone, within 25 kilometers to the north at its nearest point. Geographically, Khe Sanh lay in Quang Tri, northernmost of South Vietnam's provinces. Militarily and administratively, it was within I Corps which encompassed the five northern provinces of Quang Tri, Thua Thien, Quang Nam, Quang Tin, and Quang Ngai.[3]

The Khe Sanh combat base, some 450 meters above sea level, stood on a plateau due north of a village that bore the same name. A road linked the base to Highway 9 which extended eastward from beyond the Laotian border through the villages of Lang

---

* A kilometer equals 0.62 statute miles. A meter is one thousandth of a kilometer or 39.37 inches.

Vei, Khe Sanh, and Cam Lo to meet Highway 1, South Vietnam's main north-south artery, near the town of Dong Ha at the conflux of the Cua Viet and Quang Tri Rivers. Khe Sanh was one of several major bases along Highway 9 south of the demilitarized zone. Two of the others, the Rock Pile—named for a jagged hill nearby—and Camp Carroll, lay to the northeast, some 20 to 25 kilometers from the combat base at Khe Sanh, and figured in its defense. North of the village of Lang Vei, which lay astride Highway 9 roughly half the road distance from Khe Sanh to the Laotian frontier, U.S. Army Special Forces had established a camp for a Civilian Irregular Defense Group composed mainly of mountain tribesmen native to the region. The highway, however, followed a circuitous route that for a long stretch paralleled the border, so that straight line distances were about 3.3 kilometers from Lang Vei to the

Laotian boundary and 8 kilometers from Lang Vei to Khe Sanh.

North of Khe Sanh flowed the Rao Quan River, a tributary of the Quang Tri, which provided water for the base but was scarcely a defensive barrier. South of this stream and west of the plateau on which the combat base stood were five important hills. Identified by their height in meters, they were from east to west Hills 558, 861A, 861, 881 North, and 881 South. Across the river and directly north of the base loomed Hills 950 and 1015.* Beyond them was a succession of hills and valleys that were forested or covered by dense undergrowth and which offered excellent concealment for North Vietnamese troops and supply convoys moving into South Vietnam by way of either Laos or the demilitarized zone.

---

* For detailed map, see page 24.

U.S. Marines patrol a hill near the Rock Pile (in background), November 1966

It was to impede this infiltration that U.S. troops first moved into the Khe Sanh area. In 1962, Army Special Forces, the Green Berets, began using the plateau between the Rao Quan and Highway 9 as a camp for a Civilian Irregular Defense Group. Khe Sanh was one of a network of border camps that served primarily to gather intelligence for operations in the remote areas of South Vietnam. For some 50 months, Khe Sanh remained a preserve of the Green Berets whose activities sufficiently annoyed the enemy to bring down a 120-mm mortar barrage in January 1966. Some 9 months later, in October 1966, a Marine battalion dug in on the plateau; in January 1967 the

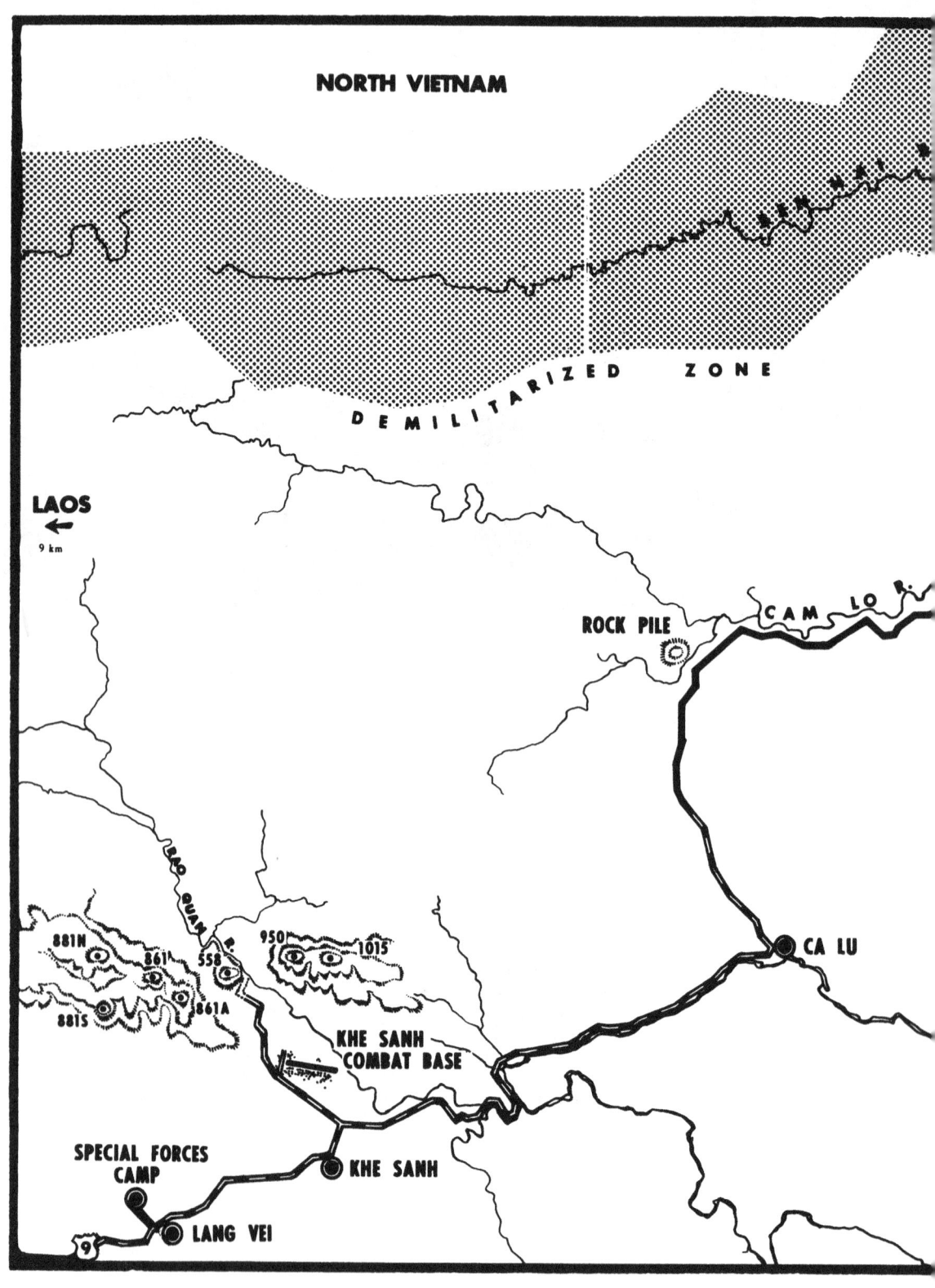

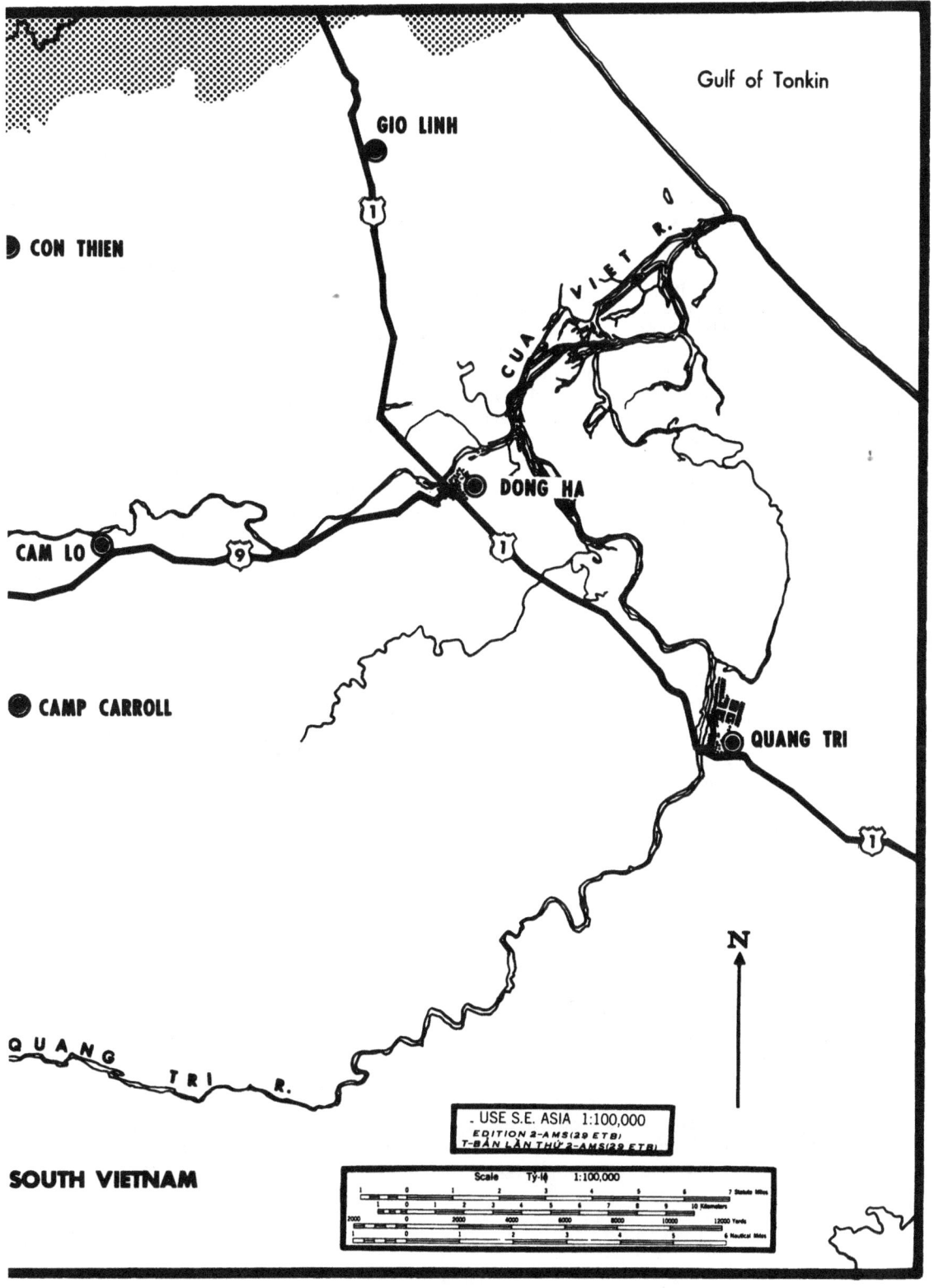

Special Forces detachment moved westward to the vicinity of Lang Vei.

After the arrival of the Marines, reduced early in 1967 to a reinforced rifle company, a naval construction detachment completed modernizing the Khe Sanh airfield. These Navy engineers, who traced their lineage to the Seabees of World War II, resurfaced the old 1,500-foot runway built by the French and improved by U.S. Army engineers, and added a new 2,400-foot extension. The Leathernecks organized a defensive perimeter to protect the airstrip and sent patrols into the hills. In April 1967, one such patrol collided with a North Vietnamese unit near Hill 861 and discovered carefully built positions that indicated the enemy was preparing to attack Khe Sanh.

The Marine high command in the northern provinces, headed at the time by Lt. Gen. Lewis H. Walt, alerted the unit in best position to reinforce Khe Sanh. Chosen for the task was the 3d Marines, two battalions strong, under Col. John P. Lanigan. Elements of one battalion reached Khe Sanh on 25 April, the day following the encounter near Hill 861, and the other, which was in action east of Quang Tri City, began arriving 2 days later. On the 28th, Colonel Lanigan's regiment commenced attacking to the northwest and within 2 weeks cleared the enemy from Hills 861, 881N, and 881S. As this struggle was drawing to a close, the 26th Marines, commanded by Col. John J. Padley, began taking over from the 3d Marines.[4]

The new regiment was greeted by heavy and frequent rains that thoroughly soaked the unstable soil beneath the airstrip. Heavily loaded Lockheed C-130 transports, with a landing weight approaching 60 tons, rolled along the pierced metal planking of the runway, compressing the spongy earth beneath them. As the plane passed, the pressure was released, and the displaced water seeped back. This pumping action soon undermined a half mile of runway, so that the 4-engine Lockheeds could no longer land safely. Canadian-built deHavilland C-7's, twin-engine transports operated by the Air Force, inherited from the larger C-130's the job of landing aerial cargo at Khe Sanh.[5]

Beginning in August 1967, Seabees once again went to work on the Khe Sanh airstrip. Some 63 construction specialists removed the metal surface, laid down 6 inches of compacted rock, covered it with asphalt, and replaced the planking. The job required 1,000 barrels of asphalt sealant and 3,000 pieces of planking for the surface. Air Force C-130's parachuted containers of asphalt to the Navy men below, but the aluminum planking was too bulky for that method of delivery. Instead, the aluminum planks were secured to metal pallets in the cavernous interiors of the turboprop Lockheeds. The planes thundered low across the plateau, and at the desired point crewmen released the restraints holding the pallet. A parachute deployed into the slipstream, opened, and snatched the cargo out of the plane. The heavy pallet fell a few yards, struck the earth, and skidded to a stop as the transport soared skyward. Although their heaviest equipment could not be delivered by this parachute extraction technique, the Seabees used what could be flown to them, completed the job, and earned the congratulations of Lt. Gen. Robert E. Cushman, Jr., Commanding General, III Marine Amphibious Force, and senior Marine officer in Vietnam.[6]

Despite the troubles experienced with water collecting beneath the runway, Khe Sanh's soil was an asset to its defenders. The main base was built on a basalt soil with remarkable adhesive properties. This meant that the Marines could dig trenches and emplacements that would require a minimum of lumber—which had to be delivered by air—for shoring. The consistency of the earth proved an advantage to the Leathernecks, even though it also would simplify North Vietnamese efforts at tunneling, a favorite enemy technique in previous sieges. Conditions within the main perimeter were not duplicated on the nearby hills which had shallow layers of a more porous soil.[7]

Before long, the runway was again able to accommodate C-123's and C-130's, but nevertheless pilots bound for Khe Sanh frequently found the field unusable, primarily because of bad weather. During the early months of the year, clouds and fog were prevalent throughout the northwestern corner of Quang Tri province. The airfield, however, seemed particularly bedeviled by fog. On many a morning when visibility was excellent from the hilltops surrounding the base, the runway remained shrouded in mist until sun and breeze combined to disperse it. A deep ravine at the east end of the runway seemed responsible, channeling warm moist air from the lowlands onto the plateau where it encountered cooler air, became chilled, and created fog.[8]

Principal Commands and Commanders

Such was the Khe Sanh battlefield upon which tens of thousands of Americans, South Vietnamese, and North Vietnamese were destined to fight. Operational control of the American forces committed there, and of all United States forces engaged in the Vietnam war, originated with President Lyndon B. Johnson, Commander in Chief of the nation's armed forces. He exercised his authority through Secretary of Defense Robert S. McNamara, Gen. Earle G. Wheeler, USA, Chairman of the Joint Chiefs of Staff, Adm. U. S. Grant Sharp, Commander in Chief, Pacific Command, and General Westmoreland, head of the Military Assistance Command in Vietnam.

President Johnson and Secretary McNamara were briefed on Khe Sanh, 29 January 1968, by General Wheeler (standing). Also present (l. to r.): Gen. H. K. Johnson, USA; Adm. T. H. Moorer, USN; Gen. J. P. McConnell, USAF; and Gen. L. F. Chapman, USMC

In January 1968 the individual members of the Joint Chiefs of Staff were Gen. Harold K. Johnson, Army Chief of Staff, Adm. Thomas H. Moorer, Chief of Naval Operations, Gen. Leonard F. Chapman, Jr., Commandant of the Marine Corps, and Gen. John P. McConnell, Air Force Chief of Staff.

As the principal commander in the Pacific at the time of the siege of Khe Sanh, Admiral Sharp was responsible for the planning and execution of operations in support of the Republic of Vietnam. His responsibility encompassed selective attacks against targets in North Vietnam as well as operations against hostile forces in the South. The ultimate American goals were to protect the people of South Vietnam, eliminate the threat to governmental stability posed by Viet Cong guerrillas and North Vietnamese regulars, and prepare South Vietnamese forces to assume the burden of their own national defense.

In carrying out his responsibilities, Admiral Sharp worked through his service component commanders and subordinate unified commanders. The former were: Gen. John D. Ryan, Commander in Chief, Pacific Air Forces; Gen. Dwight E. Beach, Commander in Chief, U.S. Army Forces, Pacific; and Adm. John J. Hyland, Commander in Chief, Pacific Fleet. General Westmoreland headed the unified, or multiservice, command in South Vietnam, which functioned as an operational headquarters despite the word "Assistance" in its title.[9]

Besides serving as the senior American commander in Vietnam, Westmoreland had to work closely with the head of the American diplomatic mission in Saigon. That is, military decisions could not be made without taking into account U.S political, economic, and social programs, which

Admiral Sharp (l.) was responsible for overall Vietnam operations. General Ryan (r.) was Commander in Chief, Pacific Air Forces

Admiral Hyland (l.) was Commander in Chief, Pacific Fleet. General Beach (r.) commanded U.S. Army Forces, Pacific

were under the aegis of the U.S. Ambassador. Because of the close relationship of civil and military matters, frequent consultation between soldier and diplomat was essential. "That this arrangement worked smoothly" was, in Westmoreland's opinion, "a tribute to the succession of prominent and talented ambassadors" appointed to the post. During 1968 the incumbent was Ellsworth Bunker.[10]

Initially, the embassy had been directly responsible for American support of Saigon's pacification campaign to extend its authority throughout South Vietnam. General Westmoreland was given increasing authority over this aspect of the war until, in May 1967, the embassy's pacification office and the equivalent section of Westmoreland's staff combined to form a single agency within the assistance command. Robert W. Komer, a former member of President Johnson's staff, assumed the rank of Ambassador and became Westmoreland's Deputy for Civil Operations and Revolutionary Development Support. The American contribution to the pacification effort thus became an exclusively military responsibility. "We are," wrote General Westmoreland, "now organized to pursue a 'one war' strategy." [11]

The U.S. Military Assistance Command embraced several subordinate organizations, among them Seventh Air Force, Westmoreland's Air Force component command. Gen. William W. Momyer headed the Seventh Air Force and also served as Westmoreland's Deputy for Air Operations. From his headquarters at Tan Son Nhut Air Base near Saigon, Momyer directed Air Force operations over the southernmost portion of North Vietnam and all of South Vietnam, in accordance with Westmoreland's directives. Targets deeper in North Vietnam were attacked by Air Force planes based in Thailand or Navy aircraft assigned to carriers of Task Force 77.

General Westmoreland (l.) and Ambassador Ellsworth Bunker (r.) greet General Wheeler at Tan Son Nhut Air Base, upon his arrival in February 1968

Operational control of the Air Force fighter-bombers in Thailand was vested in Momyer, who employed them as directed by Admiral Sharp through General Ryan's headquarters in Hawaii. Admiral Sharp directed Task Force 77's strikes against the North, operating through his Navy component commander, Admiral Hyland.[12]

A component of Seventh Air Force of vital importance to Khe Sanh's defenders was the 834th Air Division, commanded by Brig. Gen. Burl W. McLaughlin. When he assumed command of the air division in November 1967, he found himself confronted by one of those organizational peculiarities so common to the war in Southeast Asia. Although the C-7 and C-123 squadrons serving in South Vietnam were assigned to the 834th Air Division, the C-130's that did most of the heavy hauling were on temporary duty from the 315th Air Division and based in the Philippines, Okinawa, Taiwan, or Japan. Periodically, the C-130 squadrons returned to their home bases to be replaced by other aircraft on temporary assignment.

There were several reasons for this policy. Bases in Vietnam were crowded and could not easily accommodate the C-130 ground crews, administrators, and equipment that would have been part of a permanent change of station. Since the C-130's flew missions throughout the western Pacific, Air Force planners preferred to adjust the number of aircraft in Southeast Asia according to existing needs rather than risk the possibility that planes permanently assigned there might be idle at a time when other C-130's were being overworked in, for example, South Korea. Another possible motive for temporary assignment was to avoid having to transfer housekeeping units to an area where a troop ceiling was in effect.[13]

Among the Vietnam war's deadliest weapons was the Boeing B-52 Stratofortress, a massive 8-engine jet designed originally for dropping nuclear bombs from high altitudes. Assigned to the 3d Air Division with headquarters at Andersen Air Force Base, Guam, the planes operated from that island, from U Tapao Air Base in Thailand, and occasionally from Kadena Air Base on Okinawa. Maj. Gen. Selmon W. Wells commanded the air division during the siege of Khe Sanh.

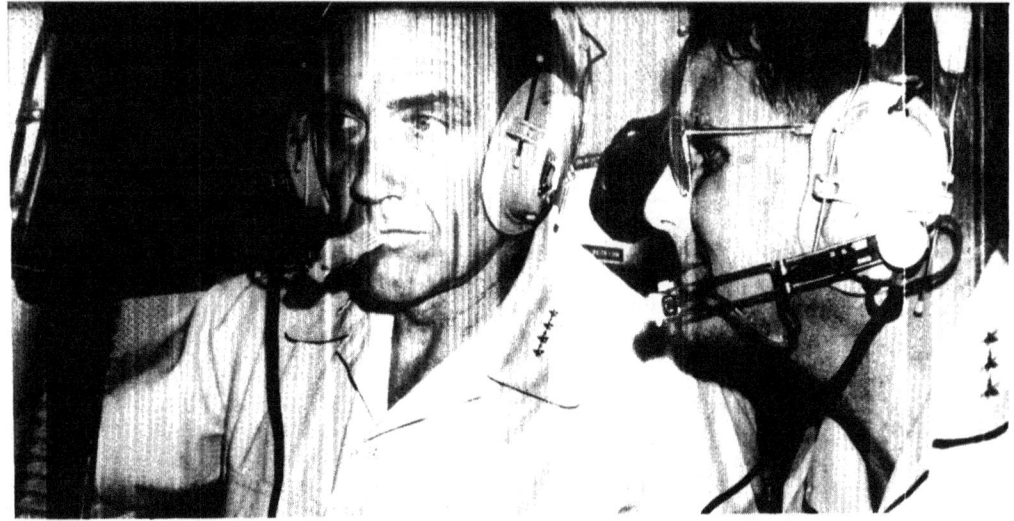

Generals Ryan (l.) and Momyer are shown in a C-130 airborne battlefield command and control center, monitoring a 1967 tactical strike. Momyer pinned on his fourth star at year's end.

The Strategic Air Command was responsible for providing B-52 strikes as requested by General Westmoreland. Besides the bombers themselves, B-52 operations required the deployment of Boeing KC-135 aerial tankers and ground radio relay stations. The command also assigned liaison officers to Seventh Air Force headquarters to coordinate the bombings with other operations. "During the Khe Sahn emergency," reported General Westmoreland, "I slept in my headquarters next to the combat operations center" and, after consulting intelligence and operations officers, "personally decided where the B-52's would strike" [14]

Despite an influx of Army units into I Corps during 1967, operational responsibility rested with Lieutenant General Cushman, commander of the III Marine Amphibious Force. The equivalent of a corps commander under General Westmoreland, he had at his disposal the 1st and 3d Marine Divisions and the 1st Marine Aircraft Wing. Maj. Gen. Rathvon McCall Tompkins commanded the 3d Marine Division and provided the reinforced regiment, the 26th Marines led by Col. David E. Lownds, that defended Khe Sanh. All three officers had fought the Japanese in the Pacific in World War II, and Lownds had also seen action in Korea.[15]

The North Vietnamese general believed to be in personal charge of the Khe Sanh campaign was Vo Nguyen Giap, a one-time school teacher in Hanoi. Beginning in 1944 with 34 men, two revolvers, 17 modern rifles, 14 flintlocks, and a machine gun, he built the Viet Minh army and a decade later led it to victory over the French at Dien Bien Phu. Whether Giap was physically present and actively in command of North Vietnamese forces at Khe Sanh is unknown. Some U.S. officials, General Momyer among them, believed he had entrusted the attack to a subordinate. Whichever the case, as Defense Minister in the Hanoi government, Giap exercised the ultimate authority over North Vietnamese operations at Khe Sanh and elsewhere.[16]

The Enemy Masses

General Westmoreland believed the North Vietnamese would attack Khe Sanh. Its nearness to enemy sanctuaries and infiltration routes made it an inviting target, and American intelligence was able to verify a hostile concentration in the area. Located north of the combat base was the North Vietnamese 325C Division. In 1967, Colonel Lanigan's 3d Marines had driven two of the division's three regiments from the hills around Khe Sanh, but both had been brought to normal strength before receiving orders to seek battle once again. Southwest of the Marine stronghold was the 304th Division which had fought at Dien Bien Phu. If at peak strength, the two enemy divisions would total some 20,000 men. In addition, one regiment of the 324th Division and the entire 320th Division were within 25 kilometers of Khe Sanh and provided a ready source of North Vietnamese reinforcements.[17]

Other details of the tactical picture came slowly into focus. Once U.S. intelligence had determined the enemy order of battle, the analysts were able to calculate the number and types of weapons generally employed to support such a force. Experience indicated that the 325C and 304th Divisions would be able to call upon three kinds of howitzers, with 24 of each available. These were 105-mm and 122-mm weapons, with maximum ranges of almost 12,000 meters, and 75-mm pieces that could lob a shell 8,600 meters and beyond. Also at hand would be three sizes of mortar, the 120-mm with a maximum range approaching 6,000 meters, the 82-mm which could reach some 3,000 meters, and the 60-mm capable of firing about 1,500 meters. The siege troops would have the support of 78 of the largest type mortar, 36 of the medium size, and 108 of the smallest. The number of rocket launchers able to hit Khe Sanh was unknown, but the 122-mm variety could hit a target 10,000 meters distance and the 107-mm could fire almost half that far.[18]

The buildup of December 1967 and January 1968 was not, however, confined to the wilderness around Khe Sanh. Hostile units seemed to be materializing all along the line of bases that the Americans had built just south of the demilitarized zone. All but about 10 percent of these troops appeared to be regulars from North Vietnam, lavishly supported by artillery.[19]

As these combat units surfaced south of the demarcation line between the two Vietnams, enemy engineers and laborers were improving the roads over which supplies and reinforcements would have to pass. Early in January 1968, photo interpreters discovered a new road originating across the Laotian border and terminating some 27 kilometers northwest of Khe Sanh. Later that month, American intelligence detected another road, one that crossed from Laos into South Vietnam some 14 kilometers from the base and provided access to a network of trails.[20]

The most detailed information on the enemy buildup and its purpose came from a North Vietnamese defector, a lieutenant, who appeared white flag in hand before Marine positions on the afternoon of January 20. He later explained that he had decided to surrender because, after 14 years of service, he had been refused promotion to captain in favor of men he considered incompetent. The disgruntled lieutenant confirmed that an attack upon Khe Sanh was imminent. This effort, he declared, was part of an offensive designed to conquer every American stronghold from the Laotian border eastward to Con Thien and thus gain control of Quang Tri province.[21]

American Preparations

In anticipation of a thrust at Khe Sanh, General Westmoreland early in January 1968 had directed his staff to begin planning for the defense of the Marine base. Recalling the kind of savage U.S. aerial bombardment that in the autumn of 1967 had helped to

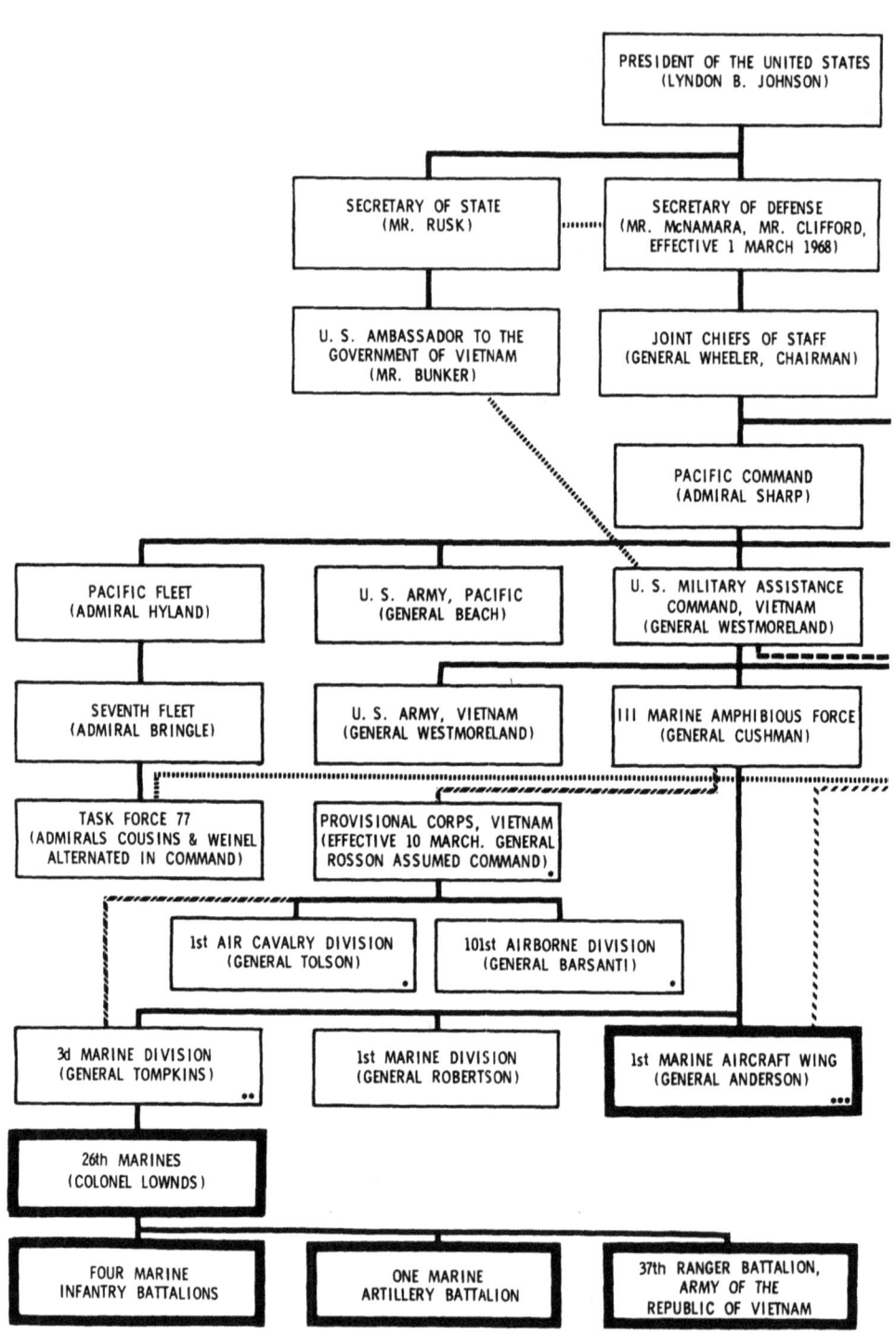

UNITS IN HEAVILY BORDERED BLOCKS TOOK PART IN THE DEFENSE OF KHE SANH, 21 JANUARY-31 JANUARY 1968

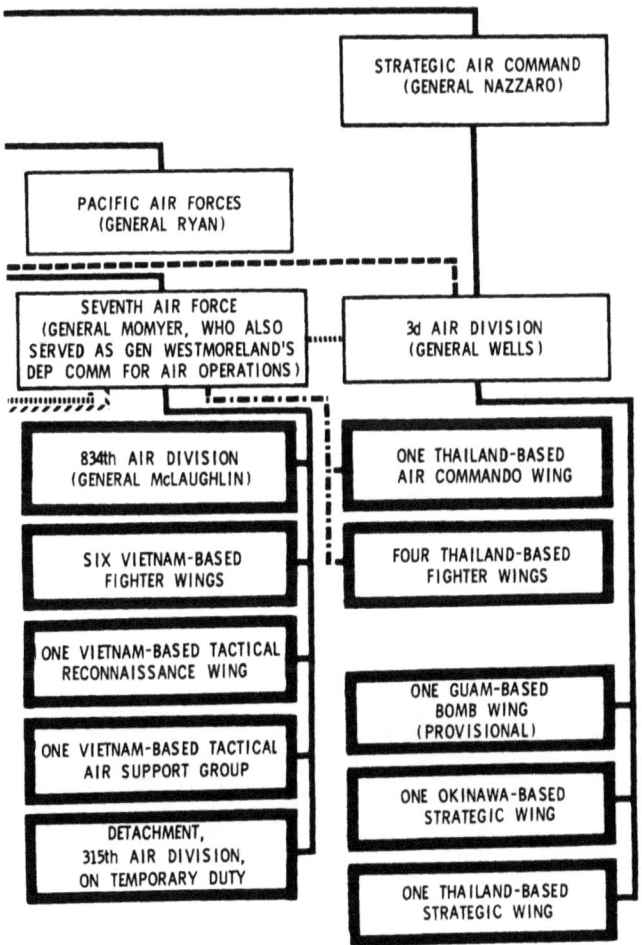

COMMAND RELATIONSHIPS FOR KHE SANH

- PROVISIONAL CORPS, VIETNAM, ESTABLISHED 10 MARCH
- 3d MARINE DIVISION AND COMPONENTS PASS TO PROVISIONAL CORPS, VIETNAM
- TO OPERATIONAL DIRECTION OF GENERAL MOMYER
- COORDINATION
- SELECTS B-52 TARGETS
- AVAILABLE FOR USE IN DEFENSE OF KHE SANH
- COORDINATION PRIOR TO 10 MARCH; OPERATIONAL DIRECTION AFTER 21 MARCH
- CONTROL EFFECTIVE 10 MARCH

destroy the hostile forces poised near Con Thien, another Marine outpost in Quang Tri province, the general decided to rely on air power rather than on large numbers of troops.[22]

Though Operation Neutralize, as the aerial effort around Con Thien was called, offered a valid precedent for the use of aerial bombardment in defense of a combat base, conditions at Con Thien had been quite different from the situation at Khe Sanh. In defending Con Thien, the Marine Amphibious Force retained its mobility and launched frequent ground attacks that, together with the aerial effort, frustrated the enemy by striking him before he was ready to move against the base. Maneuver played an important part in the Con Thien fighting, with ground combat occurring throughout an area of 20 square miles around the base. Developments at Khe Sanh indicated that the troops fighting there would rely far less upon movement than had their fellow Marines at Con Thien.[23]

If the proposed aerial onslaught against Khe Sanh's besiegers, an undertaking which Westmoreland called Operation Niagara, was to succeed, American air and ground forces would require precise, detailed, current information about enemy activities and troop dispositions. The general therefore launched a preliminary operation, Niagara I, an extensive reconnaissance effort that combined techniques as rudimentary as scouting and patrolling with the latest innovations in electronics and photography. Cameras and other complex devices contributed to the successful collection of intelligence, but men on the ground also furnished valuable information gathered while patrolling Quang Tri's hills.[24]

Reliance on air power did not rule out reinforcement, within practical limits, of the Khe Sanh garrison. The number of troops and supporting weapons dispatched to the base depended upon its capacity to accommodate them and the ability of logistical agencies to sustain them. There simply was not room at Khe Sanh and on nearby hills for more than about 6,000 men. Most of these—three infantry battalions of the 26th Marines, each with an authorized strength of almost 1,200—were already in place by mid-January 1968. When Colonel Lownds had arrived the previous August to replace Colonel Padley in command of the 26th Marines, only Lt. Col. James B. Wilkinson's 1st Battalion was located at the base. The regiment's 3d Battalion commanded by Lt. Col. Harry L. Alderman, joined its parent regiment in December, and the 2d Battalion, under Lt. Col. Francis Heath, Jr., arrived in January along with the 1st Battalion, 13th Marines, commanded by Lt. Col. John A. Hennelly. Two other battalions, one of them Vietnamese, reached Khe Sanh after the battle had been joined.[25]

Colonel Lownds did not have the number of 105-mm howitzer batteries, one for each rifle battalion, prescribed for the force he commanded. The arrival of two such howitzer units late in January brought the total number of these batteries to three, probably the most that could be supplied with ammunition in the circumstances that then prevailed. These recently arrived batteries brought Lieutenant Colonel Hennelly's artillery battalion to full strength.

Besides the 18 105-mm weapons capable of firing almost 12,000 meters, the base boasted six 155-mm howitzers accurate up to 14,600 meters, and six 4.2-inch mortars with a range of 4,020 meters. Army artillery, 16 to 18 175-mm self-propelled guns, could reach out beyond 32,000 meters and from emplacements at the Rock Pile and Camp Carroll bombard the approaches to Khe Sanh.[26]

Also on hand for Khe Sanh's defense were six medium tanks that mounted 90-mm guns, 10 Ontos antitank vehicles—each consisting of six 106-mm recoilless rifles mounted on a tracked chassis—and four "dusters" mounting either two 40-mm cannon or four .50-caliber machine guns. These last, designed almost a generation before as antiaircraft weapons, were prized for their murderous effect against ground troops.[27]

President Johnson Takes a Hand

The mounting threat to Khe Sanh caught the eye of President Johnson. As early as mid-December 1967, he had become aware that an enemy offensive was in the making and that a likely objective was Khe Sanh. Thereafter, he took a personal interest in the adequacy of American measures to protect the endangered base.[28]

The burden of keeping the President informed about what the enemy could do was carried by W. W. Rostow, Mr. Johnson's Special Assistant for National Security Affairs. To accomplish this, Dr. Rostow, a well-known economic historian, set up an informal intelligence evaluation section consisting of himself, an Air Force general, and two civilians. The officer was Brig. Gen. Robert N. Ginsburgh, a World War II Army artillery officer and Harvard Ph.D. who had transferred to the Air Force in 1949 and was serving as liaison agent between the Joint Chiefs of Staff and the White House. One of the civilians was Art McCafferty, chief of the White House situation room; the other was a secretary, Mary Lee Chaternuck, who screened the available translations of captured documents.

Each week, the President and certain of his trusted advisers lunched together and discussed the progress of the war. At these Tuesday meetings, Dr. Rostow was able to provide, among other data, the latest intelligence on what was happening at Khe Sanh.

For further information on Khe Sanh, the President turned to the Chairman of the Joint Chiefs of Staff. He asked General Wheeler whether the Marine base could and should be defended. The general answered yes to both parts of the question, but the President still had his doubts. To resolve them, he asked if this was Westmoreland's opinion. An inquiry went out to General Westmoreland, who replied that he shared this view.

Before reporting to President Johnson, General Wheeler discussed the matter with the service chiefs, who felt so strongly about the validity of General Westmoreland's opinion that they insisted on formally endorsing it. On 29 January, during the second week of the Khe Sanh battle, General Wheeler told the President that the "Joint Chiefs of Staff have reviewed the situation at Khe Sanh and concur with General Westmoreland's assessment of the situation." This apparently spontaneous vote of confidence gave rise to reports that President Johnson had insisted that each of the Joint Chiefs submit in writing his view on the wisdom and feasibility of standing firm at Khe Sanh.[29]

Not all the President's advisers favored making a stand at Khe Sanh. Most prominent among the doubters was Gen. Maxwell D. Taylor, USA, who had preceded General Wheeler as Chairman of the Joint Chiefs of Staff and who had served as U.S. Ambassador to the Saigon government. General Taylor cited the infantryman's adage that a commander could take any defensive position if he was willing to pay the price. The North Vietnamese, he warned, might be willing to make the necessary sacrifice in lives to overwhelm the Marine garrison.[30]

As the drama at Khe Sanh increased in intensity, the President became more deeply involved. According to a Washington newsman, "The White House took on the atmosphere and trappings of a military command post before a siege." Dominating the situation room were a detailed terrain model and up-to-date aerial mosaics of the Khe Sanh battleground.[31]

Once the fighting began, President Johnson received frequent reports on both the tactical and logistical situation. During a particularly determined attack on a Marine outpost, the interval between reports to the White House on the fighting was as little as 50 minutes. Summaries of supplies on hand at Khe Sanh were prepared each day until the stockpile became large enough to see the garrison through any likely emergency.[32]

President Johnson studies a terrain model of the Khe Sanh battleground. Looking on (center) is Brig. Gen R. N. Ginsburgh, USAF, liaison officer between General Wheeler and W. W. Rostow (r.), the President's Special Assistant for National Security Affairs

II. THE PRECEDENT OF DIEN BIEN PHU

Khe Sanh stirred memories of another battle, the fight for Dien Bien Phu in 1954, a struggle in which Viet Minh artillery and infantry had conquered a French base that also had depended on aircraft for supplies and reinforcements. In choosing the battlefield of Dien Bien Phu, the French tried to apply lessons they had learned in earlier actions. Unfortunately, those lessons either were poorly understood or were no longer applicable.

The French Prepare

The course of action that ended in disaster for the French at Dien Bien Phu began with a series of three Viet Minh defeats.[1] In January 1951, General Giap decided that his recently organized combat divisions were adequate to the task of capturing French-held Hanoi. Between the Viet Minh and their objective lay a well organized defensive barrier that included some 900 mutually supporting pillboxes plus medium and heavy artillery. Three times Giap hurled his troops against this line, and each time French firepower smothered the attack. Giap at last realized that his lightly armed formations could not prevail against these skillfully prepared defenses. He then marched the survivors back into the highlands and resumed guerrilla warfare until a better opportunity should appear.[2]

As a result of their three victories, the French tried to lure the Viet Minh into another battle in which firepower would again be decisive. General Giap refused the bait, however, until the French in their eagerness made a mortal error. Instead of choosing an easily supported defensive position, the high command selected Dien Bien Phu, a valley in remote northwestern Vietnam which took its name from a large village located there.[3]

At Dien Bien Phu, the French hoped to establish a *base aero terrestre* from which to mount attacks upon Viet Minh supply lines. The heart of this air-ground base was a flying field where transports could land supplies and fighter-bombers and observation planes take off to locate and destroy the enemy.

The all-important airstrip lay in a valley measuring 9 by 16 kilometers. Its security depended upon two outposts set up to keep the Viet Minh from moving within artillery range of the runway and aircraft parking areas. The large garrison, some 10,000 troops when the siege began, was believed to have sufficient artillery of its own to silence the few batteries the enemy was expected to emplace nearby.

Few of the French expectations actually came to pass. The warplanes available to them did not disrupt Viet Minh supply lines. Over these routes came battalions, rather than batteries, of artillery and antiaircraft guns.

Even as he was completing his plans and massing troops, General Giap undertook feints toward Seno and Luang Prabang in Laos and Pleiku in central Vietnam. In each instance, his enemy reacted by establishing blocking positions. In addition, the French leadership at Hanoi voluntarily tied down still other troops by launching an amphibious operation in the vicinity of Tuy Hoa, a thrust that General Giap ignored.[4]

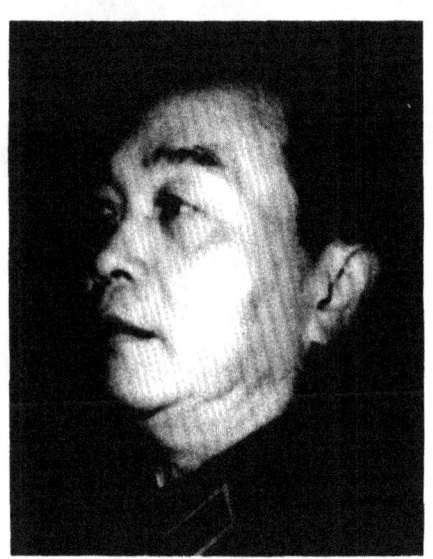

Massing his forces against Khe Sanh, General Giap (r.) tried unsuccessfully to repeat his Dien Bien Phu victory

The Viet Minh buildup was completed by 13 March 1954, when General Giap inaugurated the siege with a sudden and devastating artillery barrage. After 2 days, the Viet Minh held both outposts that were to have protected the airfield.

French headquarters at Hanoi responded by scraping together as many transports as it could—including twin-engine Fairchild Flying Boxcars flown by American civilians—and trying to parachute supplies, equipment, and reinforcements* to sustain the garrison. Air strikes, however, failed to suppress murderous fire from Communist antiaircraft guns that were appearing all around the besieged valley. These weapons prevented the transports from flying straight, level, and low to parachute their loads into the gradually contracting drop zone. The French fought valiantly but the Viet Minh tightened the noose around the garrison. On 7 May 1954, having expended their last ammunition, the French were overrun by the enemy force. Incomplete records indicate that French casualties during the battle totaled about 5,000 dead, with some 10,000 troops, half of them wounded, taken prisoner. Giap's losses were an estimated 23,000.

---

* A cumulative total of 16,500 defenders served at Dien Bien Phu during the siege.

Comparison with Khe Sanh

The decision to defend Khe Sanh was made with Dien Bien Phu in mind and the defenses of the Marine base were strengthened accordingly. Comparisons of the status of the Marines at Khe Sanh and the plight of the French at Dien Bien Phu revealed that the Americans enjoyed a marked superiority in two essential categories—firepower and logistic support.

To augment the firepower of the Dien Bien Phu garrison, the French were able to muster fewer than 200 planes on a daily basis. These included such diverse types as Morane 500 light observation planes, compact Grumman F8F fighters, and 4-engine Consolidated Privateer patrol craft that had evolved from the wartime Liberator bomber.

In defense of Khe Sanh, the Americans could draw upon a Southeast Asia armada of 2,000 planes and 3,300 helicopters. These aircraft, moreover, benefited from reliable communications, and many of them had the ability to destroy a target con-

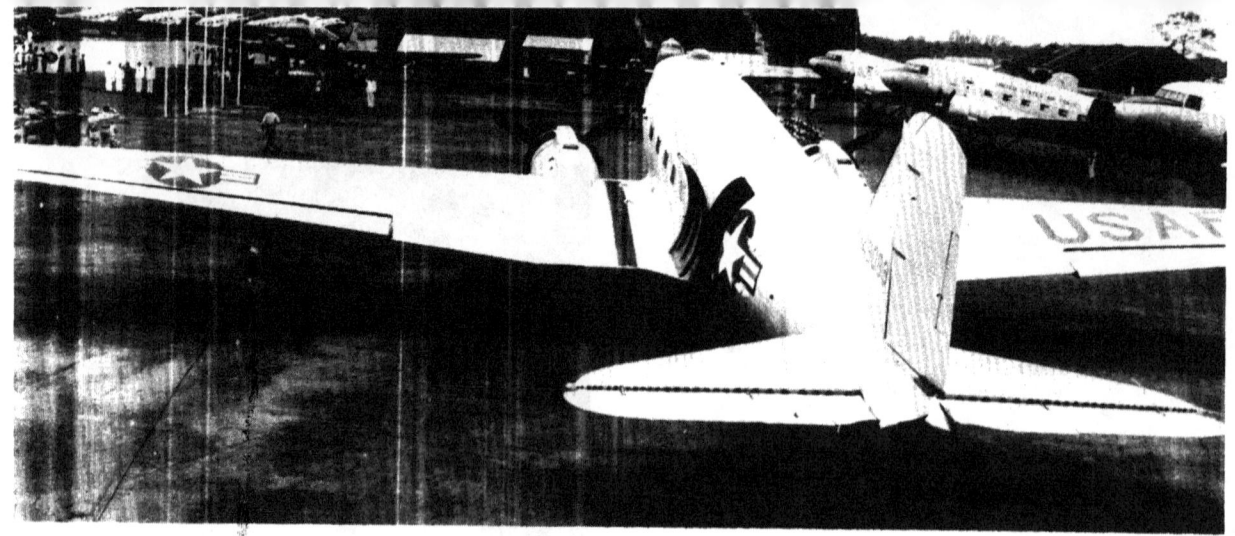

Above are some of 21 USAF C-47's flown to Nha Trang Airfield in December 1952 to bolster French airlift operations.

After the fall of Dien Bien Phu, victorious Viet Minh troops—accompanied by French officers—cross the Doumer Bridge into Hanoi (below r.)

cealed by fog or darkness using internal equipment—as in the case of the Marine and Navy Grumman A-6's—or by relying on radar direction provided by control facilities on the ground. The ability of Army gunners at the Rock Pile and Camp Carroll to support the Marines with 175-mm barrages promised the Khe Sanh garrison a source of assistance that could not be affected by bombardments of the Marine base itself.

The Marine advantage in logistical matters was even more striking than the difference in firepower. Radar enabled transports to parachute cargo accurately in any weather, a kind of versatility unknown at Dien Bien Phu. Cargo extraction equipment developed by the U.S. Air Force also permitted the delivery of items too bulky to drop by parachute. In addition, the transports flying to Khe Sanh in 1968 were vastly improved over those of 14 years earlier. The most efficient of the Air Force transports was the C-130, credited with a maximum payload in excess of 20 tons, which actually delivered an average of some 13 tons per sortie during the battle. Also available were Fairchild C-123's, considered capable of carrying almost 8 tons, and de Havilland C-7A's built to deliver 3 tons of cargo. Like the C-130, both of these types operated at about 60 percent of rated capacity. By comparison, in 1954 the French flew a small number of Fairchild Packets, twin-engine transports with a 7-ton maximum payload. They had relied primarily, however, upon old Douglas C-47's originally designed to carry 3 tons, the same maximum load as the smallest and least used of the Air Force transports available to the Khe Sanh garrison.

These advantages seemed to outweigh by far the problems the Americans could expect to encounter. Like the French, they would have difficulty silencing the cleverly camouflaged antiaircraft guns certain to be encountered at Khe Sanh. These weapons could take a heavy toll of transports making deliveries to the Marine base. In addition, the weather would definitely be a handicap.[5]

Why Khe Sanh?

Khe Sanh was a valuable base for allied ground operations against infiltration routes entering South Vietnam and, as events would prove, for attacks on North Vietnamese supply dumps located across the Loatian border. By January 1968, the base had evolved into a well organized defensive position with a runway that could accommodate the largest American tactical transports. Moreover, the base had become a symbol of U.S. determination to see the war through. Intelligence officers were convinced that the enemy, aware of this symbolism, would lay siege to the base and attempt to overwhelm its defenders in the same way he had crushed the French and their auxiliaries at Dien Bien Phu. Westmoreland's staff recognized that an attack on Khe Sanh might be part of some even more ambitious scheme—combined perhaps with a thrust from Laos through the A Shau Valley toward Hue or Da Nang to isolate a portion of I Corps—but they were certain that Giap, whether directing operations from Hanoi or actually in command on the battlefield, fully intended to repeat along Highway 9 the kind of triumph he won 14 years before in the wilderness far to the north.[6]

Yet the possibility existed that by massing troops against Khe Sanh, General Giap or his field commander might be putting a pistol to his head. Ever since 1966, General Westmoreland had been fighting what amounted to a war of attrition. He used his remarkably mobile forces to strike suddenly, attempting to engage the enemy so that America's awesome firepower, everything from M-16 rifles to B-52 bombers, could be brought to bear. His objective was not to capture hill or ridge line, but to destroy enemy soldiers and hostile units.[7]

Since Giap would have to concentrate large numbers of troops in northwestern South Vietnam, where there

were comparatively few civilians to inhibit the use of American air and artillery, Westmoreland felt free to make unstinting use of bombs and shells. Once this firepower had shattered the North Vietnamese divisions the highly mobile U.S. ground troops could exploit the situation. The Americans, it seemed, might well be able to do at Khe Sanh what the French had tried and failed to do at Dien Bien Phu.[8]

The war in South Vietnam, where intensive firepower was used against enemy forces, was but one part of a U.S. strategy that included bombing of selected targets in North Vietnam. In March 1967, in a speech before the Tennessee legislature, President Johnson listed three objectives of the bombing campaign. They were "to back our fighting men by denying the enemy a sanctuary," to "exact a penalty" for North Vietnam's violations of the 1954 agreement that had ended the war between the French and Viet Minh, and finally "to limit the flow or substantially increase the cost of infiltrating men and supplies into South Vietnam."

The goal of the United States in fighting in the South, bombing the North, and pursuing other military measures was the negotiation of an honorable peace that would enable the nations of Southeast Asia to concentrate upon economic and social needs. The President believed that successful military operations in Southeast Asia would convince Ho Chi Minh, the leader of North Vietnam, that peace was preferable to fighting. Mr. Johnson also maintained that American success would serve as "a concrete demonstration that aggression across international frontiers or demarcation lines is no longer an acceptable means of political change."[9]

Ho Chi Minh, North Vietnamese leader

III. ENCIRCLEMENT

In January 1968, while plans were being set in motion to send reinforcements to Khe Sanh, the troops already there hurried to complete shelters to protect themselves against the deluge of shells they were certain would come. By mid-month, for example, men of the 26th Marines had virtually completed bunkers to house their operations section and the communication center, and eight other similar shelters were almost one-third finished. Enough timber and sandbags were on hand to complete the construction already underway. Additional materiel stood beside the C-130 loading ramp at Da Nang Air Base for delivery as needed.[1]

On the ground, contact between Marines and North Vietnamese became more frequent and more violent. On 17 January, a reconnaissance patrol from Khe Sanh triggered an ambush that cost the lives of its patrol leader and his radioman. Two days later, a rifle platoon combed the ambush site, a ridge some 700 meters southwest of Hill 881N. Hidden amid the dense vegetation, about 25 North Vietnamese opened fire on the Marines, who promptly fired back, then called down artillery on the concealed enemy, and returned to the combat base.

A rifle company probed the enemy occupied ridge the following morning. While elements of another company, lifted to Hill 881S by helicopter, set up a defensive perimeter, Capt. William H. Dabney, USMC, led his company toward Hill 881N. Fog slowed the men, but visibility was rapidly improving as they started up the two fingers of ground that extended southward from Hill 881N. On these approaches, Captain Dabney's Marines encountered prepared defensive works manned, it appeared, by a North Vietnamese battalion.

Air strikes—especially one by napalm-carrying jets that caught the enemy as he was counterattacking—and fire from artillery and recoilless rifles enabled the Marines to seize a hillock that dominated the enemy defenses. Such was the situation when orders arrived directing Captain Dabney to fall back to Hill 881S. The company was being recalled in anticipation of an imminent enemy attack, to which the Marines had been alerted by the North Vietnamese lieutenant who had defected earlier in the day.[2]

The Battle is Joined

The predicted attack began in the early hours of 21 January with a mortar bombardment of the Marine position on Hill 861, following which enemy sappers tried to blast passages for attacking infantry through the defensive barbed wire. Some of the attackers actually penetrated the curtain of protective fire, but they were contained in the vicinity of the helicopter pad and killed. Surprisingly, the North Vietnamese ignored Hill 881S during the storming of Hill 861 and paid in blood for this oversight, being scourged throughout the battle with fire from the higher ground.[3]

Repulsed at Hill 861, the enemy turned his attention to the combat base itself. At about 0530 on the morning of the 21st, mortar and artillery

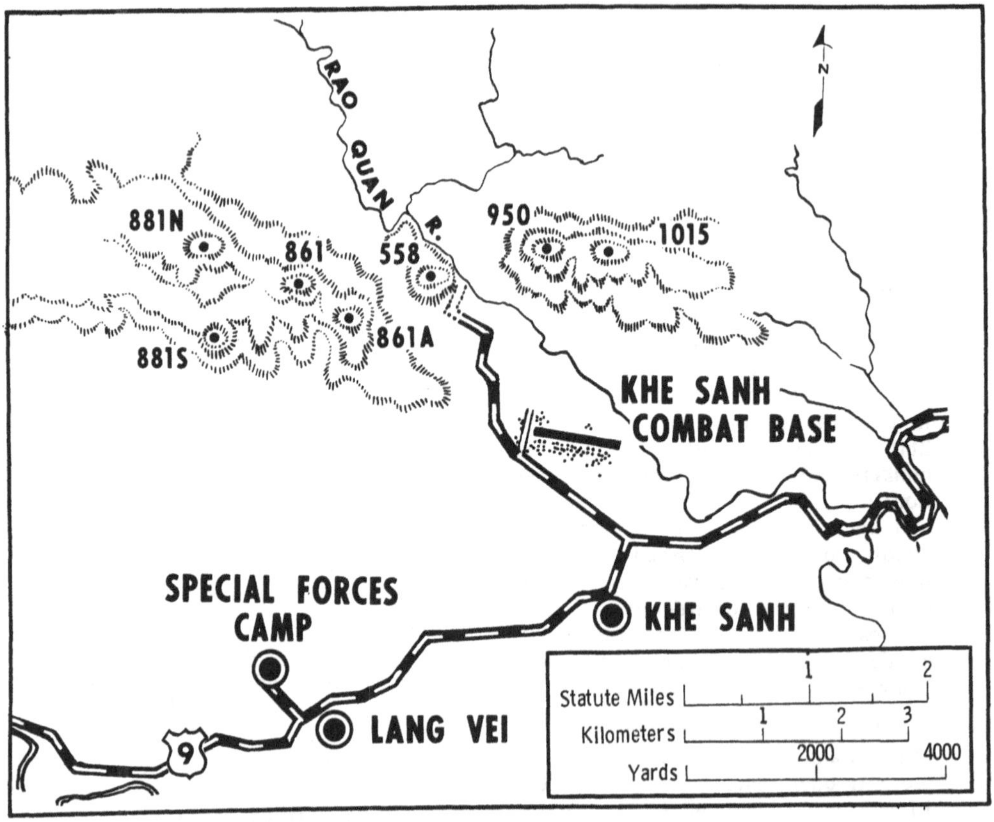
RAO QUAN R.
881N
861
558
950
1015
861A
881S
KHE SANH
COMBAT BASE
SPECIAL FORCES
CAMP
KHE SANH
LANG VEI
9
N
Statute Miles
Kilometers
Yards
1
2
1
2
3
2000
4000

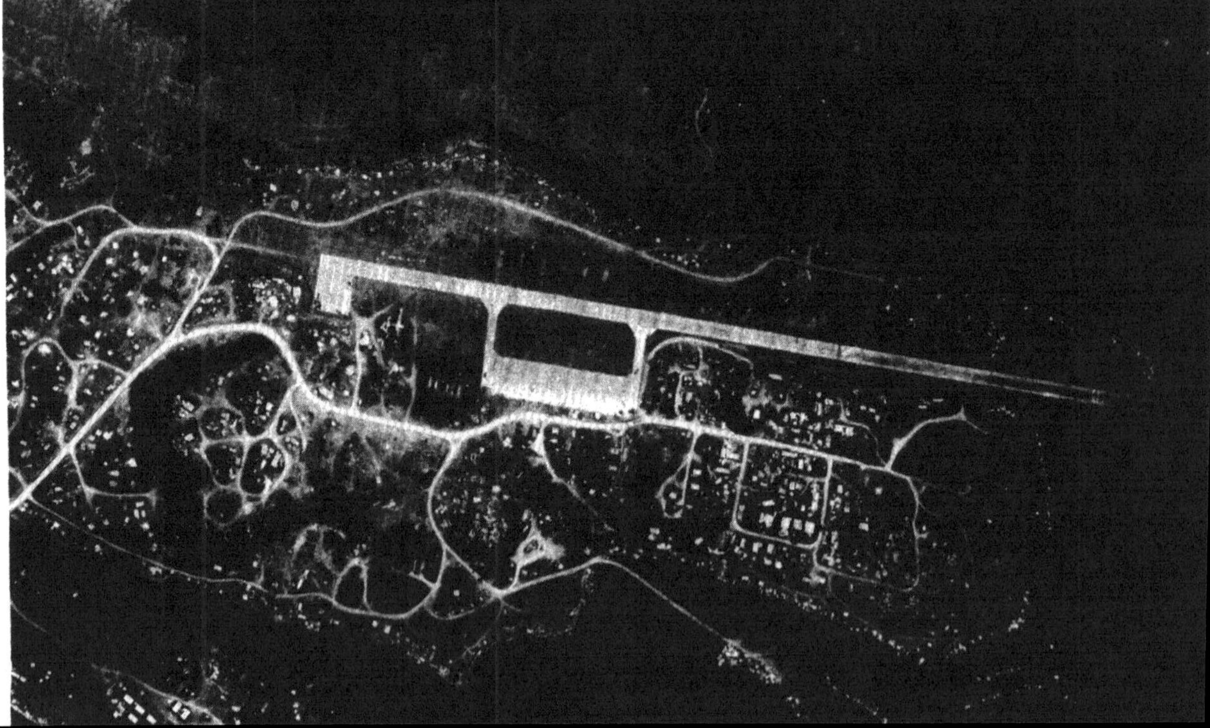

shells and rockets began exploding among the bunkers, trucks, and helicopters atop the plateau. The barrage started fires and caused explosions in the largest base ammunition dump. Almost 1,500 tons of ammunition were destroyed, about 98 percent of what was stored there. North Vietnamese gunners also demolished one parked helicopter, damaged five others, and gouged holes in the runway surface. A Seabee maintenance unit at Khe Sanh helped reopen 2,000 feet of runway so that Air Force C-123's could continue to land while further repairs were being made.[4]

The attack on Khe Sanh triggered a flurry of aerial activity. On the 22d, for example, B-52's bombed four targets in the vicinity of the base. By midnight on 23 January, pilots of Marine, Navy, and Air Force fighter-bombers and attack craft claimed to have touched off 40 secondary explosions and 28 secondary fires, killed 39 North Vietnamese soldiers, and collapsed five bunkers built by the enemy—all this in the area immediately surrounding Khe Sanh.[5]

Meanwhile, Marine helicopters brought to Khe Sanh the 1st Battalion, 9th Marines, under Lt. Col. John F. Mitchell. The first of Mitchell's riflemen stepped from their helicopters on the afternoon of 22 January and, in slightly more than 24 hours, the last member of the rear echelon of battalion headquarters had set foot on the airfield at Khe Sanh. During those hectic hours, a 2-helicopter section led by Capt. T. A. Bowditch of Marine Medium Helicopter Squadron 164, airlifted 254 men in four flights to the base. Like most of the aircraft operating around Khe Sanh during this period, the captain's section encountered hostile fire whenever it landed or took off from the plateau. Miraculously, neither craft was hit.[6]

General Cushman decided against an attempt to clear the enemy from the high ground that dominated Highway 9 because progress would have been too slow and casualties too numerous. The job of replenishing the garrison's ammunition supply was assigned to aviation.

While helicopters and fighter-bombers swarmed around Khe Sanh, elements of General McLaughlin's 834th Air Division tackled the problem of landing enough ammunition to enable the Marines to fight on despite the destruction of much of their munition stockpile. The task was truly formidable. The garrison had thus far repaired only 2,000 feet of the 3,900-foot runway. The lighting system for night landings no longer worked. Each transport as it approached or departed Khe Sanh had to run a gauntlet of North Vietnamese .30- and .50-caliber machine guns, concealed on the hills and ridges around the base. Finally, the enemy directed his mortars against the planes as they were being unloaded beside the damaged runway.

The largest plane in Vietnam that could use the bobtailed runway at Khe Sanh was the elderly C-123, a twin-engine, conventionally powered craft, first built by Fairchild in the mid-1950's. Some of them had been fitted with auxiliary jet engines that greatly improved performance. Replenishment of the munition stockpiles at Khe Sanh fell in the category of tactical emergency, which meant that cargo planes could be diverted from less important missions to deliver the ammunition so desperately needed by Colonel Lownds' men. Six C-123's became available on the afternoon of the 21st, and began delivering slightly more than 24 tons of munitions, their initial contribution to the defense of

(L.) Aerial view of the Khe Sanh Combat Base

Khe Sanh. Landings continued throughout the night despite low-lying clouds and enemy fire, as by the whitish light of flares the C-123's touched down and safely unloaded. Again on the 22d, the C-123's returned, flying 20 sorties that pushed the amount of ammunition delivered to the neighborhod of 130 tons, enough to meet the emergency and to gain time for establishing routine deliveries to sustain the Marines for as long as the fight should last.[7]

Almost from the outset, Colonel Lownds had to cope with a refugee problem. The first noncombatants to appear at the combat base came from the Khe Sanh village, overrun by a North Vietnamese battalion. These refugees, few in number, were evacuated in planes that had unloaded at Khe Sanh, but as the enemy extended his control on both sides of the Laotian border, additional civilians and irregular troops sought a haven with the Marines. Khe Sanh's defenders thus came to face a particularly difficult situation in which humanitarian impulses had to be weighed against the possibility of enemy infiltration, the limited space available on the plateau, and the danger from enemy fire.[8]

To the untrained eye, Khe Sanh might have seemed all confusion during the first weeks of the battle. Supplies and reinforcements arrived; refugees departed. Despite fog and antiaircraft fire fighter-bombers swept low to attack the siege force, while in the distance tons of B-52 bombs converted green hills into a moonscape. Amid all this activity, Colonel Lownds made the final adjustments in the disposition of his troops. To the north he set up a line of outposts extending from Hill 950 across the Rao Quan River to Hill 881S. In addition, he placed the newly arrived 1st Battalion, 9th Marines, around a rock quarry west of the base. His last reinforcements, men of the 37th Ranger Battalion, Army of the Republic of Vietnam, reached the base on 27 January and took over a segment of the main perimeter.[9]

Before the fight was a week old, American airmen reported seeing tanks across the Laotian border, west and slightly south of the base. If the enemy actually used armor, it would mark a major tactical innovation in the Vietnamese war. Nevertheless, the Marines were prepared for such an eventuality. To cover the one approach to Khe Sanh suitable for armored vehicles, the garrison could employ as many as needed of the 180 3.5-inch rocket launchers and 32 106-mm recoilless rifles divided among the four Marine battalions. Also available were the 10 Ontos antitank vehicles and the handful of M-48 tanks.[10]

As January drew to a close, the Khe Sanh Marines seemed well prepared for the ordeal to come. Colonel Lownds had received reinforcements and deployed them to improve the base's defense. Repairs of battle damage done to the runway enabled C-130's to resume using the airstrip. Air strikes were proving effective, as were the mortar and artillery concentrations fired in support of the defenders. For example, on 23 January napalm dropped a half kilometer northwest of Khe Sanh flushed from cover 10 North Vietnamese soldiers, all of whom were then killed by Marine 81-mm mortars. Similarly, in a somewhat bizarre action, Marine artillery scattered an enemy pack train in which the beasts of burden were elephants.[11]

There were ominous portents, too. The enemy's bombardment continued, although he ceased for a time to probe Marine defenses. Also, in nearby Laos tank-supported North Vietnamese had routed a lightly armed Laotian battalion located at Ban Houaysan along Highway 9. Both victors and vanquished seemed headed for the Special Forces camp at Lang Vei.[12]

(Above) Fuel dump hit by one of numerous North Vietnamese mortar attacks on Khe Sanh
(Below) Refugees being evacuated from Khe Sanh

The Tet Offensive

By 31 January, a major attempt to overwhelm Khe Sanh appeared imminent. The North Vietnamese had deployed a powerful infantry force in the northwestern corner of South Vietnam, furnished it with artillery and antiaircraft guns, and introduced tanks into the region. In the hills around the Marine base, the enemy had established supply points, dug in his artillery, and begun work on trenches and bunkers that would be required by an assault force.[13]

When the next blow fell, however, it was directed not against Khe Sanh but against Saigon, five other major cities, 34 provincial capitals, and a scattering of towns, villages, and military installations. Thousands of South Vietnamese civilians and soldiers on leave took advantage of an announced ceasefire (which the Allies cancelled in I Corps because of the threat to Khe Sanh) to travel to their ancestral homes to celebrate Tet, the lunar New Year. The heavy road traffic helped conceal the movement of tens of thousands of North Vietnamese and Viet Cong soldiers.

As might be expected in so ambitious an offensive, coordination was less than perfect. Shells, for example, burst over Da Nang airfield and at the nearby Marble Mountain air facility some 24 hours before the main attacks. Also, the enemy's success varied from place to place, indeed from hour to hour. At Saigon, the attackers scored a psychological triumph at the very outset by blasting their way into the U.S. Embassy grounds. Local security forces—U.S. Army military police, Marine embassy guards, and Vietnamese police—rallied quickly, however, and kept the assault units from gaining their major objectives. Although the enemy caused a great deal of destruction at Bien Hoa and Tan Son Nhut airfields near Saigon, the defenders uprooted them. South Vietnamese and American troops cleared the city and both air bases, but hostile forces remained for a time in the area.[14]

At Da Nang the enemy's luck was all bad. Following the premature shelling of the airfield, the North Vietnamese 2d Division advanced on the city from the hills to the southwest. Reconnaissance elements of the 1st Marine Division detected the move and called for artillery and aerial bombardment. Nearer Da Nang, General Cushman spotted an enemy contingent from his command helicopter. Two Marine battalions moved out, rescued a beleaguered group of South Vietnamese irregulars, and routed the enemy. Another unit tried to seize Hoi An, south of Da Nang, while still others made a stab at I Corps headquarters. In both instances, the attackers were frustrated by the determined resistance of Americans and South Vietnamese.[15]

On the other hand, the North Vietnamese achieved complete surprise at the ancient capital of Hue, a large city halfway between Da Nang and the demilitarized zone. In the absence of an American garrison, the national police were primarily responsible for protecting the city. Other units available to assist them were: the headquarters of the South Vietnamese 1st Division; the Black Panther Company, one of the Vietnamese Army's elite units; the 3d Regiment, Army of the Republic of Vietnam, located northwest of the city; and a South Vietnamese battalion to its southwest.

The enemy, moving as individuals or in small groups, slipped into Hue amid the holiday throng. His presence did not become known to the defenders until he opened fire with rockets and mortars. By that time, 31 January, the infiltrators controlled all of the Citadel—the old walled city north of

Can Tho, one of many cities struck by the Viet Cong during the Tet offensive

the Perfume River—except for the South Vietnamese 1st Division's headquarters. South of the river, the advisory compound of the U.S. Military Assistance Command held out as did a few other pockets of resistance.

Help soon arrived. Elements of two U.S. Marine battalions reached the city on the 31st, punched through to the assistance command compound, and crossed the river, only to fall back when they could not breach the Citadel's massive walls. The Americans, reinforced to regimental strength, concentrated on clearing the area south of the river. In carrying out this task, which they completed on 9 February, the Marines sought to minimize civilian casualties and destruction of property by using tear gas and employing direct fire weapons that could be aimed precisely. The fighting south of the river, the Marines reported, resulted in 1,053 enemy dead.

In the old city, Vietnamese forces did most of the fighting, though a Marine battalion assisted for a time. On 24 February, the flag of the Republic of Vietnam was raised over the battered Citadel. Mopping up—killing or capturing the North Vietnamese troops who held out among the rubble—lasted until 2 March.

Recapturing Hue required 13 Vietnamese and three Marine battalions. Five U.S. Army battalions assisted by disrupting the enemy's routes of supply and reinforcement. Clouds and rain prevented air power from being of much assistance during the fighting.[16]

The extent of the enemy's Tet offensive—that it was carried out on so vast a scale—had not been anticipated. According to General Ginsburgh, who was working with Dr. Rostow in the White House situation room, "We probably did not pay sufficient credence to . . . the element of their campaign which talked about an uprising in the cities. We paid less attention . . . than we should have probably because it didn't look like such a campaign would be effective."[17]

Precisely what the enemy had in mind as the goal of the Tet offensive was not clear. The general uprising in which the North Vietnamese seem to have placed their hopes, proved more myth than reality. However, the notion that a society or social class can be maneuvered into a situation where revolution is inevitable has been common to both European and Asian Communism. After their successful revolution in 1917, the victorious Bolsheviks had also expected a spontaneous and successful uprising of the German proletariat. Similarly, the Vietnamese Communists may have really believed the South Vietnamese people were on the verge of revolt.[18]

Whatever Hanoi's actual hopes and beliefs, the Tet Offensive failed to trigger a general uprising. It did, however, disrupt South Vietnamese society, destroying thousands of homes, and creating 470,000 frightened refugees whose needs for food and shelter threatened to inundate the Saigon government. At Hue, hardest hit of the republic's cities, reporter Robert Shaplen found destruction and despair worse than he had encountered during World War II or the Korean conflict. Nearly 4,000 civilians had perished in the fighting there, 2,800 of them executed by the North Vietnamese and Viet Cong, and 90,000 persons required food or shelter. The Communists, moreover, had looted the city treasury, sabotaged public utilities, and made away with important records. "Not only is Hue's spirit broken," Shaplen wrote, "it is a bureaucratic mess."

The administrative tangle was soon unsnarled, however, and the destitute

Aerial view of Hue shows the six-square-kilometer Citadel surrounded by three-meter-thick walls. Shiny aluminum roofs show where dwellings were repaired or replaced after the Tet offensive

of Hue received not only food but more than $1.5 million in construction materials for building new homes. After a year's absence, Mr. Shaplen returned to Hue and found that the North Vietnamese, as a result of their Tet savagery, "had lost more than they gained." This judgment held true, he believed, not for Hue alone but for all of South Vietnam.[19]

The moral impact of the Tet offensive thus worked to the disadvantage of the North Vietnamese and Viet Cong. But the physical results of the fighting may have been even more damaging to the Communist cause. American intelligence estimated that 37,000 of the 68,000 troops who launched the nationwide series of attacks were killed during the first 30 days. The Tet offensive also had an effect on American policymakers, and this will be discussed in a later chapter.[20]

The widespread Communist attacks upon South Vietnam's cities and towns raised questions as to the enemy's objective at Khe Sanh. One observer, Sir Robert Thompson, a participant in Britain's successful pacification of Malaya, subsequently suggested that the enemy's purpose in massing forces in the farthest reaches of I Corps was to lure U.S. units away from South Vietnam's cities, which then became vulnerable to the Tet attacks. President Johnson, however, did not believe Hanoi was making a feint in the northwest; as late as mid-February he alluded to a "Route 9 offensive" in which the enemy hoped "to plant his flag on the free soil of the Republic of Vietnam." Similarly, General Westmoreland, a year after the battle, described the siege of Khe Sanh as "an integral part of a nationwide offensive" designed to demoralize the South Vietnamese armed forces, to gain control of the cities or failing that to seize Quang Tri and Thua Thien provinces, and to "create another Dien Bien Phu which would have a demoralizing effect on the American people and cause them to lose heart."[21]

February: The Critical Month

The launching of the Tet offensive throughout South Vietnam brought no relaxation of the pressure against Khe Sanh. Reports transmitted by electronic sensors during the early hours of 5 February indicated that the North Vietnamese were moving into position for an attack against Hill 881S. Appropriately placed artillery concentrations thwarted this operation, but enemy troops that same morning stormed Hill 861A.

A heavy bombardment rocked the combat base, but the main position nevertheless fired every available artillery piece in support of the hill's defenders. Marines at the outpost blazed away with their weapons and also used tear gas as the enemy tried to penetrate the defensive barbed wire. Some of the assault troops succeeded in entering the Marine perimeter, but prompt counterattacks either killed them or drove them from the hill.[22]

As the fighting at Hill 861A was coming to an end, an Air Force C-130E, piloted by Lt. Col. Howard M. Dallman touched down at Khe Sanh with a load of ammunition. Also on board was an aeromedical evacuation team. When an enemy shell ignited some of the munitions, Lieutenant Colonel Dallman taxied the plane off the runway and ordered the medical team to take cover. Assisted by the flight engineer, Charles F. Brault, and loadmaster Wade H. Green, the pilot extinguished the flames. After a tire pierced by a shell splinter had been repaired, Lieutenant Colonel Dallman and his copilot, Capt. Roland F. Behnke, managed to start a turbine that had stalled out because of concussion from a shellburst. They got the plane into the air, and the navigator,

Lt. Col. H. M. Dallman, USAF, landed at Khe Sanh with a load of ammunition while the base was under enemy fire

Maj. Gerold O. Johnson, set a course for Da Nang where the plane landed safely.[23]

Although the shelling of Khe Sanh and its outposts continued, 3 days elapsed before the enemy again probed Marine defenses. During the interim, he struck for a second time at the Lang Vei Special Forces camp. Some 10 months earlier, in May 1967, enemy soldiers disguised as South Vietnamese irregulars had managed to enter the camp. Though they failed to capture it, the episode did persuade the Green Berets that the existing campsite was ill chosen. To obtain better fields of observation and fire, Special Forces headquarters at Da Nang decided to rebuild the camp on Highway 9 about 1,000 meters west of the old site. From this new location, South Vietnamese and Montagnards could continue to patrol the Laos-South Vietnam border.[24]

Actually patrols were few during the late months of 1967. Reports of extensive infiltration across the Xe Pone River, which here separates Laos from South Vietnam, convinced Capt. Frank C. Willoughby, commander of the Lang Vei Special Forces detachment, that first priority should go to improving the camp's defenses. The wisdom of this decision was confirmed when refugees from the Laotian battalion driven from Ban Houaysan came straggling into Lang Vei.

At the beginning of February, the camp boasted excellent defenses against infantry attack and some protection against armor, which the enemy had used at Ban Houaysan. The camp consisted of five mutually supporting positions, each protected by barbed wire, trip flares, and claymore mines—the last being electrically fired weapons, mounted on standards, which spewed fragments horizontally when triggered by the defenders. The camp had its own 4.2-inch, 81-mm, and 60-mm mortars and could call for fire support from Marine batteries at Khe Sanh and from Army artillery farther to the east. Antitank defenses consisted of two 106-mm recoilless rifles, four 57-mm recoilless weapons which were of little value against stoutly armored vehicles, and 100 M-72 light antitank assault weapons—disposable, preloaded rocket launchers that in effect were 1-shot bazookas—which proved less than reliable in combat.

During the enemy buildup that preceded the siege of Khe Sanh, General Westmoreland's headquarters asked III Marine Amphibious Force and the 5th Special Forces Group to review their plans for both fire support and reinforcement of Lang Vei. At Khe Sanh Colonel Lownds kept two rifle companies in readiness to move westward to the Special Forces camp either by foot or helicopter. If circumstances warranted, other units would follow. Like the 26th Marines, the Special Forces contingent at Da Nang also maintained a mobile force to go to the assistance of Lang Vei.[25]

Lang Vei's defenses were tested on the morning of 7 February and found wanting. The weapon that made the difference was the PT-76, a 16-ton Russian-built amphibious tank mounting a long-barrelled 76-mm gun. About 11 of these spearheaded the attack, crushing wire barriers for the infantrymen who followed them and blasting defensive positions. Although this first appearance of enemy armor in South Vietnam—thundering into Lang Vei under the light of flares, raising choking clouds of dust—was a shock to the camp's defenders, they fought back gallantly with every weapon available. Fire from one of the 106-mm rifles hit two tanks, setting both on fire, and disabled a third. The M-72 light assault weapons immobilized one and with help from hand grenades destroyed another. Still another tank was abandoned when a nearby PT-76, the one destroyed by M-72 rockets and grenades, burned with its 3-man crew trapped inside.

An Air Force forward air controller checked in shortly after the enemy tanks first appeared. Accompanied by a flareship and a gunship—the former was a cargo plane modified to illuminate targets on the ground, the latter a converted transport that mounted a battery of automatic weapons arranged to fire downward as the plane banked—the controller directed fighter planes against targets radioed him by Captain Willoughby. The strike aircraft carried general purpose bombs, considered less effective in these circumstances than napalm or antipersonnel weapons but nevertheless helpful to the defenders.

Capt. Gerald L. Harrington, the second Air Force forward air controller to appear over the Special Forces camp that morning, found himself peering down at what "looked like the Fourth of July" with "everybody" firing a "Roman candle toward Lang Vei." The captain had to fly beneath a broken overcast which varied from 1,000 to 1,200 feet. He soon discovered that fire from the ground was too intense to permit leisurely scrutiny of the battlefield. "To stay in one position," he later declared, was an invitation to the North Vietnamese to "start shooting you down." Marine artillery shells fired from Khe Sanh added to the danger in the cloudy skies above the embattled camp.[26]

Locating ground targets was extremely difficult. A burning fuel dump led pilots to the camp, but neither the Green Berets nor the controllers overhead had a satisfactory device to mark targets for fighter strikes. What was needed, according to Captain Harrington, was a replacement for the white phosphorous rockets he was carrying, something that would remain clearly visible for 30 minutes. Instructions radioed from the Lang Vei bunker were not precise enough for close-in strikes, but the captain, with help from the ground and from his starlight scope—a night vision device—succeeded in locating several worthwhile targets. The Special Forces radioman told him each time a cannon fired, and he kept watch for sudden bursts of flame that could be the muzzle flash from the gun mounted on the PT-76's.

"I saw what looked like a cannon going off three times," Captain Harrington later reported, "and to the west of there I saw a flame thrower go off. So I figured these must be the bad guys."

He used a rocket to mark this particular target and summoned a twin-jet B-57 medium bomber from above the clouds. The B-57 dropped four bombs, which triggered some 15 secondary explosions and apparently destroyed three tanks.[27]

As time passed, the overcast grew worse and the plight of Lang Vei's defenders more desperate. At about 0245, one of the tanks bulled through the wire of the camp's innermost defenses to lead an attack on the Special Forces operations center and the other bunkers that were still in American hands. According to plan, Captain Willoughby asked Colonel Lownds to send the two rifle companies being kept in readiness at Khe Sanh. The request forced the Marines to choose between turning down the captain or risking serious casualties and almost certain failure. Helicopters could not be used because the North Vietnamese dominated all the night landing zones at Lang Vei. To set out along Highway 9 would invite ambush and probable disaster. To march across country would reduce the likelihood of ambush but take too long. Faced with these alternatives, Generals Cushman and Tompkins agreed to hold the two companies at Khe Sanh.[28]

Shortly after dawn, a relief force did attempt to intervene in the battle. It was organized by three Green Berets—Sfc. Eugene Ashley, Spec. 4 Joel Johnson, and Sgt. Richard H. Allen—from among the Laotian troops who had taken over the old Lang Vei camp after their retreat from Ban Houaysan. The Americans were in communication with Air Force forward air controllers directing strikes in support of their efforts. One Thailand-based controller climbed through the clouds, now extending throughout most of the region from 500 to 1,500 or 2,000 feet, rendezvoused with a flight of Navy A-1's and led the propeller-driven attack planes down through the overcast to batter enemy infantry trying to breach the walls of the command bunker with explosive charges. The A-1's opened fire with 20-mm cannon, blasted the North Vietnamese off the shelter, and followed up with bombs and napalm. Strikes such as these enabled Ashley's group to gain a foothold within the campsite, but fire from enemy-held bunkers forced abandonment of the attack after four heroic but unsuccessful attempts to reach the besieged Americans.[29]

Captain Willoughby decided to make a break for safety at the very time a 50-man Green Beret relief force was preparing to fly to the vicinity of Lang Vei in Marine helicopters and bring out the survivors. In late afternoon, the captain called for air strikes, then dummy runs to keep the enemy's face in the dirt as he and his men fled the shattered bunker. Another survivor, who had been separated from Captain Willoughby's command group, emerged from cover in time to see a helicopter landing part of the relief force at the old Lang Vei camp. He, too, made his way to safety, one of 14 survivors from the 24-man detachment.

Many of the mountain tribesmen who had been based at Lang Vei now sought the protection of the Marine base at Khe Sanh. The defenders, however, had to take into account the same considerations—danger from hostile fire, lack of space, and possibility of enemy infiltration—that had caused misgivings about sheltering earlier groups of refugees. The Leathernecks decided to disarm the irregulars and hold them in a reasonably safe place outside the base until Green Berets arrived to determine which ones were genuine members of Civilian Irregular Defense Groups and therefore eligible to be evacuated.[30]

The capture of Lang Vei was followed by a probe of the quarry position manned by Lieutenant Colonel Mitchell's 1st Battalion, 9th Marines. The enemy objective was an outpost

A Navy A-1 Skyraider is positioned for launch from the attack carrier USS Coral Sea to fly combat missions over Vietnam

some 500 meters west of the battalion's main position. Despite inroads by North Vietnamese foot soldiers, the Marines clung to part of the outpost, and a counterattack after sunrise on 9 February routed the enemy. In this action, the last major ground attack for some 2 weeks, the Marines lost 21 killed but claimed at least 124 North Vietnamese dead.[31]

Besides continuing to pummel Khe Sanh's ground forces with mortars, rockets, and artillery, the enemy made life exceedingly dangerous for the crews of cargo planes bringing in supplies. On 11 February, a Marine KC-130F, loaded with flexible bladders containing jet fuel for use in turbine-powered Marine helicopters, was hit by enemy fire as it approached the runway. Fuel appeared to be streaming from the plane as the pilot made a normal landing, but before worried onlookers could relax, the rolling Lockheed burst into flame and veered from the runway. Pilot and copilot escaped through an overhead hatch, suffering only minor burns, and firefighters rescued at least six passengers or crewmen who were more seriously hurt. Six others burned to death.[32]

This was the most spectacular and deadliest in a series of incidents in which transports, either landing or unloading, were hit by gunfire or shell fragments. Through 10 February, seven Air Force C-130's had thus been damaged, though none were destroyed.[33]

The first of the two Hercules transports hit on 11 February was immobilized but escaped destruction because of the bravery and skill displayed by the pilot, Capt. Edwin Jenks, his crew, a detachment of airmen stationed at Khe Sanh, and a mechanic flown to the Marine base from Da Nang. Captain Jenks' aircraft came under fire as soon as it had begun unloading. Shell fragments severed a hydraulic line in the tail section, and the leaking fluid caught fire. Captain Jenks and his crewmen escaped from the crippled plane and, acting on the instructions of Lt. Col. William R. Smith, senior Air Force officer at the base, took cover from the shells that continued to fall within the Marine perimeter.

SSgt. Robert Mahaffy, a member of Lieutenant Colonel Smith's Air Force detachment, aided by another airman, used a fire extinguisher to put out the flames. However, the airman holding the nozzle was overcome by the chemical fumes and let it slip from his grasp. The hose flopped about, spraying chemicals in the sergeant's face and blinding him. Smith led Mahaffy to the nearby Marine aid station where a member of the Navy medical corps washed out his eyes. Neither of the two men suffered permanent injury.

Once the flames were out and the injured cared for, Lieutenant Colonel Smith moved Captain Jenks and the others from the C-130 to an underground bunker where he distributed among them the detachment's last few cans of beer.

Next, Smith radioed Da Nang for an experienced mechanic and a "rudder package" to replace the damaged portion of the transport's hydraulic system. The mechanic arrived but the parts somehow went astray. Captain Jenks realized that he could not wait for a second hydraulic component to be shipped to Khe Sanh, since each hour spent on the ground multiplied the chances that the $2.5 million aircraft would be destroyed. The pilot therefore decided to try flying the C-130 to Da Nang, after the mechanic had made emergency repairs using tools and materials available at Khe Sanh.

The flight to Da Nang would be a dangerous task since a loss of fluid from the patched hydraulic system at a critical moment could mean death for all on board. Near noon on 13 February the repairs were finished. Jenks and his crew boarded the plane for a takeoff attempt. They succeeded in coaxing the craft into the air, taking advantage of wretched weather—a 50-foot ceiling and horizontal visibility limited to 1,000 feet—to frustrate enemy gun crews. When the C-130 was safely on the ground at Da Nang, mechanics counted 242 holes in the battered transport.[34]

By this time General Momyer had become concerned about the danger to which the C-130's were being exposed in landing at Khe Sanh. The rugged, powerful Lockheeds were, as he later termed them, a "make or break resource" too valuable to risk unnecessarily. From 12 February through the end of March, Air Force C-130's landed at the Marine base on only four days, though they continued to deliver cargo by parachute or by means of extraction systems. Fairchild C-123K's,

Lt. Col. W. R. Smith, USAF, in front of Khe Sanh's base operations and control tower

(Above) A C–123 hit by enemy mortar fire at Khe Sanh

(Below) Air Force medics move a casualty from the aid station on Khe Sanh to a waiting C–130 Hercules, for a flight to Da Nang hospital

the model with auxiliary jet engines, not only took part in the air drop but also landed cargo. Smaller and lighter than the C-130, this plane required less runway to land than did the Lockheed, spent less time taxiing, and therefore offered a poorer target for hostile gunners. It could carry more than 5 tons of cargo, roughly a third of what a C-130E usually landed at Khe Sanh. Also permitted to land at the base were C-7A's with payloads of no more than 3 tons.[35]

By digging trenches, constructing bunkers, and wearing the armored vests issued them, the Marines saved many lives that would otherwise have been lost. But men continued to die at Khe Sanh. On Washington's birthday, for example, a random shell scored a direct hit on a bunker, killing Chaplain Robert B. Brett and his clerk. An estimated 1,300 shells battered Khe Sanh on 23 February, a record for a single day, and one of them detonated an ammunition dump destroying more than 1,500 90-mm and 106-mm rounds. This day's holocaust killed eight of the defenders. Several days later, on the 25th, 26 Marines died when a patrol was ambushed.[36]

The 1,300 rounds fired into Khe Sanh on the 23d represented the heaviest enemy bombardment of the war to that date. Prior to the Khe Sanh fight, the greatest daily concentration of enemy rockets and shells had been the 1,065 rounds that fell on 2 July 1967 during fighting around Con Thien, a Marine base just south of the demilitarized zone. The North Vietnamese, however, had divided the shelling between Con Thien—hit by some 700 shells—and a similar strongpoint at nearby Gio Linh.[37]

Great as the weight of metal and high explosive hurled at Khe Sanh was, the North Vietnamese proved unable or unwilling to mount an assault on the main base. Although they did push trenches to within 350 feet of Marine lines, on occasion digging farther than 100 meters in a single night, the anticipated all-out attack did not materialize. Indeed, a probe of the sector held by the South Vietnamese 37th Ranger Battalion ended in disaster for the enemy. After removal of some mines from in front of the Ranger position—a task done with such cunning that not a single trip flare was ignited—a North Vietnamese battalion surged forward into a maelstrom of bursting shells, automatic weapons fire, and exploding bombs. Halted well short of his objective—the point of farthest advance was marked by seven corpses in and around the defensive wire—the North Vietnamese broke off the action before daylight of 1 March, leaving behind 60 to 70 dead.[38]

Within the base the troops remained alert. Rumor had it that the North Vietnamese were burrowing beneath the plateau and would emerge at a designated time within the perimeter as their comrades rushed the outer defenses. Another concern was that the besiegers of Khe Sanh might deny the Marines the use of the Rao Quan River, which served as the sole source of drinking water for the main base and wandered for miles through enemy-held territory.[39]

Despite misgivings such as these and the continued shelling, by 1 March Khe Sanh had endured the worst of the battle, even though the enemy had not yet begun to fall back. Air power had sustained the Marines in bad weather and now the cloud cover was breaking up. Strange to say, the brightening of the skies over Khe Sanh coincided with a pall of gloom that settled over elements of the American press.

Press Reaction to the Continuing Siege

The continuing battle for Khe Sanh inspired many American commentators to compare, somewhat belatedly, the situation at Khe Sanh with conditions at Dien Bien Phu. *Life* magazine, for example, listed three events that had "cast doubt on the usefulness of our military might as an instrument of our Asian policies." They were North Korea's capture of the U.S. intelligence ship *Pueblo* on 23 January 1968, the Tet offensive, and the "looming bloodbath at Khe Sanh."[40]

Arthur Schlesinger, Jr., historian and onetime member of President John F. Kennedy's staff, wrote an open letter urging that: "Whatever we do, we must not re-enact Dien Bien Phu." Mr. Schlesinger's letter, printed in the *Washington Post* on 22 March, dismissed as folly the notion that an American-held Khe Sanh could have any effect on infiltration as long as the Marines were immobilized there. After noting that air power had thus far

View of Khe Sanh from the cockpit of a C-130 transport delivering supplies to U.S. Marines

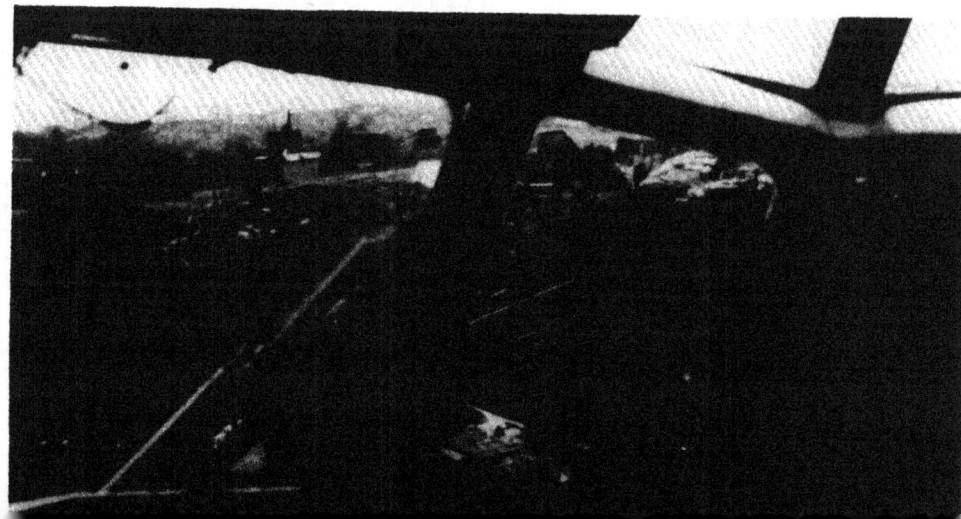

made the difference at Khe Sanh, he recommended that the Air Force evacuate the Marines before the airfield was so churned up by shell fire as to become useless. He reminded his readers that enemy antiaircraft could dominate the aerial approaches to Khe Sanh and fend off American planes while "shock troops" overwhelmed the defenders. "Let us not," he pleaded, "sacrifice our brave men to the folly of generals and the obstinacy of Presidents." [41]

In a *New Republic* article, Oliver E. Clubb, Jr., a specialist in the field of Asian politics, joined Mr. Schlesinger in pointing out that a besieged Khe Sanh could not impede enemy infiltration through the northwestern corner of South Vietnam. He concluded therefore that the base was being defended for reasons "not worth the life of a single Marine," and that the decision to make a stand there "could easily end in a military disaster unprecedented in the Vietnam War." [42]

James Burnham, a member of the staff of William F. Buckley's *National Review*, strove for balance as he declared that "Khe Sanh looks like a mistake for our side." He based this somewhat tentative judgment on his belief that a "static defense"—especially one that tied down Marine units trained expressly for offensive operations—was a "defective concept." He refused, however, to abandon hope, raising the possibility that General Giap himself might have fallen "into a trap that has caught many another

aging commander: the dream of replaying a triumph of his earlier days—in Giap's case the dream of a second Dien Bien Phu." He also called attention to an interview, reported originally by Gene Roberts of the *New York Times*, in which an American officer had cited control of key terrain, "massive air power, and adequate artillery" as being the difference between failure at Dien Bien Phu and eventual victory at Khe Sahn.[43]

Although some individuals like Mr. Schlesinger gave way to gloom and others were cautiously hopeful like Mr. Burnham, still others were confident of an American victory. Among this last group was S. L. A. Marshall, an army reserve brigadier general as well as a syndicated columnist. He complained that some commentators looked at Khe Sanh and thought only of Dien Bien Phu. For his part, he endorsed the view, which he attributed to General Walt, that the Marine base was "a viable position with little or no risk of entrapment.[44]

Even as these writers were issuing their conflicting pronouncements, the actual threat to Khe Sanh had begun to recede. The Marine defenders were poised on the threshold of victory, brought there in large part by air power. Intelligence obtained through such varied means as reconnaissance patrols and electronic sensors enabled fighter-bombers and B-52's to ring the base with bursting bombs. While this heavy pounding of the besieging force went on, cargo planes continued to defy weather and the enemy to sustain Khe Sanh's 6,000 men.

IV. AN AERIAL HIGHWAY

When the siege of Khe Sanh began, General McLaughlin's 834th Air Division consisted of some 7,500 men and 240 transports, including planes and crews on temporary duty in South Vietnam as well as those performing other duties but available for emergency airlift missions. On hand in late January were six C-7A squadrons with 81 aircraft, four C-123 squadrons totalling 58 planes, and three C-130 detachments with 72 transports. All Air Force C-130's in South Vietnam were on temporary duty from the 315th Air Division, with headquarters at Tachikawa, Japan. After the start of the enemy's Tet offensive, Air Force C-130 strength was increased to 88 planes in February and 96 in March. Had the Khe Sanh situation grown worse, another 21 planes—UC-123's used to spray herbicide in the defoliation program—could have been reconverted to serve as transports.

By way of contrast, in November 1953 the French had been hard pressed to find 65 C-47's to drop paratroops at Dien Bien Phu; in March of the following year, when the siege actually began, only 124 transports were available to them. The French managed to parachute a daily average of 100 tons to the beleagured garrison throughout its 56-day ordeal. Theoretically, General McLaughlin could deliver six times as much, but maintenance requirements, the time needed to rig loads, and other considerations would cut this tonnage about in half.[1]

About one-third of the airmen serving under General McLaughlin were members of an aerial port group. Made up of three squadrons, this organization furnished cargo handling detachments at 42 locations throughout South Vietnam. Keeping track of the network of port detachments and the rapidly shuttling transport planes was the job of McLaughlin's airlift control center, which had operating elements at 18 airfields where large amounts of cargo were shipped or received.[2]

Principal source of supplies destined for the Marines in I Corps was Da Nang. Air Force C-123's and Marine KC-130's based there were only half an hour by air from the embattled base. General McLaughlin's command sent maintenance specialists and mission coordinators to Da Nang to permit more efficient use of that crowded airfield, but most C-130 missions continued to originate at Tan Son Nhut, Cam Rahn Bay, Tuy Hoa, and Nha Trang, where crew quarters and aircraft maintenance facilities were located. Although the home bases had facilities for crew rest and C-130 refurbishment, the flight time from Tan Son Nhut was 95 minutes, Cam Ranh Bay 75 minutes, and Tuy Hoa 1 hour. By way of comparison, during the Dien Bien Phu fighting, French C-47's taking off from Bach Mai airfield near Hanoi reached the battlefield in an average time of about 75 minutes.[3]

Whatever the distance covered, Air Force and Marine crews sooner or later had to fly those last deadly miles through a ring of antiaircraft fire. The danger was present whether the incoming planes actually touched wheels to runway, parachuted cargo from an altitude of a few hundred feet, or skimmed low over the airstrip to use a cargo extraction system. Enemy gunners would even fire through smokescreens into the flight path they thought an approaching cargo craft might follow. American strike aircraft helped reduce the volume and accuracy of flak but could not silence the guns completely. One C-130 navigator, who served for more than a year in South Vietnam, stated that the "ground-to-air fire was . . . heavier and closer to the aircraft during a landing approach at Khe Sanh than at any other time and place" during his tour.[4]

Even before the North Vietnamese encirclement, landing a C-130 at Khe Sanh was no easy task. In good weather pilots sometimes found it difficult to judge distance when their final approach carried them over the deep ravine at the east end of the runway. In bad weather, Khe Sanh became surprisingly hard to locate. As late as December 1967, airborne radar had picked up a fairly good return from structures built on the surface of the plateau, but as the likelihood of a prolonged battle increased, the Marines burrowed into the soil, and the echo became progressively poorer.[5]

Fortunately, pilots could rely for assistance on a ground controlled approach radar installed at Khe Sanh, operated by a Marine air traffic control unit. Another Marine radar, a TPQ-10 set, was available in case of emergency. An air support radar team normally used the TPQ-10 to direct air strikes.

General McLaughlin, commander, 834th Air Division. He won his second star in August 1968

Landing under Fire

When the fight for Khe Sanh began, Air Force transports and Marine aerial tankers were able to land to unload their passengers and cargo. For a short time after destruction of the ammunition dump on 21 January, damage to the runway closed the field to planes larger than C-123's, but the C-130's soon were back on the job. As the tempo of combat picked up, landings became increasingly hazardous until the Marines were calling the transports "mortar magnets" and "rocket bait" because they unfailingly attracted hostile fire as they taxied to the unloading area.[6]

Even after the aircraft had landed safely, men and planes remained vulnerable to small arms and shell fire. Crews of C-123K's enjoyed a slight advantage over those who flew the larger C-130's. The lighter Fairchild could lose enough momentum within 1,400 feet of touching down near the eastern threshold of the runway to permit a 90-degree turn. Seldom did one of these planes miss the first of two turnoffs that led to the unloading area,

a narrow metal-surfaced lane parallel to the main runway and located near its western terminus.

The Lockheeds, however, required a roll of almost 2,000 feet which meant that these Hercules transports frequently screeched past both turn-offs, had to continue to the west end of the runway, risk hits from enemy small arms while turning around, and taxi back to one of the exits. Thus, the enemy had repeated opportunities to destroy the C-130's.[7]

The transport crews used a technique called "speed offloading" to reduce the time they spent on the ground at Khe Sanh. The key piece of equipment was a pair of 7-foot metal runners fitted to the ramp at the rear of the cargo compartment. Within that compartment, the individually bundled loads were attached to pallets, measuring 108 by 88 inches, which rested upon metal rollers built into the floor. Two parallel guide rails kept the platforms centered and, on C-130's, contained a locking system that held the loads firmly in place. The C-123's had no such locking device; its pallets were secured by chains.

After a transport landed, the loadmaster could attach the metal runners and lower the ramp as the pilot taxied toward the unloading area. At Khe Sanh, however, the procedure was different. Usually a member of the Air Force detachment at the base selected a pair of runners stored beside the taxiway and attached them to the plane. This was necessary because the runners were in short supply and might not be carried by every transport landing at the base.

In the unloading area, the loadmaster unlocked the pallets or released the chains so that the forward motion of the aircraft—aided if necessary by a vigorous shove—sent the pallets to the rear of the cargo compartment out the open hatch, and down the ramp to the ground. Unloading a transport with forklifts could take between 5 and 10

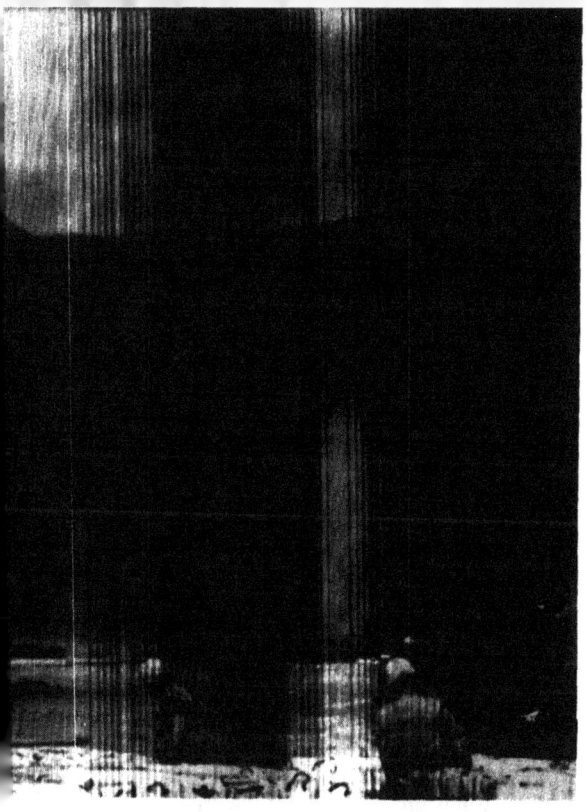

A C-130 lands with a load of ammunition while fighter aircraft attack enemy forces spotted moving along the mountainside

minutes; speed offloading could be finished in as little as half a minute.

Both C-123's and C-130's used the same pallets, made of aluminum and plywood for a standard cargo handling system. The cargo hold in the C-123 was too narrow to accommodate the 108-inch width of the pallet. Since the plane could handle a width of 88 inches, the platforms were simply turned and loaded sideways.[8]

Khe Sanh Marines found the light and sturdy platforms ideal for use in roofing bunkers. Because incoming planes seldom had time to reclaim the empty pallets, a large number of the expensive platforms, worth roughly $350 each, accumulated near the taxiway. The Air Force contingent at the base tried, with the help of Marine guards, to prevent their loss but the prevailing fog made this extremely difficult. Visibility often was so limited that individuals could spirit away the platforms with practically no likelihood of being detected.[9]

Being struck by a bullet or shell fragment was not the only hazard awaiting aircraft landing at Khe Sanh. Shells bursting on the runway left shards from their casings and jagged chunks of metal planking that could pierce the tires of taxiing planes. Among the most important work done by Air Force personnel at Khe Sanh was changing tires, often at considerable risk, so that the transports could get back into the air before shells or rockets converted them to junk. Some indication of the rigors of landing at the base may be gleaned from the fact that during the 10-week siege the life expectancy of C-130 tires in use throughout Vietnam declined from 30 sorties to 18.[10]

The dangers encountered on the ground by the C-130's, the newest and largest Air Force tactical transports, persuaded General Momyer to forbid landing the valuable planes at Khe Sanh, a ban that remained in force from 12 through 25 February. During this period, 58 C-123K sorties landed almost 300 tons of cargo, and C-7A's landed eight times to deliver 13 tons. On 25 February, the C-130's resumed landing, but only until the end of the month. This 4-day burst of activity consisted of 14 C-130 landings which deposited slightly more than 160 tons in the Khe Sanh unloading area. During March, C-123K's were the only cargo craft to touch down at the Marine base. The C-130's, however, continued to deliver cargo either by parachute or using an extraction system.[11]

The men who flew the C-123K's —only this model, with its pod-mounted auxiliary jet engines, landed at the base—depended for their survival on speed and precision. The pilot had to use a steep landing approach to reduce exposure to enemy fire. He would begin his descent about 5 kilometers from the field, dropping with flaps extended at the rate of 3,000 feet per minute along a 4½ degree glide path. All fliers preferred to approach from the east because the unloading zone lay near the west end of the runway. A transport pilot landing from the west could not slow down in time for either turnoff leading to the unloading zone. He would have to turn around at the eastern end and taxi almost the length of the flight strip before unloading.

Once on the ground, a C-123K pilot could not reverse his propellers because this would automatically shut down the two jet powerplants needed for the steep ascent that would get him quickly out of range of hostile gunners. While the rolling plane lost momentum, the loadmaster went through the speed offloading procedures as the pilot turned from the runway and taxied slowly through the unloading area.

The outward bound passengers crouched behind cargo handling equipment, or whatever else offered them protection until the transport was empty, then hurried aboard. The pilot continued to the western taxiway, turned into the runway facing east, and took off in the opposite direction from which he had landed. Three minutes was the usual time between touchdown and retraction of the landing gear as the plane again rose skyward, but a rare C-123K could land, unload, take on passengers, and take off in 1 minute or slightly less.[12]

Sometimes speed and precision were not enough. On 1 March for instance, a mortar shell burst near a C-123K that was gathering speed for its takeoff. Fragments struck one of the piston engines, the propeller began windmilling, and the plane veered from the runway to burst into flame. The transport was destroyed, but incredibly the only casualty was the loadmaster, who hurt his back. Not long afterward another C-123K incurred damage that kept it at Khe Sanh overnight. Before repairs could be made, a North Vietnamese mortar crew scored a direct hit, starting a blaze that consumed the plane.[13]

Weather permitting, fighters directed by a forward air controller flew flak suppression runs as the cargo planes approached Khe Sanh. Without these strikes, transport losses would have soared and Khe Sanh's survival might have been imperiled. Even with fighter protection, landing was a dangerous and exhausting job. There were days when clouds kept the fighters grounded but did not prevent the transports—large, alone, and vulnerable—from making radar-controlled approaches.[14]

On the afternoon of 6 March, a C-123K bound for Khe Sanh took a hit in its port jet engine even before it had begun its descent. The pilot advised the base control tower that he was turning back to Da Nang, but within minutes a cloud of smoke rose over the hills east of the combat base. A forward air controller and helicopter pilots investigated but found no survivors. The crash claimed 48 lives— the 4-man Air Force crew, 1 Navy man, and 43 Marines.[15]

Supply by Parachute

The battle had scarcely begun when General McLaughlin and his staff realized that because of weather and enemy opposition they would be unable to land enough cargo-laden transports to supply the Khe Sanh garrison and that sizeable quantities of supplies would have to be dropped by parachute. This method of delivery employed the so-called container delivery system, something of a misnomer since the item dropped was actually a bundle—a ton of ammunition, food, or fuel—covered with a shroud and lashed securely to a wooden pallet. A C-130 could carry from 14 to 16 of these loads, which rested on the rollers in the floor of the cargo compartment. The loadmaster released the restraints holding the bundles in place, and the pilot raised the nose of the plane just slightly, increased power, and let the cargo roll out the open door. A small parachute attached to each bundle opened in the slipstream and deployed a larger canopy that lowered the cargo to earth.[16]

On 25 and 28 January C-130's parachuted 67 tons of ammunition, petroleum products, and rations to the men defending Khe Sanh. These five missions demonstrated that large quantities of bulky items could be delivered rapidly by parachute. The Marines, however, continued to harbor doubts concerning two vital aspects of parachute delivery—accuracy in bad weather and the ability of the garrison to recover enough of the bundles to make the drops worthwhile.[17]

Obviously radar in some form would solve the accuracy problem. A possible solution was a ground-radar aerial delivery system which had been the subject of experiments at Pope Air Force Base, North Carolina. Unfortunately, this system required drops from high altitude, which led inevitably to greater dispersion than was acceptable at Khe Sanh.[18]

The principles of the system tried at Pope—radar guidance from the ground combined with precise timing by the plane's navigator—could, however, be applied at Khe Sanh. Operators of the ground-controlled approach radar at the Marine base were able to provide the incoming pilot with a westward heading and prescribe a path of descent that would bring the plane over the runway's eastern threshold at a specific altitude.[19]

Here the navigator would take over. He used the plane's doppler navigation system and a stopwatch to guide the craft to a computed release point where the loads were to be dropped. To reach this point, the navigator first needed to calculate the wind speed and direction and the ground speed of the aircraft. After thus compensating for drift, he had to consult a timing chart that showed the time to release point at various ground speeds—24.8 seconds, for example, from runway threshold to release point at 135 knots. While timing the run, the navigator would give the pilot heading corrections to keep the plane aligned with the plot of earth where the cargo was to fall. Because the drop zone was only 300 yards long, an error of 1 second in timing, or a similarly small mistake in alignment could cause the load to miss completely. So important was team work that each pilot and navigator had to fly a training mission to Khe Sanh in order to become acquainted with instrument procedures before they were allowed to attempt an actual delivery.

At the release point, the pilot would increase power, thus nudging the unsecured cargo to the rear and out the door. He could not pull up, as was usually done in good weather, because experience at Khe Sanh indicated that smooth acceleration made for better accuracy under instrument conditions than did changing the altitude of the aircraft.[20]

The first use of this improvised system took place on 13 February. A spell of bad weather soon demonstrated the value of radar control. On the 17th and 18th, the only planes in the air over Khe Sanh were the Air Force transports which delivered 279 tons of supplies in 18 drops.[21]

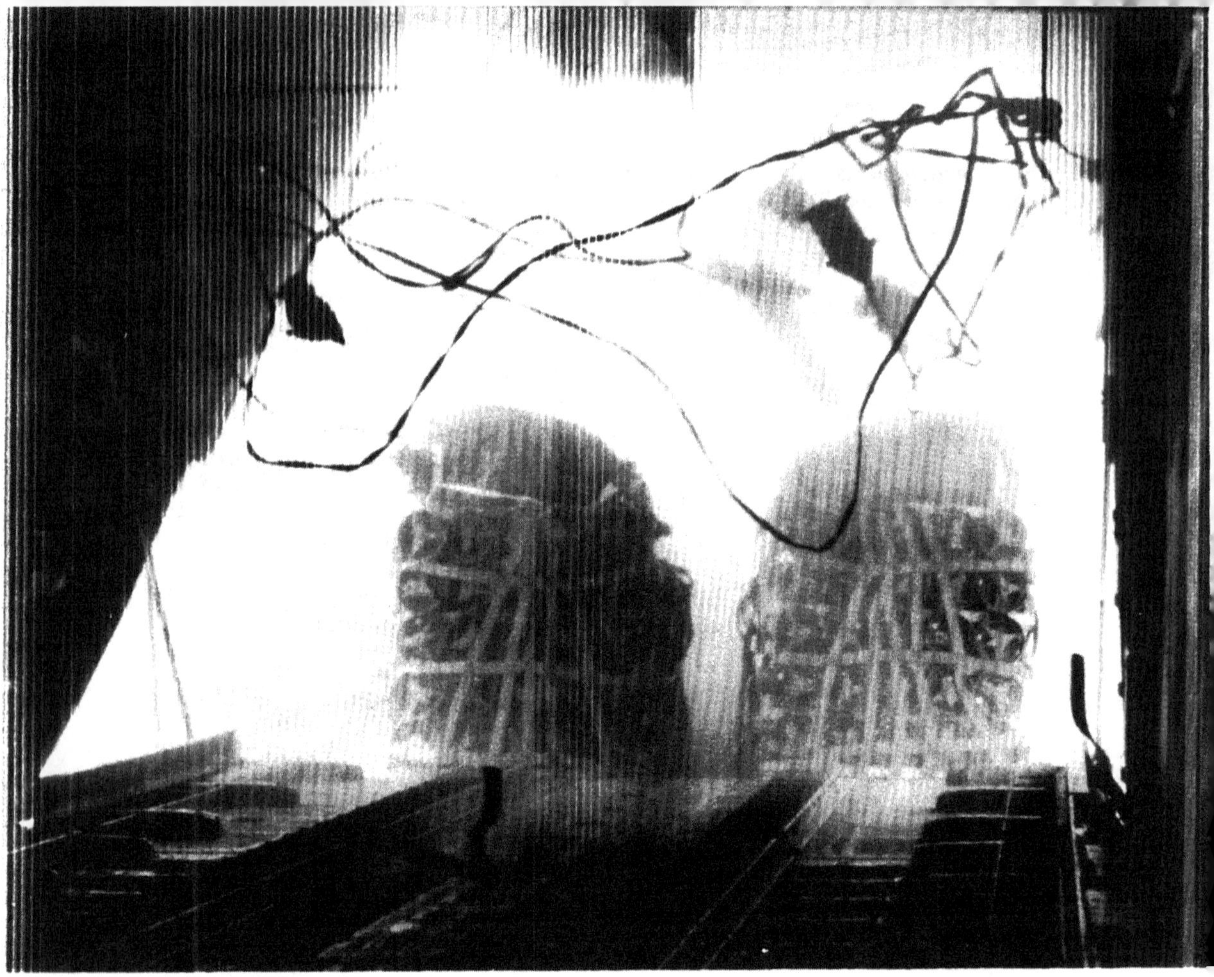

Aerial
Resupply
of
Khe Sanh

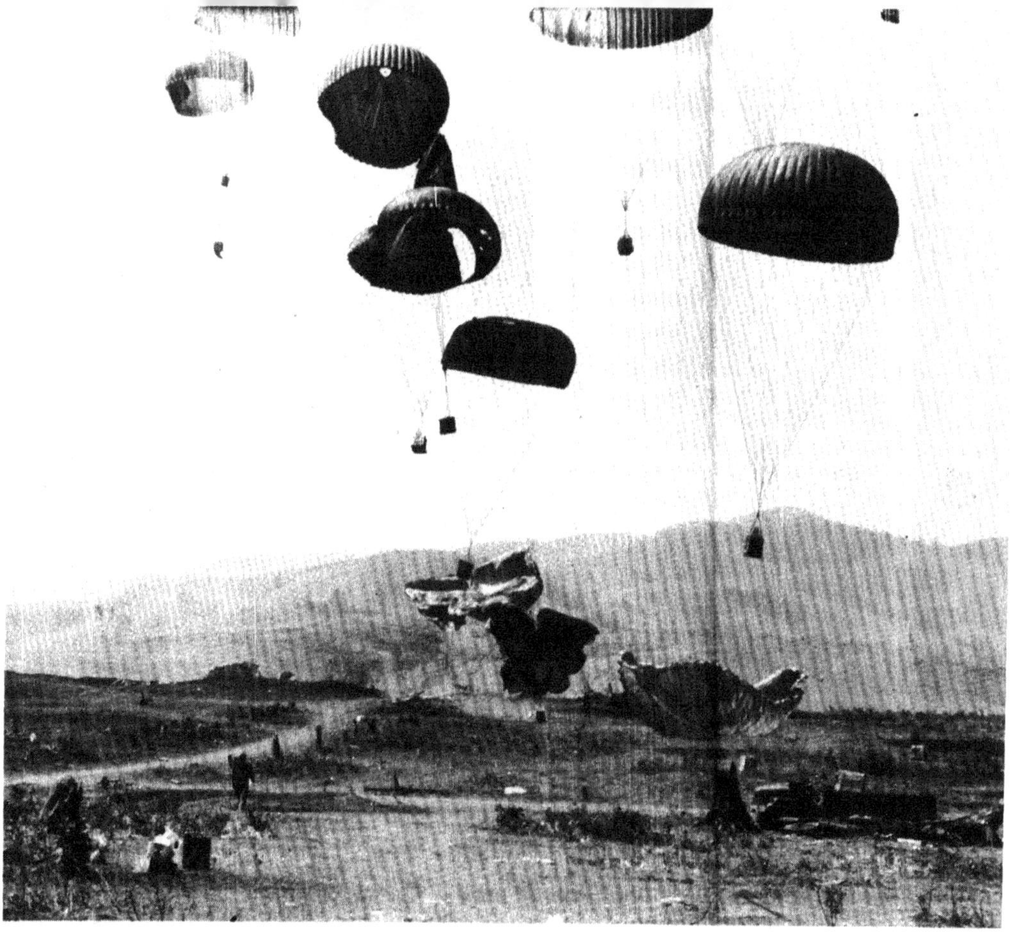

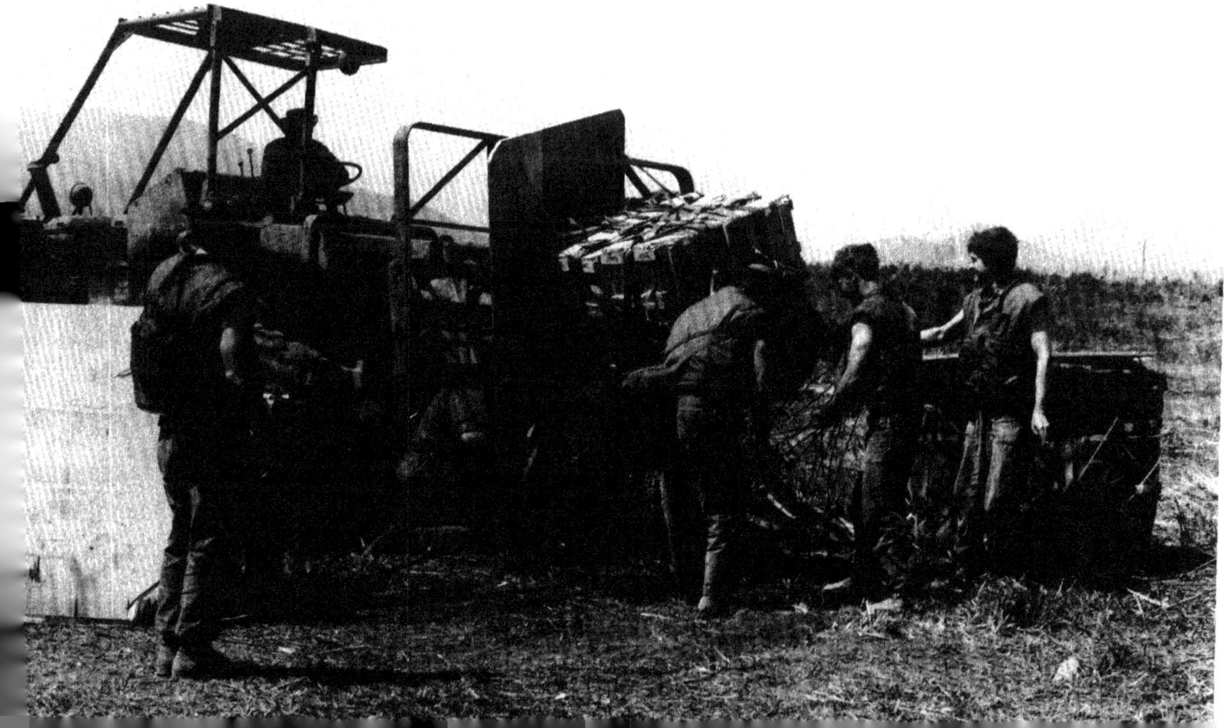

Such was the procedure for dropping cargo when flying on instruments. A typical foul weather drop of this sort was made on 16 February by a C-130 from the 779th Tactical Airlift Squadron. The plane, piloted by Capt. Ronald C. Spivey, crossed the runway threshold at 130 knots airspeed and 400 feet altitude. During the few seconds between threshold and release point, the navigator, Capt. Peter F. Drugan, spotted an error in the heading prescribed by the ground controller, and the loadmaster, SSgt. George Arleth, Jr., noticed that the loads were not properly rigged. Around came the plane for a second pass, boring through what the squadron historian described as "a hail of lead thrown up from entrenched machine guns," to release at precisely that invisible point in the sky which brought the cargo to earth within the selected target area. Other crewmembers who contributed to this success were 1st Lt. John Howder, the copilot, and TSgt. Lawrence R. Ervin, flight engineer.[22]

This method was accurate, with a circular error average of 83 yards in drops on 17 and 18 February. On the following day, however, a North Vietnamese shell destroyed the radar upon which the system depended. This setback came as no surprise. Tests conducted in anticipation of just such an event had shown that the Marine TPQ-10 radar, installed at Khe Sanh to control fighter strikes, could serve as an adequate substitute, even though it could not by itself guide an approaching transport to the desired point above the east end of the runway. Needed supplementary aids were readily available. Radar reflectors placed along the runway improved the accuracy of the sets installed in the cargo planes. TACAN (Tactical Air Navigation) readings, which located the aircraft in relation to broadcasting stations on the ground, were an additional help, as were a radio beacon transponder and low frequency beacon installed at Khe Sanh.[23]

The Air Force, using Marine radar, thus solved the weather problem, but there remained still another major difficulty in delivering cargo by parachute—providing an adequate drop zone. The ideal solution was to drop within the main perimeter, but not enough space was available. The location finally chosen lay beyond the western end of the runway between the base itself and the position manned by 1st Battalion, 9th Marines. Responsibility for protecting the drop zone rested with this battalion which, with the assistance of Marine engineers, checked each morning for mines planted by the enemy under cover of darkness.[24]

Because the security of the drop zone was so precarious, the Marines could not leave bundles of cargo lying there overnight lest the North Vietnamese seize the chance to plant booby traps. Loads had to be retrieved quickly, but the garrison had few trucks or forklifts. As a result, the Marines insisted that one drop be cleared away before the next began and also that there be ample time for a final cleanup at day's end. Initially the Marines called for 1 hour between drops with no cargo dropped after 1500, but they came to accept a half-hour interval with no drop after 1600.[25]

The C-130's and C-123's that parachuted supplies onto the Khe Sanh drop zone attained enviable accuracy. The C-130's, for example, boasted a circular error average of 110 yards for 496 sorties in good weather and bad. The Lockheeds made 148 sorties on instruments for a circular error average of 133 yards, and 308 in good weather for an average of only 95 yards.[26]

Yet, some bundles did miss the drop zone. Those that drifted into enemy territory were destroyed by bombs or shells to prevent the North Vietnamese from seizing the supplies they carried. Others that strayed over Marine positions could land with a devastating impact, as happened on 2 March when errant containers flattened bunkers and injured five men in the perimeter held by the 1st Battalion, 9th Marines.[27]

When there were inaccurate drops, officers at 834th Air Division headquarters—navigators whenever possible—conducted post-mortems. On occasion these investigators found errors in correcting for drift, but at other times the fault could only be attributed to "abnormal crosswinds" in the ravine at the end of the runway. Still others were the result of failure by the ground radar to position the plane accurately before yielding control to the navigator.[28]

Cargo Extraction Systems

McLaughlin's staff also searched for a method of delivering heavy timbers for the garrison's construction projects. Loading the timbers into a C-130 transport, landing at the base, and unloading was out of the question. Landings had become too hazardous and there was no suitable unloading equipment at Khe Sanh. Some thought was given to delivering the timbers by large parachutes designed for exceptionally heavy loads, but this proved infeasible. The existing drop zone was too small for the purpose and too far from the construction sites. Manhandling the cargo from the drop zone to the main perimeter would certainly draw fire and result in casualties. Airmen and Marines agreed that the only solution was to use an extraction system, as had been done the previous year when the Seabees were repairing the runway.[29]

Available for immediate use was the low altitude parachute extraction system, used at Khe Sanh in the summer of 1967 and reintroduced on 16 February 1968. The system required the pilot to bring his C-130 down the axis of the runway at an airspeed of 130 knots and an altitude of just 5 feet. Trailing through the open unloading door was a parachute reefed to a diameter of 48 inches. Upon reaching a point calculated to deposit the cargo on the westernmost 750 feet of the runway, the crew electrically fired a squib that burst the reefing line and allowed the parachute to open to its full diameter of 28 feet. The sudden drag created by the chute broke the restraints holding the load inside the airplane. The pilot, in effect, flew from under the special sled-like pallet to which cargo and parachute were attached, allowing the load to drop to the runway and skid to a halt.[30]

The low altitude parachute extraction system was accurate but not foolproof, and an accident could turn the packaged cargo into a 10-ton missile. On one mission, for example, the parachute opened fully, but the pallet did not budge. The loadmaster, who had little experience with this system, jettisoned the chute but not quickly enough, for the load was by now moving through the open door. With no parachute to slow it, the pallet slid a distance of 1,500 meters, crashed into a bunker, and killed a Marine.[31]

Parachute extraction could be dangerous for air crews as well as the men on the ground. The wreckage of the C-123 destroyed on 1 March lay on the southern edge of the runway, in such a position that it was an obstacle to an unwary pilot employing the parachute extraction technique. Besides weather and enemy fire, the men who flew the transports had to contend with the possibility of collision.

From the outset, the Marines had expressed concern over the punishment inflicted on the runway by the heavy

The Air Force employed a low altitude parachute extraction system (above) and a ground proximity extraction system (lower r.) to resupply Khe Sanh

loads extracted from the C-130's. Lt. Col. William R. Smith, USAF, mission commander at this time, went to the heart of the matter when he asked: Why save the runway and lose Khe Sanh? The defenders agreed to use the extraction system and, as they had feared, within 4 weeks the heavily-loaded pallets were playing havoc with the runway. Nearly every load gouged out portions of the surface planking and bent the surviving metal so badly that it could not be straightened. The damage was confined, however, to a single 700-foot section at the far western end of the runway and did not pose a threat to the use of the airstrip.[32]

Low altitude parachute extractions continued throughout the siege, with the last two sorties being flown on 2 April. By that time, however, the 834th Air Division had introduced a supplementary method of cargo extraction. The change was necessary because of a lack of equipment for low altitude parachute extractions. The electrical gear used to fire the squib that released the reefing line was critically scarce and there was a less acute shortage of the special steel pallets.[33]

To supplement or, if necessary, replace the parachute extraction system, General McLaughlin and his advisers recommended the ground proximity extraction system, in which cargo was yanked from a rolling aircraft when a hook extending from the cargo compartment engaged an arrester cable rigged across the runway.[34]

In 1966, the Air Force and Army had retired an experimental ground proximity extraction system and ordered replacement equipment that had been redesigned to eliminate the defects that had appeared during testing. Because the low altitude parachute extraction system seemed more versatile, the new gear was never used. Fortunately, 10 sets were located, including one in the hands of the manufacturer, and flown to the western Pacific.[35]

The Army logistic specialists who would rig the loads to be extracted were less than enthusiastic about the assignment. No manuals existed on how the system should function but the Army agreed to do what it could using standard pallets and following whatever rigging procedures might emanate from General McLaughlin's headquarters. A message from the Office of the Commanding General, U.S. Army, Vietnam, warned the 834th Air Division that "the U.S. Army cannot assume/share responsibility for the performance of the system to include damage to aircraft, ground personnel and facilities, or delivered materiel." [36]

After a brief training session at Naha Air Base, Okinawa, the C-130 crews were ready to try the extraction equipment just installed at Khe Sanh. On 30 March, a C-130 approached the airstrip, touched down, and rolled swiftly along the runway. A boom, to which a hook was attached, extended from a loaded pallet through the opening at the rear of the cargo compartment. The huge transport rolled across an arresting cable which then rose to engage the hook and pull the load out of the plane. As soon as the pallet was gone, the pilot accelerated and took off.[37]

However, an unexpected problem arose on this first mission. The Marines who installed the arrester mechanism had drawn fire and were driven to cover before finishing the job. As a result, the load—though probably weighing less than the usual 25,000 pounds—uprooted the moorings that held the cable in place. Luckily, the extraction equipment did its job prior to being itself extracted.[38]

In a congested area like the main base, the ground proximity extraction system had definite advantages over low altitude parachute extraction. With the hook and cable arrangement, the load was always under control. The pallet could not escape from the cargo compartment unless the hook was engaged, and once the load was on the ground the arrester equipment checked its movement. This method, then, was safer than parachute extraction because there was no way to release the pallet too late or too soon, and no parachute to malfunction. Also, the cargo came to rest each time in almost the same place, thus eliminating even the remote possibility of widespread damage to the runway surface.[39]

Airmen on the Ground at Khe Sanh

Present at Khe Sanh during the fighting was a small Air Force contingent that helped control airlift operations, assisted in handling cargo, and made emergency repairs to aircraft. The senior Air Force officer at the base was the mission commander, whose normal tour lasted about 2 weeks, almost all of which was spent at Khe Sanh. A lieutenant colonel, the mission commander had control over all 834th Air Division transports in the area, any emergency maintenance performed on them, and their unloading at Khe Sanh. He also served as liaison officer between the air division and Colonel Lownds' regiment.[40]

The Air Force control element at the base, called a combat control team, began its day by preparing the drop zone to receive cargo. Sometimes the team members set out markers even though ground fog, which raised the possibility that friendly troops might fire at each other, had prevented the Marines from conducting their usual thorough sweep of the area. In such instances, the need to begin supply drops outweighed the risk of ambush. As the C-130's or C-123's approached, the team stood by to assume control of the incoming traffic if either the Marine-operated Khe Sanh control tower or the recently activated Hue-Phu Bai control element should lose radio contact. In serving as emergency replacement for both of these facilities, the team monitored four different radio frequencies whenever transports were en route to Khe Sanh. Any time that a C-123K landed on the pockmarked runway, the control team, operating from a radio-equipped jeep, told the pilot where to taxi, what outbound cargo or passengers were waiting, and when to takeoff.[41]

Lt. Col. Donald M. Davis, USAF, mission commander during the latter part of March, reported certain difficulties that the control team had encountered. Some of the radios, for instance, failed to survive the punishment they received at Khe Sanh. The generators used there required fueling after only 2 hours of operation, and refilling the tank was a dangerous undertaking amid hostile fire.

Davis also expressed disappointment in the performance of a low frequency beacon used to assist navigators bound for Khe Sanh. He said the item was too fragile for use at a combat base and reported that it interfered with signals from nearby radios. Although every one of the three beacons used during the battle sustained damage from enemy fire, experience at the Marine bastion had shown that burying as much of the beacon and its generator as possible would reduce vulnerability.[42]

The maintenance done on aircraft at Khe Sanh was strictly of an emergency nature—that is, just the work that would enable a plane to get into the air before North Vietnamese gunners demolished it. If complex and time-consuming maintenance was necessary, mechanics were flown in from Da Nang to do it. Changing tires was the most common activity, since the Seabees—responsible for keeping the field open—had neither machines to sweep away shell fragments nor metal planking to repair shell holes adequately.[43]

Cargo handling was divided between the Marines, who were responsible for supplies delivered by parachute into the drop zone, and airmen who retrieved cargo deposited on the runway. Both the Air Force and Marine Corps used specially trained persons for this work. The Leathernecks were assigned to Company A, 3d Shore Party Battalion, whose title and duties originated during the amphibious campaigns of World War II when such

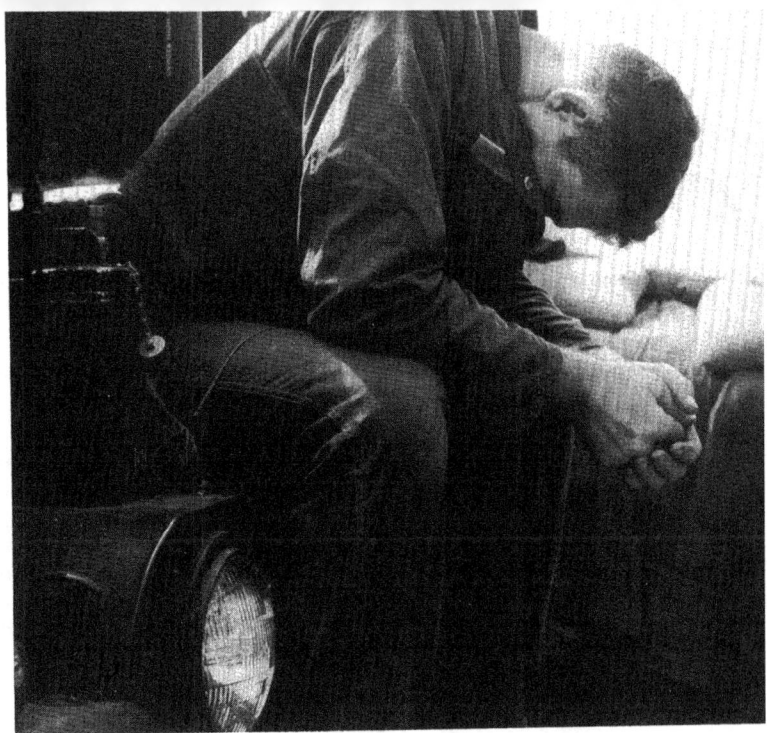

An airman of the combat control team at Khe Sanh catches 40 winks between duties at the beleaguered outpost

units had gathered supplies dumped along the beach and moved them to storage areas. The airmen, who were commanded by an officer, were members of an aerial port mobility team consisting of 7 to 14 enlisted men. The mobility team helped plan outbound loads, prepared manifests for cargo and passengers departing from Khe Sanh, and assisted in unloading and recovering cargo.[44]

On 11 March, North Vietnamese forward observers began directing fire into the drop zone whenever Marine retrieval teams moved onto it. Lieutenant Colonel Davis, who assumed the post of mission commander shortly after the enemy adopted these tactics, declared that the drop zone had become "probably the most hazardous area at Khe Sanh."[45]

Nevertheless, members of Company A, 3d Shore Party Battalion, did most of their work on that dangerous ground. These Marines employed forklifts and mechanical mules to recover supplies that landed in the drop zone. They also retrieved the parachutes and platforms used in the container delivery system. Marine helicopters then flew the parachutes out of Khe Sanh, but until space was available in outbound transports, the platforms had to be stored near the taxiway. According to an Air Force officer, these plywood pallets were fairly safe from the larcenous impulses of Khe Sanh's defenders. Like the platforms used with parachute extraction gear, they were awkward to carry off.[46]

Even though they were not responsible for clearing the drop zone, airmen frequently ventured into it in quest of what Lieutenant Colonel Davis called "supplemental rations or 'goodies'" that were attached to bundles delivered by parachute. If no airman was present to remove these packages, the contents went to the Marines instead of to the intended recipients. Rather than have his men continue to risk death or injury in the drop zone, he recommended that luxuries of this kind be delivered by the C-123K's that landed atop the plateau and were unloaded by the aerial port mobility team.[47]

55

One of the many essential tasks performed by mobility teams was to load casualties onto aircraft for evacuation and hospitalization. Early in the battle, team members had determined the number of men to be evacuated and radioed the approaching plane to rig for a specific number of litters. As the flight strip became more dangerous, the walking wounded hurriedly boarded and took seats, while men of the mobility team placed the litter patients on the cargo deck.[48]

Had an airman serving on the ground at Khe Sanh kept a diary, he would have recorded a series of events involving both mere inconvenience and mortal peril. During the 10 days ending on 3 March, for example, the mission commander reported that his jeep had been hit three times by shell fragments. Punctured tires or gasoline tanks had temporarily disabled three forklifts. Two men were wounded seriously enough to be evacuated, while four others remained on the jobs despite wounds that would entitle them to Purple Hearts. In only 10 days, 6 of 14 men in the aerial port mobility team had sustained wounds of varying severity.

During this fairly typical period, the mission commander, Lt. Col. John F. Masters, Jr., had requested numerous items for the safety and comfort of his men. He called for pierced steel planking and sandbags to build a bunker exclusively for the team and some of its equipment. He asked for fire extinguishers, toilet paper, and insecticides. Finally, after a man who shared the team's sleeping quarters was bitten by a rat, he sent word he needed rat poison. At the end of Masters' tour as mission commander, not one of these requests had been honored.[49] The lack of response may have been due to the overwhelming priority assigned the delivery of ammunition, food, and similar cargo. What seemed vital to a man crouched beside Khe Sanh's runway may have appeared a luxury to someone at Da Nang who was trying to make the most efficient use of available transports.

Supplying the Outposts

Supplying the outposts around Khe Sanh was an arduous task. The enemy could easily ambush supply columns bound from the main base to the hills nearby. Moreover, the hilltop defensive perimeters were too small to double as drop zones. The only feasible method of delivering food, water, and munitions—and of evacuating the wounded—was by helicopter.[50]

When Colonel Lownds was organizing Khe Sanh's defenses, Marine helicopters took on cargo that had been flown into the main base and delivered it directly to Hills 950, 558, 861, and 881S. The bombardment which began on 21 January became too destructive to permit loading the helicopters on the exposed surface of the plateau. Dong Ha therefore replaced Khe Sanh as supply point for the Marine-held outposts. As antiaircraft fire became more intense around Khe Sanh, helicopter gunships flew flak suppression missions in support of the cargo helicopters. During February the enemy took advantage of mists that clung for days at a time to the hills and ridges to set up still more automatic weapons. As a consequence, the rotary-wing gunships could no longer suppress the volume of fire that could be focused on the approaching helicopters.[51]

The Marines responded by devising what they called the "Super Gaggle," a tactical innovation that made its debut in the last week of February. This was simply a formation of supply-carrying helicopters escorted by the usual gunships plus McDonnell Douglas A-4 Skyhawk attack planes. A Marine controller riding in a TA-4, the

2-seat trainer version of the Skyhawk, was in charge. He checked the weather around Khe Sanh and reported if the ceiling permitted effective flak suppression. If the report was favorable, a dozen A-4's took off from Chu Lai, while 12 to 16 twin-rotor CH-46 helicopters and their escort of UH-1 gunships left Quang Tri City for Dong Ha where the larger helicopters loaded the cargo destined for the outposts.

The helicopters left Dong Ha on a schedule that would bring them over their destination just about the time the A-4's had hit known and suspected antiaircraft emplacements with bombs, napalm, and tear gas. Two A-4's laid a smoke screen to conceal the final approach of the helicopters, during which four other Skyhawks again battered the North Vietnamese with cannon, bombs, and rockets. As the CH-46's, their loads stowed in nets that swayed beneath the fuselage, approached and departed, the helicopter gunships stood ready to rescue the crew of any that might fall victim to enemy fire. Seldom was this necessary, for adequate escort drastically reduced CH-46 losses.[52]

At times, the weather had completely isolated the outposts. Early in February, Marines on Hill 881S went without food for 3 days until the fog dissipated. Similarly Hill 950 was swathed in clouds for 9 days during which no helicopter could land. The men exhausted their supply of water and a patrol had to probe the enemy-infested wilderness to fill canteens at a stream. Fortunately, the weather began improving as the Super Gaggle commenced operating.[53]

A Marine helicopter heads for outposts on a resupply mission

Tour of duty over, U.S. Marines prepare to board an Air Force C-130 at Khe Sanh

Although they made their greatest contribution to the supply effort in sustaining the outposts, Marine helicopter pilots flew in and out of Khe Sanh throughout the battle. They brought in reinforcements during the buildup, delivered fragile items that could not be parachuted, and carried away the wounded, sometimes flying them to a hospital ship off the coast.[54]

The Task Completed

The magnitude of the Khe Sanh airlift was staggering. The number of supply drops made there by 15 March exceeded the total for all of Vietnam before that time. Between 21 January and 8 April, 8,120 tons of cargo were parachuted to the defenders in 601 individual sorties by C-123's and C-130's. Lockheed C-130's landed 273 times, C-123's 179 times, and C-7's eight times to unload a grand total of 4,310 tons of cargo and 2,676 passengers. Flown out of the base were 1,574 persons, at least 306 of them wounded. Air Force C-130's took part in 15 ground proximity extractions and 52 low altitude parachute extractions.[55]

The men who planned and executed this impressive effort paid a price both in lives and in planes destroyed. Forty-four passengers and an Air Force crew of four perished in the 6 March crash of the C-123 hit by ground fire as it neared Khe Sanh. Two other C-123's fell victim to mortar fire while on the ground at the combat base, and eight planes of this type sustained varying degrees of battle damage during supply missions. There was, however, no further loss of life among C-123 crews or passengers. None of the jealously-hoarded C-130's was destroyed, but at least 18 incurred damage and two passengers were killed as they left their plane. The few C-7's that participated emerged unscathed as did their crews.[56]

During the action, Marine helicopters transported 14,562 passengers and

4,661 tons of cargo to the main base and its satellite outposts. Losses among helicopters bound for the outpost line numbered as many as three in a single day until a deadlier escort was provided. After the introduction of the Super Gaggle, only two cargo-carrying helicopters succumbed to hostile gunners. The most serious accident suffered by Marine aviation at Khe Sanh was the 10 February crash of a KC-130 which killed six men.[57]

These statistics, fragmentary though they are, support two conclusions. First, Air Force cargo planes sustained the main base until troops were available to open Highway 9. Second, Khe Sanh's outposts could not have survived except for Marine helicopters.

V. TACTICAL TEAMWORK

Teamwork between the services, as the airlift story makes clear, was vital at Khe Sanh. Airmen on the ground worked in harmony with the Marines, while overhead Air Force, Navy, and Marine pilots cooperated in a joint effort to deliver damaging blows to the enemy forces surrounding the base. On occasion, Air Force F-100 pilots were directed to targets by the Marines, and Navy A-1's bombed on instruction from Air Force officers. Pilots occasionally complained of unfamiliar procedures used by another service, but this was a minor annoyance that did not hamper air support of the Khe Sanh Marines.[1]

Cooperation Among the Services

Operational planners took advantage of every break in the weather to mass strike aircraft over the base. On 16 March, for instance, the recently arrived 355th Tactical Fighter Squadron dispatched 15 F-100 sorties within 4 hours. Five aviators—Air Force Majors Joe C. Robinson, Abner Prophett, Charles R. Peters, and Windall K. Dalton, along with a Navy exchange pilot, Lt. Clifford Martin—delivered a telling blow, touching off 36 major explosions and starting 100 fires in an attack on a supply point. This Air Force squadron had deployed to South Vietnam from Myrtle Beach, South Carolina, releasing a Vietnam-based F-4 unit for services in Korea during the *Pueblo* crisis.[2]

Among the aircraft that saw service in defense of Khe Sanh was the North American T-28, a 2-place, conventionally powered trainer modified for counterinsurgency missions and used for daylight strikes in Laos. On 8 February, three of these planes, diverted from their assigned targets, bombed enemy positions not far from the Khe Sanh airfield and then landed to refuel. One T-28 blew both main tires and had to be left overnight. Its pilot, Air Force Major John Pattee, returned the next day with two tires and two skilled mechanics. While replacing the tires, the three men discovered additional damage, the most serious of which prevented use of the nosewheel for steering. Despite this, they shoehorned themselves into the plane, took off, and landed successfully at Nakhon Phanom in Thailand.[3]

Of special value during the periods of bad weather were Marine A-6A's, Grumman-built attack planes fitted with electronic gear that permitted effective operation regardless of visibility. At night these planes carried out armed reconnaissance in the vicinity of Khe Sanh and also bombed known and suspected enemy concentrations.[4]

Another Marine contribution to the air campaign was the M-21 aircraft arresting gear installed at Da Nang. The device was an adaptation of the arresting gear used on aircraft carriers, basically a cable stretched across the runway at its midpoint to engage a hook trailing from a rolling aircraft. This equipment enabled Air Force F-4's to land safely even though the runway was dangerously slick from rain. The Air Force had arresting gear of its own at the end of each runway, and this equipment could handle a faster-moving plane than could the Marine va-

T-28 (above) and Marine Corps A-6 (below) strike aircraft joined the fight at Khe Sanh

riant. But the Leatherneck system had two main advantages: it engaged the plane after a comparatively short roll, thus reducing the chance of skidding off the wet pavement; and it could be reset in half a minute, rather than the 10 minutes it was taking to disengage one aircraft and ready the Air Force equipment to receive another. The M-21, therefore, was much better suited to handling formations of F-4's when the planes had to land in rapid succession.[5]

The Navy's air contribution at Khe Sanh reflected developments in North Vietnam. In January 1968 carrier planes and Air Force fighter-bombers were engaged in a campaign to isolate the port of Haiphong by severing the transportation lines leading inland. Unfortunately, the weather was so bad that visual strikes were possible only on an average of 3 days per month during the first 3 months of the year. Of the three, February was the most dismal, offering weather that Admiral Sharp characterized as the worst since systematic bombing of North Vietnam began back in 1965.[6]

Naval aviators managed, however, to conduct successful strikes during February. One target was a radio and radar installation that controlled the Russian-built interceptors defending Haiphong and Hanoi. Carrier-based Grumman A-6's, with all-weather bombing equipment, shattered this link in the enemy's defenses.[7]

Despite attacks such as this one, the storms that shrouded the North forced a reduction in the number of Navy sorties dispatched there and released planes and munitions for use in defense of Khe Sanh. As a result, during February Task Force 77 was able to divert some 2,800 of its 3,672 planned sorties—about 77 percent—against enemy targets in northern South

Vietnam and portions of southeastern Laos. In March, approximately 3,100 or 67 percent of 4,711 carrier sorties hit targets in these areas.[8]

The extent of naval participation in the defense of Khe Sanh was far greater than its role in Operation Neutralize, the successful 1967 air action against Communist forces around Con Thien. During the last 3 weeks of September 1967, planes from Task Force 77 conducted 1,604 strikes against enemy positions inside the demilitarized zone that threatened Con Thien and other nearby U.S. outposts. The Navy's principal assignment, however, was carrying the war to North Vietnam, a mission that required 8,540 sorties during the month of September.[9]

Typical of the Navy's work at Khe Sanh was an attack on 10 February by A-4's against a North Vietnamese machine gun that had been firing on Marine helicopters trying to deliver supplies to Hill 881S. Located in a ravine, the weapon was not an easy target. The flight leader, Comdr. Lowell F. Eggert, reported that his pilots had trouble finding it but, once they did, promptly knocked it out.[10]

As February gave way to March, General Westmoreland became concerned about enemy trenches, and possibly tunnels, that were probing closer to the Marine perimeter. "It is imperative," he told General Momyer, "that any opportunity be taken of weather breaks to obtain FAC [forward air controller] coverage and directed . . . strikes against these."[11] The Seventh Air Force commander joined the commander of the 1st Marine Aircraft Wing in calling a meeting of their staffs to "plan concentration of maximum controllable tactical air into the area immediately surrounding Khe Sanh."[12]

Out of this discussion came a decision that Air Force and Marine fliers would respond to the immediate emergency, with Navy aviators joining in on 3 March. The naval liaison officer who attended the meeting advised the commander of Task Force 77 that General Momyer requested the carriers to provide flights of from two to six aircraft for each of 18 time-on-target strikes per day during the crisis. The planes were to check in with the airborne battlefield command and control center which would assign them either to a forward air controller or to a radar operator on the ground.[13]

Lt. (jg.) William S. Orris, one of the Navy aviators who attacked the trench system, described the detonation of his 1,000-pound delayed action bombs as resembling the eruption of volcanoes. A forward air controller told Comdr. Paul A. Peck, another Navy participant in the attack, that the bombs had collapsed 50 meters of trench and killed at least two men who had sought shelter there. The enemy soon abandoned the building of assault trenches.[14]

The Navy air support effort, however, did not always go this smoothly. There were occasions when neither the forward air controller nor the radar operator could get around to the circling Navy planes before their fuel ran low. In such cases, the pilots jettisoned their ordnance over the ocean as they returned to their carrier.[15]

Escorting the Transports

The North Vietnamese antiaircraft guns dug in around Khe Sanh were no larger than 37-mm, and their exact number was never determined. Despite the absence of heavier weapons, the enemy's guns were numerous enough, and his crews sufficiently accurate, to menace the existence of the aerial highway that supplied the Marine base. By the first week in March, the danger was so acute that an escort became necessary for all transports approaching

Khe Sanh in any but the worst weather.[16]

In preparing to escort a supply mission into Khe Sanh, planners first drew on their maps a line indicating the ground track of a cargo plane from the time that it dropped below 3,500 feet above ground level until it regained that altitude after takeoff. On the basis of this line, they then calculated the potential danger area, the terrain from which a 37-mm gun could hit a plane performing a particular mission— either landing, parachuting cargo, or using an extraction system.

A typical escort mission began when the transport made rendezvous with fighters and observation craft some 18 miles from Khe Sanh. All the planes checked in with an Air Force airborne command and control center which issued last-minute instructions. In theory, transports could proceed unescorted only when clouds or fog denied the enemy visual observation of the approaches to the airfield. If visibility was good, they were to receive an escort even though it was necessary to wait for fighter protection. In actual practice, however, the senior Air Force officer on the ground at Khe Sanh and the pilot of the incoming plane evaluated the probable intensity of hostile fire and decided whether or not to await an escort if none was on hand. Seldom did the cargo planes postpone their approach.

If an escort was both necessary and available, forward air controllers took positions on each side of the transport. Their job was to locate previously uncharted gun positions, direct fighter-bombers against them, and also to prevent the fighter escort from accidentally bombing the Marines. The fighters, which flew a racetrack pattern around the cargo craft, responded to instructions radioed from the two forward air controllers and also attacked known antiaircraft sites within range of the transport's flightpath. These strikes, made with 20-mm cannon and fragmentation bombs, usually began when the plane being escorted was about 1,500 feet above the ground.[17]

If neither fog nor clouds offered concealment, two fighters put down smokescreens on both sides of the incoming transport throughout the last 3 miles of its approach. Flying at 480 knots no more than 300 feet above the earth, each fighter carried four smoke dispensers. This number provided a margin in case of malfunction, since three dispensers would create an adequate screen.[18]

The approach of a transport was not the only occasion when antiaircraft sites came under attack. During the siege of Khe Sanh, every identified 37-mm emplacement was repeatedly hit until intelligence showed the gun to be destroyed or abandoned. Weapons of lesser size were attacked whenever

An A-4 Skyhawk aboard the USS Coral Sea

A USAF F-4 Phantom enroute to target

they posed a threat to American aircraft. In all, more than 300 antiaircraft positions were reported destroyed.[19]

The introduction of radar-directed surface-to-air missiles could have greatly complicated the task of defending Khe Sanh, but none of these weapons appeared in the immediate vicinity of the base. In mid-January, four such missiles proved ineffectual against B-52's flying over the demilitarized zone. There were no similar incidents around Khe Sanh, and no further missiles were spotted near the demarcation line until late in May.[20]

Enemy fighters might have intervened with deadly effect against the vital but vulnerable transports, a possibility that American commanders kept always in mind. When considered necessary, cannon-equipped Air Force F-4's that had bombed targets near Khe Sanh remained in the area to provide combat air patrol against any incursion from the North. A fighter unit commander, who took part in these missions, claimed that the F-4's burned so much fuel prior to dropping their ordnance that only one flight in seven could furnish effective fighter cover. The practice of designating a combat air patrol, with no bombing assignment, was preferable. Carrier planes helped meet the threat of North Vietnamese MiG's by bombing those airfields that the short range enemy fighters would have had to use.[21]

The Falconers

Air Force forward air controllers —tactical air controllers (airborne) in Marine parlance—played a role similar to that of the medieval huntsman who sighted his prey, removed the hood from his trained falcon, and launched it to make the kill. These controllers were essential to the successful defense of Khe Sanh. In general, tactical aircraft sent to assist the Marines reported initially to the airborne battlefield command and control center which then assigned them to forward air controllers on station over the base. Although more than one controller was usually on hand, the volume of aerial traffic was such that flights of fighters often had to wait their turn to attack. In these circumstances, the planes entered a holding pattern—which on occasion could extend as high as 35,000 feet—and gradually descended as plane after plane dropped its bombs.[22]

When the fight for Khe Sanh began, four Air Force light observation planes were operating from the base airfield. One was a Cessna O-1, a single-engine, high-wing monoplane used by both the Air Force and Marine

Corps. The others were O-2A's, also high-wing monoplanes but constructed with twin booms extending rearward from the wings to the horizontal stabilizer. This planform, vaguely reminiscent of the World War II Lockheed P-38, permitted the mounting of two engines, tractor and pusher, fore and aft of a stubby fuselage. All four planes sustained damage during the initial bombardment but were flown to safety. Despite the departure of the light aircraft, two Air Force officers, Majors Milton Hartenbower and Richard Keskinen, remained behind to serve as air liaison officers in Colonel Lownds' headquarters.[23]

In the best of weather, the forward air controller's job was difficult and dangerous. Flying through the clouds which had prevailed during the flight at Lang Vei, the controller had to penetrate the overcast, which might be concealing a hilltop or ridge line, identify a target that could well be shooting at him, climb above the cloud cover, and lead the waiting fighters downward through the murk.

Beneath the overcast, the controller radioed instructions to the attacking planes. He told them what the target was—a bunker, perhaps, or trenches—whether it was defended, where it lay in relation to friendly troops, and from which direction attacking aircraft should make their runs. He then used a white phosphorous rocket or perhaps a smoke grenade to mark the target, and the strike commenced.[24]

In addition to bad weather and hostile fire, forward air controllers also had to worry about friendly artillery. Careful coordination was necessary to avoid straying into the path of shells fired from Camp Carroll, the Rockpile, or the Marine base itself.[25]

Because of the Tet offensive and the siege of Khe Sanh, air operations beyond South Vietnam's borders declined in relative importance. Pilots who had been flying interdiction missions outside the country were diverted to attack targets only a short distance from friendly positions.[26]

When all went well, an air strike directed by a forward air controller could achieve spectacular destruction. One controller reported the existence west of Khe Sanh of what appeared to be an ammunition supply point for enemy artillery. He summoned fighters beneath an overcast to strafe, launch rockets, and drop napalm, and was rewarded by the sight of hundreds of secondary explosions as crated rounds detonated.[27]

Soviet-built 37-mm anti-aircraft gun used against tactical aircraft at Khe Sanh

On the morning of 8 February, a forward air controller was responsible for stopping a proposed bombardment that would surely have killed innocent civilians. Word had reached Khe Sanh that several hundred people were moving westward along Highway 9 from the vicinity of the Marine base toward the ruins of the Special Forces camp at Lang Vei. The fact that they were bucking the normal tide of refugees aroused suspicion and gave rise to talk of shelling the column. Luckily, Air Force Captain Charles Rushforth "went down and made a good low pass to see who they were." Skimming just above the treetops, he determined that these were actual refugees, "mostly old men and women and children," who evidently "figured they could go back to Lang Vei village or maybe even back into Laos."

Unfortunately, the enemy used war victims such as these for his own purposes, so that a forward air controller might find himself in a situation where his best instincts had to yield to military necessity. Such was the case on 10 February when a second column of refugees appeared on Highway 9. Aerial reconnaissance revealed North Vietnamese soldiers among the noncombatants forcing them to act as supply porters. The immediate military situation dictated an attack to prevent the movement of supplies.[28]

Radar Control

Two types of radar were used to control strikes in defense of Khe Sanh: the Marine TPQ-10 located at the base, and the Air Force Combat Skyspot system for which there were several stations in Southeast Asia. The Marine radar operated 20 hours per day. Major Hartenbower, an Air Force Liaison officer at Khe Sanh, was generous in his praise of the Marine operators who routinely directed strikes as close as 500 meters from friendly troops. These skilled specialists, he believed, could bring the strikes to within 50 meters of Marine positions in an emergency. The major maintained that without this radar, close-in strikes would have been impossible in bad weather.[29]

The other radar was the Air Force MSQ-77 Combat Skyspot which had been operating in Southeast Asia for almost 2 years. Back in 1966, the Viet Cong had taken advantage of impossible flying weather to overrun a Special Forces camp in the A Shau Valley. During the fight for the important patrol base, the only assistance available to fighter-bomber pilots was that provided by forward air controllers flying

O-1's. A ceiling of 300 to 500 feet complicated the controllers' task of guiding strike aircraft to worthwhile targets and also restricted the jets to shallow approaches in which the pilots could not bomb with the required accuracy. The failure of tactical aviation in this action led to the adoption of Combat Skyspot as a means of putting bombs on target regardless of the weather.

Progenitor of Combat Skyspot was a radar bomb scoring unit used by the Strategic Air Command to test the proficiency of bomber crews in mock raids staged against cities in the United States. Even before the A Shau defeat, tests conducted in Texas had shown that the scoring unit could also control strikes by fighters or bombers. A van-mounted computer accepted such factors as altitude, wind velocity and direction, aircraft speed, temperature, and ballistic traits of the ordnance carried. On the basis of this information, the computer furnished the heading, altitude, and airspeed that the plane should maintain. As the craft approached that point in the sky at which its bombs would have to be released in order to hit the target, the operator on the ground began a countdown. Course corrections and the actual signal to release bombs were broadcast from the Skyspot van.[30]

In the defense of Khe Sanh, Combat Skyspot provided remote control for attack planes, fighter-bombers, and B-52's. Because of the complexity in operating a large number of planes in the immediate vicinity of the base, delays and some confusion were inevitable. On 24 February, for example, an F-4 flight commander realized just in time that he was being directed into an area where Skyspot-controlled B-52's were dropping their bombs from high altitude. Other incidents had less potential for disaster, but the Skyspot system did at times acquire control of more aircraft than it could handle. A pilot might be directed to a succession of holding points only to end up, after burning a great deal of fuel, exactly where he had started and with his full load of ordnance still on board. Sometimes, an aviator ran low on fuel before his turn came and had to jettison his bombs and return to base. These failings, however, were outweighed a thousandfold by the successful strikes that Combat Skyspot made possible.[31]

The O-1 (l.) was used by Forward Air Controllers to mark targets. Below is a Combat Skyspot facility, used to direct strike aircraft to targets in Vietnam

VI. APPOINTMENT OF A SINGLE MANAGER FOR AIR

During the battle for Khe Sanh, General Westmoreland appointed his Deputy for Air Operations, General Momyer, as single manager for tactical combat aviation throughout South Vietnam. The Air Force had long favored centralized control, and the concentration in the skies above Khe Sanh of large numbers of different kinds of aircraft made such a move seem imperative from the Air Force point of view. The selection of a single manager late in the Khe Sanh fighting was, according to General Momyer, "the culmination of a long series of discussions about control of air assets in I Corps."[1]

First Steps toward Centralization

The Marine Corps, whose fighter-bombers and attack planes were among the air assets to which General Momyer referred, was satisfied with the existing method of control. It strongly opposed surrendering its authority over the 1st Marine Aircraft Wing to an Air Force headquarters at Tan Son Nhut, some 400 miles to the south. General Cushman, whose headquarters was at Da Nang, exercised operational control over his air arm in I Corps. The Marines insisted that this arrangement ensured the fastest possible response to requests for air strikes throughout the corps area and that any change would therefore be a change for the worse.[2]

But General Westmoreland had the authority to place Marine aviation under Momyer's operational control if so drastic a change appeared necessary. Since the impending action at Khe Sanh seemed critical, he instructed his Deputy for Air Operations to draw up a plan for massing all available aerial firepower around the imperiled Marine base. The idea was to be able to shift strike aircraft quickly throughout Quang Tri and Thua Thien provinces to meet changes in enemy troop dispositions. Specifically, Westmoreland instructed Momyer to "coordinate and direct the employment of tactical air, Marine air, diverted air strikes from out of country air operations, and such naval air as may be requested." In addition, B-52 strikes were to be "coordinated through him."

The degree of control initially entrusted to General Momyer was limited. Westmoreland merely directed General Cushman to place at Momyer's disposal "all tactical bomber sorties not required for the direct support of Marine units," and the sorties thus released were to be "initially committed in the Niagara operation." The Marines, however, interpreted this as a definite step toward centralization of operational control, which they believed was General Westmoreland's ultimate goal. They saw their I Corps control network becoming just another link in the more extensive Air Force system and their Da Nang-based squadrons coming under the exclusive authority of an Air Force headquarters.[3]

To Reconcile the Irreconcilable

General Westmoreland had undertaken a formidable task. His stated objective was to centralize control of Marine and Air Force squadrons without

Lt. Gen. R. E. Cushman commanded the III Marine Amphibious Force from his headquarters at Da Nang

destroying the integrity of the Marine air-ground team. The Marines believed, however, that the close relationship between air and ground could not exist unless the unified team was controlled by Marines. The Air Force sought efficiency by bringing Marine squadrons under centralized direction; the Marine Corps worked for the same goal by avoiding centralization under Air Force control. General Westmoreland, it appeared, was trying to reconcile the irreconcilable.⁴

The extent to which the Marine Corps and Air Force differed on centralized control was reflected in their contrasting attitudes toward the exercise of command during the Korean War. In Korea, the Fifth Air Force had exercised operational control over Marine air units. To General Momyer this arrangement seemed logical and desirable. "If the battle for Khe Sanh develops," he declared, "it may be the event to get the air responsibilities straightened out as we had them in Korea and WWII." ⁵

Centralized operational control was a prospect that Marines viewed with foreboding. Lt. Gen. Keith B. McCutcheon, USMC, a onetime director of Marine aviation who later commanded III Marine Amphibious Force in Vietnam, stated that opposition to the appointment of an Air Force general as a single manager for tactical combat aviation was based to a great extent on concern that "it would recreate the Korean War situation." Whereas General Momyer endorsed the command relationship set up in Korea, Marine leaders remembered it as depriving the 1st Marine Division, only Marine ground force in actual combat, of control over the aviation units organized, equipped, and trained to support it.

Some Marines saw unified management as a threat to the future as well as a retreat into an unsatisfactory past. They feared that any shift of operational control for the Vietnam war could serve as a precedent for breaking up the air-ground team. Since Leatherneck ground commanders relied upon Marine aviation much as they did upon artillery, loss of the air arm would require extensive changes in tactics, organization, and armament. Furthermore, a breakup of the air-ground team would definitely affect the mission of the Marine Corps.⁶

On 18 January, Admiral Sharp received word of General Westmoreland's intention to meet the emergency in I Corps by imposing closer control over Marine air power. The admiral replied almost immediately, cautioning the general against any change that might violate existing doctrine and trigger an interservice debate over roles

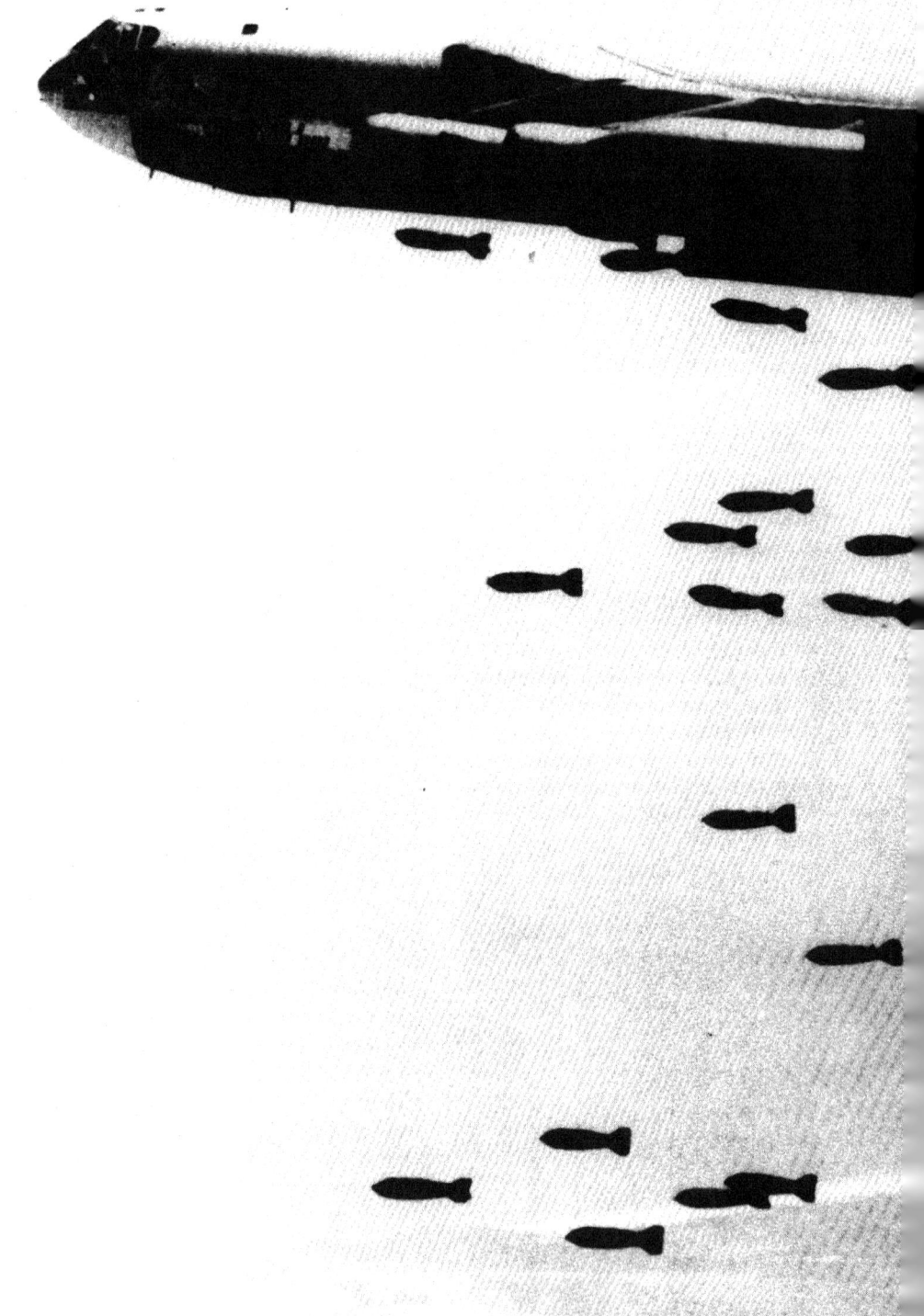

"... the thing that broke their backs was ... the fire of the B-52's."

—General Westmoreland

and missions. He declined to approve a radical alteration in the status of Marine aviation in Vietnam and suggested further discussion with General Cushman and his staff. He did not, however, rule out future consideration of a formal proposal affecting operational control of the 1st Marine Aircraft Wing.[7]

The 22 January Agreement

Rather than insist on an immediate transfer of operational control, General Westmoreland went ahead with an arrangement designed to improve cordination between Seventh Air Force and the Marine wing. On 22 January, representatives of General Momyer's headquarters conferred with General Cushman and his staff and fashioned an agreement that, whatever its failings, governed Marine-Air Force relations throughout most of the Khe Sanh battle. In essence, the conferees agreed to link the Seventh Air Force and Marine control networks, using an Air Force airborne battlefield command and control center to achieve coordination.

This airborne battlefield command and control center consisted of a C-130 whose cargo compartment had been fitted with an air conditioned capsule containing electronic equipment capable of storing information, displaying data for controllers, and furnishing reliable communication with ground stations and other aircraft. The gear crammed into the airborne command and control center constituted a "central nervous system providing data for on-the-spot decisions in fluid tactical situations."[8]

The Air Force conferees had maintained that this control center, besides ensuring the orderly and effective application of air power, could also coordinate aerial attacks with artillery bombardment and make certain that

Interior of a C–130 airborne battlefield command and control center

Maj Gen. N. J. Anderson commanded the 1st Marine Aircraft Wing during the defense of Khe Sanh

friendly bombs did not endanger the Marines below. To do all these jobs, however, the airborne command and control center would have to be incorporated in the control network that originated in the Khe Sanh fire support coordination center.⁹

The fire support coordination center, which resembled in purpose the installation housed in the converted C-130's operating above the base, was headed by Lieutenant Colonel Hennelly of the 1st Battalion, 13th Marines. Located within the fire support coordination center were the fire direction center, which with the aid of a computer converted requests for artillery support into fire commands, and a direct air support center through which requests for air strikes reached the 1st Marine Aircraft Wing's tactical air direction center. Planes from this wing normally flew the missions requested by Marine units in the field. But when it was fully committed, liaison teams at the direct air support center could call upon Air Force or Navy aircraft to deliver the necessary attacks. The demands of Operation Niagara were such that before the battle ended, the Khe Sanh direct air support center, in conjunction with the airborne battlefield command and control center, had obtained the assistance of planes from all services, Army aviation included.¹⁰

The 22 January agreement also established rules for the coordination of air strikes. Maj. Gen. Norman J. Anderson, commander of the 1st Marine Aircraft Wing during the defense of Khe Sanh, later described the compact as an acknowledgement that "close air support of Marine ground forces was a job to be accomplished by the specialized members of the Marine air-ground team, while other air resources took on more distant targets." The location of the target did play a role in the 22 January agreement, with the Marines insisting on concentrating their aerial firepower against the targets closest to Khe Sanh, but geography was not the only concern in assigning targets.¹¹

Another key consideration was control. The agreement represented a plan, however imperfect in practice, to exert the firmest control in those areas where the danger of accidentally bombing friendly units was greatest. For this reason, all strikes in the sector closest to Marine positions were to be cleared through the Khe Sanh fire support coordination center and directed by either a Marine airborne tactical air controller or an Air Force forward air controller. Procedures also required that the fire support cordination center

73

review requests for air strikes in areas where there was the possibility of collision between aircraft and artillery shells. Certain tracts beyond artillery range were designated free fire zones in which pilots could initiate attacks, or simply jettison bombs, without prior approval.[12]

Air Force Dissatisfaction

Air Force participants saw two major flaws in the 22 January agreement for coordinating air strikes in defense of Khe Sanh. First, they thought it put too much emphasis on geographical considerations. General Momyer insisted that air power had to be free to go where the targets were, regardless of area boundaries. As he saw it, the 1st Marine Aircraft Wing was tied to I Corps and unavailable for use against important targets elsewhere in South Vietnam.

The second Air Force complaint was that Marine airmen were fighting a private war at Khe Sanh. Leatherneck pilots assigned targets in the zone nearest the base were accused of ignoring the airborne battlefield command and control center. If the principal coordinating agency was thus bypassed, Air Force officers declared, the Marine contribution to Operation Niagara could not be fitted into the overall air campaign. Unless there was close coordination between Marine Corps and Air Force, the flow of aircraft into the Khe Sanh area could not be regulated to avoid long delays for fuel-hungry jets and extended periods when aircraft were unavailable.

No such objections emanated from General Cushman's headquarters. The Marines were satisfied that their comrades at Khe Sanh were receiving prompt, accurate, and effective air support. Once again there was a difference of opinion which defied compromise. By mid-February, however, increasing enemy pressure on Khe Sanh persuaded General Westmoreland to try once again to give General Momyer greater control over Marine tactical aircraft. Because of Westmoreland's continuing interest, the question of selecting a single manager for air remained under discussion.[13]

Appointment of a Single Manager

During meetings held throughout the remainder of February, Momyer and his staff devised a form of control that would give him sufficient flexibility to shift aircraft throughout South Vietnam, massing them wherever their bombs would have the deadliest effect. Rather than have the Marine aircraft wing deal directly with Marine ground units, he desired that Cushman's headquarters submit its requests for planned air strikes to the tactical air support element at Tan Son Nhut. This element was the agency through which Army ground commanders fixed the priorities that governed the allocation of scheduled air strikes. The Seventh Air Force would then notify the 1st Marine Aircraft Wing of the sorties required by III Marine Amphibious Force and at the same time advise General Anderson's headquarters of priority missions in support of non-Marine units. General Momyer's tactical air control center would have the authority to divert Marine or Air Force sorties from scheduled strikes to emergency targets. It could also commit planes of either service that were on ground alert.[14]

General Cushman considered such an arrangement unacceptable. He argued that the appointment of a single manager with that degree of authority would replace "my aviation commander," General Anderson, and hand "control over his assets" to General Momyer, who was not "directly under my command." This loss of control over the aircraft wing did not, Cushman pointed out, alter "my overall operational responsibilities." He therefore declared his unalterable opposition

MARINE CORPS POSITION ON COMMAND AND CONTROL
KHE SANH
JANUARY 1968

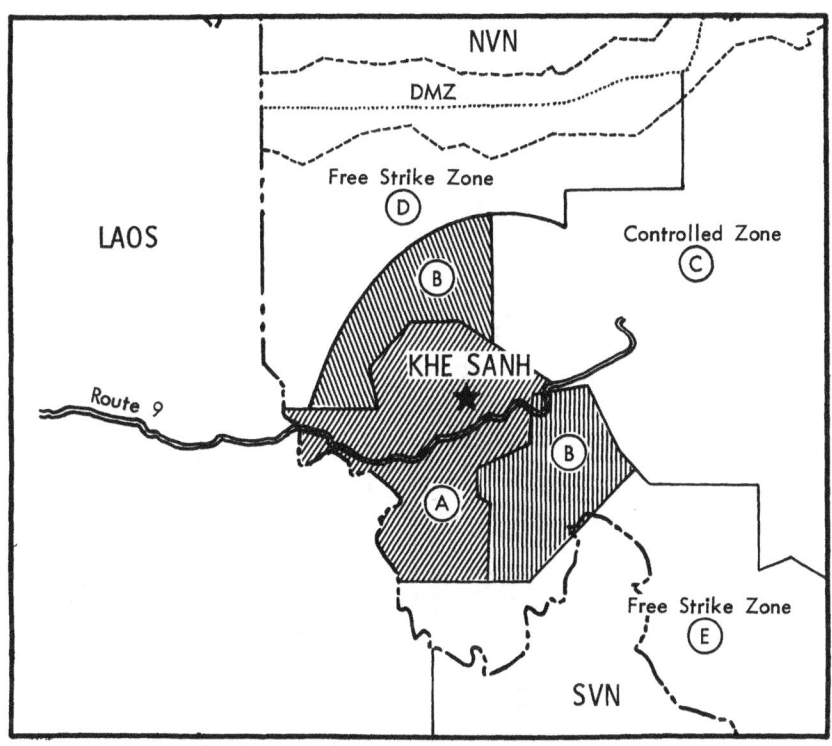

A-B RESTRICTED FIRE AREAS. AIR AND ARTILLERY SUPPORT COORDINATED AND CONTROLLED BY THE MARINES AT KHE SANH

C   RESTRICTED FIRE AREAS. AIR AND ARTILLERY SUPPORT COORDINATED AND CONTROLLED BY THE MARINES AT DONG HA

D-E FREE STRIKE ZONES. AIR STRIKES CONTROLLED BY THE SEVENTH AIR FORCE AIRBORNE BATTLEFIELD COMMAND AND CONTROL CENTER

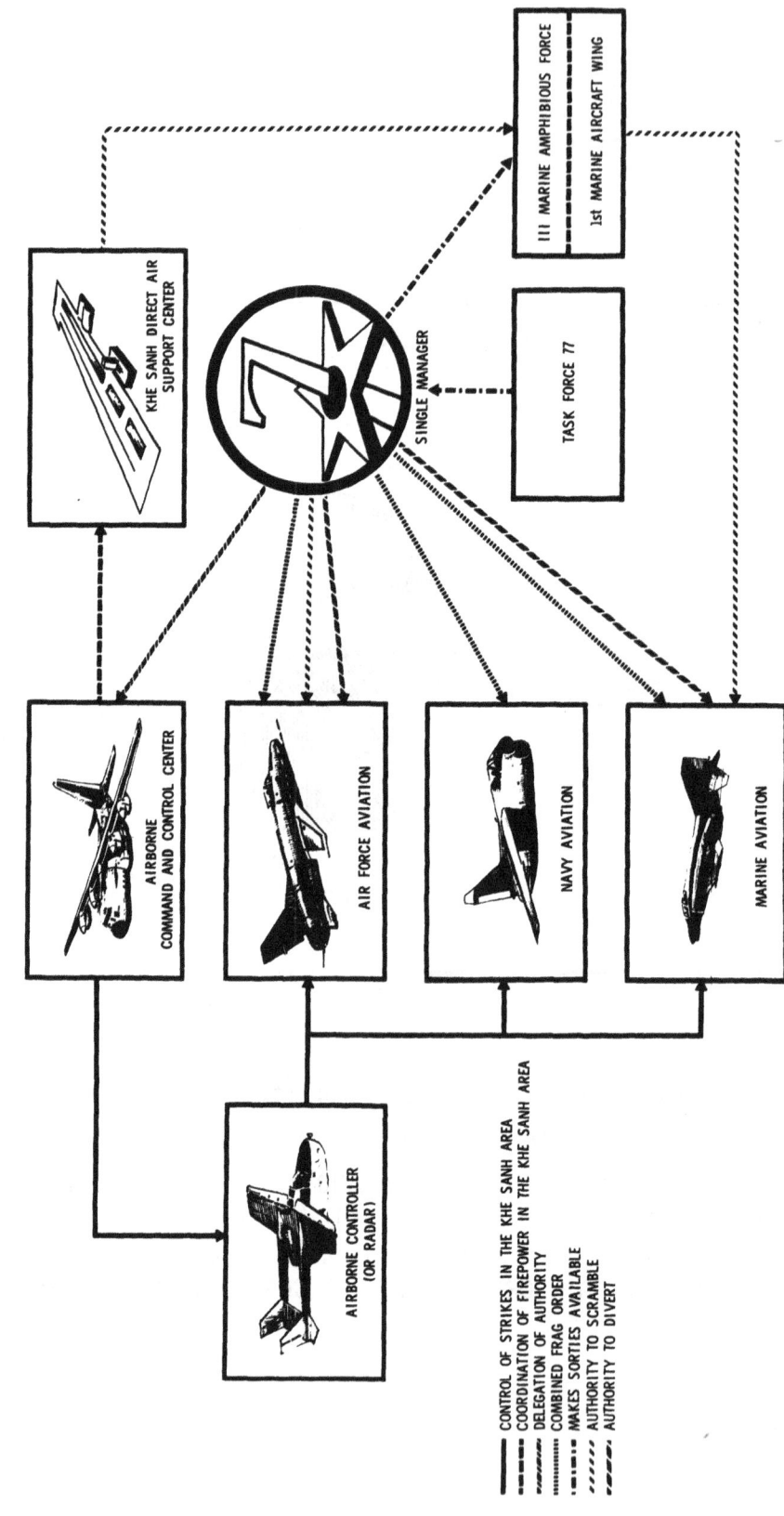

"to any fractionalization of the Marine air-ground team." [15]

As the discussions continued, it became clear that Westmoreland was determined to unify control over air power in South Vietnam. "The question," General Momyer said, "was not whether there should be one man responsible for all air operations but how best to accomplish this arrangement while preserving the principle of Marine air units supporting Marine ground units whenever the tactical situation permitted." [16]

Despite abiding Marine reluctance, General Westmoreland forwarded to Admiral Sharp a plan to appoint Momyer as single manager of tactical combat aviation throughout all of South Vietnam. This formal proposal was revised at Pacific Command headquarters. Admiral Sharp satisfied himself on two points: first, that Marine emergency calls for air support would not have to be submitted to Seventh Air Force headquarters; and, second, that General Cushman and his Marine superiors would have the right of appeal. This done, he approved the single manager plan on 2 March. [17]

Admiral Sharp, later commenting on this decision, stated that he had approved selection of a single manager because of the recent introduction of large numbers of Army troops into I Corps. "I didn't think the single manager concept necessary as long as Marines were the only troops in I Corps," he explained, but, as Army numbers increased, "it got to the point where a single manager got to be a reasonable thing to do." [18]

As Admiral Sharp indicated, the number of Army units in I Corps was increasing dramatically. In January 1967 there had not been one U.S. Army combat battalion in the entire area, but by year's end Westmoreland had dispatched 16 such units to join 21 Marine battalions, 33 South Vietnamese, and 4 South Korean. This moreover, was a continuing trend, so that in April 1968 I Corps Army battalions outnumbered Marine battalions 30 to 24. Because of the changing composition of forces within the corps tactical zone, General Westmoreland established an Army headquarters—initially designated Provisional Corps, Vietnam—to exercise control over all American forces in the two northernmost provinces, Quang Tri, where Khe Sanh was located, and Thua Thien. On the organizational charts, the provisional corps, commanded by Lt. Gen. William B. Rosson, USA, occupied a box between III Marine Amphibious Force, to which it was subordinate, and the three divisions assigned to it. These were the 3d Marine Division, involved in the defense of Khe Sanh, the 1st Cavalry Division, counted upon to reopen the highway to Khe Sanh, and the reinforced 101st Airborne Division. [19]

On 8 March, the same day that he announced the creation of Rosson's corps, General Westmoreland formally designated his Deputy for Air Operations as single manager for tactical combat aviation in all of South Vietnam. General Momyer assumed responsibility for "coordinating and directing the tactical air effort throughout South Vietnam, to include I CTZ [I Corps Tactical Zone] and the extended battle area." At the same time, General Cushman received instructions to place Marine fighter-bombers, attack planes, and reconnaissance craft, as well as the Marine air control system, under the "mission direction" of Momyer. [20]

In carrying out the directive, General Momyer selected the III Marine Amphibious Force direct air support center at Da Nang as the principal coordinating agency for I Corps, enlarged it, and arranged to have non-Marines assigned there to give the center stronger multi-service character. A

General Momyer, Seventh Air Force commander, was appointed single commander for tactical combat aviation in all of South Vietnam. Above he is being checked out in the cockpit of an A-37 at Tan Son Nhut

similar interservice organization was established at General Rosson's corps. The Marine divisions retained their direct air support centers as did the reinforced regiment holding Khe Sanh.

Planning for scheduled air strikes began at rifle battalion headquarters and moved up the chain of command, with consolidated target lists being prepared at regiment and division. Rosson's headquarters submitted to III Marine Amphibious Force a consolidated request covering its assigned Army and Marine units, and Cushman's staff combined this list with ones prepared by units under the direct control of the Da Nang headquarters. The combined requests then went to Tan Son Nhut for approval by the tactical air support element, which now included Marines in its operations and intelligence sections. Final stop for the combined I Corps target list was the Seventh Air Force tactical air control center, where Marine representatives also were stationed. This agency matched available units and ordnance with selected targets and issued appropriate operation orders, called "frag orders" because a rigid format permitted very sparse or fragmentary wording with no loss of meaning.[21]

The 1st Marine Aircraft Wing no longer merely advised the Seventh Air Force tactical air control center of any excess sorties. It now reported its total capacity calculated on the basis of one sortie per day by each jet aircraft. Da Nang forwarded this data to Tan Son Nhut along with the compilation of requests for air support.[22]

Single management had to provide for immediate strikes to meet battlefield emergencies (see Chart p. 79). When a division or one of its components needed air support in an emergency, its call for help went to a Marine or Air Force direct air support center which could divert any aircraft under orders to hit a target within the division zone of action. If nothing was available, division turned to corps which had similar authority in its area of operation. Should nothing be available in the five provinces that

IMMEDIATE AIR REQUESTS
STRIKE AND RECONNAISSANCE SUPPORT

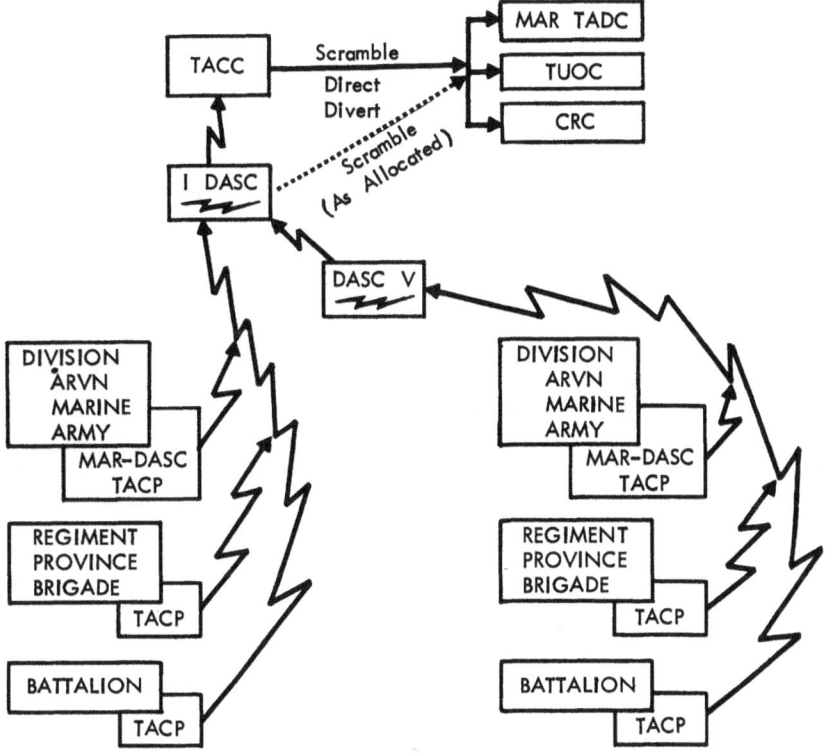

NOTES: 1. ⚡ is Divert Authority for Internal air.
2. Requests go direct to DASC where communication permits; intermediate levels monitor; silence means consent.

made up I Corps, General Cushman's headquarters would contact Tan Son Nhut where the tactical air control center, relying on the tactical air support element for coordination, could divert strikes across corps boundaries or launch emergency strikes. At Admiral Sharp's insistence, the direct air support center at III Marine Amphibious Force retained the authority to launch on its own initiative any aircraft that it might have available. An alert force could thus be maintained at Da Nang despite the centralization of control over tactical aviation.[23]

Naval aviation had only peripheral contact with the single manager system. Restricted by the location of the carriers to strikes in I and II Corps, the task force submitted to the tactical air control center at Tan Son Nhut a daily schedule of strikes in South Vietnam. The control center near Saigon forwarded this information to the appropriate direct air support centers which then assumed responsibility for assigning forward air controllers to the Navy flights. The carriers launched attacks against previously chosen targets and did not normally respond to emergencies, though Navy aircraft might be diverted from the primary target if the tactical situation so required.[24]

A Look at the Results

Although the battle for Khe Sanh provided irresistible impetus toward the selection of a single manager for tactical combat aviation, the arrangement actually went into effect late in the struggle for the Marine base. On 10 March, 3 weeks before Operation Niagara came to its successful conclusion, emergency requests began being handled according to the new procedures. The first frag order combining all Air Force, Marine, and Navy tactical air strikes did not emanate from Tan Son Nhut until 21 March. The single manager system thus approached full operation with strikes delivered on 22 March; slightly more than 13 percent of all Niagara tactical sorties took place from that date through 31 March, when the operation ended. Training the new men assigned to the jointly manned direct air support centers and complete incorporation of Rosson's corps into the III Marine Amphibious Force communication net were not finished until 1 April, the day after Niagara's termination and just a week before the siege was broken.[25]

General Momyer later declared that the fight at Kham Duc, a town near the Laotian border, "was the real test of the single management system," rather than Khe Sanh. In May 1968, in order to cover the withdrawal of friendly forces from Kham Duc, his headquarters had to plan, on short notice, to "commit a large fighter force to bring the enemy under heavy strikes throughout the operation." Marine and Air Force fighter-bombers, "large numbers of FAC's," and a "responsive reconnaissance effort" were involved in this action. Kham Duc was, in the general's words, "a situation that required speed, concentration, and deployment of diversified resources in a highly congested air and ground space."[26]

The Marines continued to express dissatisfaction with unified management. Service spokesmen claimed that the change was unneeded, arguing that the 1st Marine Aircraft Wing had provided adequate support during the Army's 1967 buildup in I Corps and could continue to do so. General Westmoreland, however, was not persuaded that centralized control was unnecessary.

When the Marines complained that the unified system was time-consuming and unresponsive to the needs of ground units, Seventh Air Force reacted by assigning sorties on a weekly basis whenever feasible, rather than insisting on an all-inclusive daily frag order. Responsiveness improved with experience and with the adoption of practices that gave General Anderson control of enough sorties to support Marine helicopter operations and also to have a reserve available for battlefield emergencies.[27]

Concern over the future of the air-ground team continued to motivate much of the Marine Corps opposition to unified management. For this reason, the Corps took full advantage of the right of appeal that Admiral Sharp had considered so important. The complaints at last reached the Office of the Secretary of Defense and, in May 1968, Deputy Secretary of Defense Paul Nitze handed down what essentially was a compromise decision.

He upheld the appointment of a single manager for air, declaring that the "Unified Commander on the scene should be presumed to be the best judge of how the combat forces assigned to him are to be organized, commanded, and deployed." Mr. Nitze did not, however, believe that "the assignment of Marine air units under the single management of the Deputy

COMUSMACV for Air should constitute a precedent for centralized control of air operations under other combat conditions, or need pose a threat to the integrity of the Marine air/ground team." He observed that unique circumstances had spawned unified management and declared that General Westmoreland should "revert to normal command arrangements for III MAF when the tactical situation permits." [28]

Once the future of their air-ground team seemed secure, some Marines tended to modify the harsh initial judgment of centralized management that had been based upon operations at Khe Sanh. Writing in 1970, General McCutcheon conceded that "when three Army divisions were assigned to I Corps and interspersed between the two Marine divisions, a higher order of coordination and cooperation was required than before." Single management provided this and, in his opinion, was "an overall improvement as far as MACV as a whole was concerned." [29]

The Air Force and Marine Corps had differed over the issue of unified management but, when General Westmoreland imposed his solution, they cooperated in carrying out his wishes. "The system worked," declared General McCutcheon. "Both the Air Force and the Marines saw to that. But the way it was made to work evolved over a period of time, and a lot of it was due to gentlemen's agreements between on-the-scene commanders." [30]

Khe Sanh radar equipment and the control tower played a vital role during the battle for Khe Sanh

VII. "THE THING THAT BROKE THEIR BACKS"

The integration of B-52 raids—known as Arc Light strikes, the term applied to Stratofortress operations in the Southeast Asia war—into a support plan that included tactical aviation and artillery did not originate with the defense of Khe Sanh. The 3d Air Division, commanded by General Wells from his headquarters at Andersen Air Force Base on Guam, had taken part in just such an aerial campaign when it lent its destructive power to Operation Neutralize, carried out in northeastern Quang Tri province in September and October 1967. The purpose of Neutralize was to force the enemy to relax his pressure against American bases at Camp Carroll, Dong Ha, and Con Thien. During the operation, daily photo reconnaissance flights provided the data upon which to plan two B-52 missions each day, morning and evening, and at least 3 dozen daily sorties by fighter bombers.[1]

Increasing the Tempo

General Wells' B-52's began their contribution to Khe Sanh's defense a week before the Marine base came under siege. From 14 through 21 January, 94 B-52's hit 12 North Vietnamese targets, mainly storage areas, bivouacs, and infiltration routes, that lay some distance from the Marine base itself. As if to prove that proximity to Khe Sanh did not alone determine the importance of a target, the B-52's on 30 January flew the largest strike of the war to that time, a blow delivered against a target complex in Laos. During the day, 36 of the big bombers attacked an enemy command and control facility; nine other sorties were flown after dark. Thunderous explosions collapsed caves, caused 85 secondary detonations observed by aircrews, and may have disrupted enemy attack plans. By the end of January, 463 B-52 sorties had hit 65 targets related to the survival of Khe Sanh.[2]

At this very early stage in the battle, the prime concern was to increase the weight of ordnance dropped in support of the Marines. To do so, General Wells adopted the so-called Bugle Note procedures, which went into effect on 15 February for Niagara missions and later were extended to strikes elsewhere in South Vietnam.

The new procedures were based on a grid system, superimposed on a map of the Niagara area, in which each block represented a 1- by 2-kilometer box, the area that a cell of three B-52's could blanket effectively with high explosives. Every 90 minutes on the average, a 3-plane cell would arrive at a chosen point where it could be picked up by a Combat Skyspot control unit and directed through a series of check points to its particular target block. Subsequent cells could be directed to other blocks as desired, and each cell had an alternate target in case the primary could not or need not be hit.[3]

Obviously Bugle Note could not have the bombers beginning their runs exactly 90 minutes apart. To avoid establishing a pattern that the enemy could take advantage of, the plan allowed for varying the time between

Lt. Gen. Selmon W. Wells, USAF, commander of 3d Air Division based on Guam

cells. The interval could be an hour, 90 minutes, or 2 hours.[4]

The arrival by 7 February of 26 additional B-52's—a detachment sent to the far Pacific in reaction to North Korea's capture of the intelligence ship *Pueblo* off Wonsan harbor—simplified the task of providing a grand total of 48 sorties per day. Fifteen of the bombers landed at Kadena Air Base, Okinawa and brought to three—Guam, Thailand, and Okinawa—the areas from which Stratofortress strikes might originate. On 12 February, the Joint Chiefs of Staff advised Admiral Sharp that bombing missions against targets in Southeast Asia could originate at Kadena.[5]

After only a day's Bugle Note operation, General Wells' headquarters proposed a major change, to provide six B-52's every 3 hours rather than three every 90 minutes. Adoption of this proposal would permit even more devastating target coverage. Also, fewer launches would mean greater ease in scheduling maintenance, a less hectic pace for mechanics, and a better opportunity to photograph and analyze bombing results. The change went into effect on 25 February.[6]

Close Support

A routine B-52 mission flown from U Tapao, Thailand, on 12 November 1967 contributed quite by accident to an important tactical innovation. Nine B-52's took off from U Tapao to hit troop concentrations and rocket batteries in the vicinity of Con Thien, but one of the planes failed to observe the 3-kilometer safety zone established to keep bombs from falling accidentally among friendly troops. This particular plane—there is doubt as to which one—dropped its explosives within the safety zone about 1.4 kilometers from Marine lines.

Neither the men defending Con Thien nor their fortifications suffered harm from this error. Indeed, the results from the misdirected bomb load verged on the astonishing, as secondary explosions blossomed near the defensive perimeter. The enemy was clearly taking advantage of the safety zone imposed on the Stratofortresses, a fact that lent greater urgency to an idea discussed the previous summer, the use of B-52's in what amounted to close air support.[7]

The successful, though accidental, close-in bombing at Con Thien served as an example of what the B-52's could do in defense of a combat base such as Khe Sanh. As early as 8 January 1968, the topic arose during a meeting of representatives of the Strategic Air Command's advance echelon in Vietnam and officers from III Marine Amphibious Force. Air Force conferees were reluctant to encourage B-52 strikes within the customary safety zone except in emergencies. The Marines then suggested a series of tests that, if successful, would gradually bring the B-52 salvos to a distance of only 1,000 meters from friendly forces. To reduce to a minimum the risks involved, General Cushman's headquarters urged the installation of new radar beacons at both Con Thien and Khe Sanh to help guide the planes to targets within the 3-kilometer safety zone surrounding the latter base.[8]

The 3d Air Division for a time endorsed the installation of this equipment as a further aid to B-52 accuracy. Additional study, however, led General Wells to reverse his stand. The

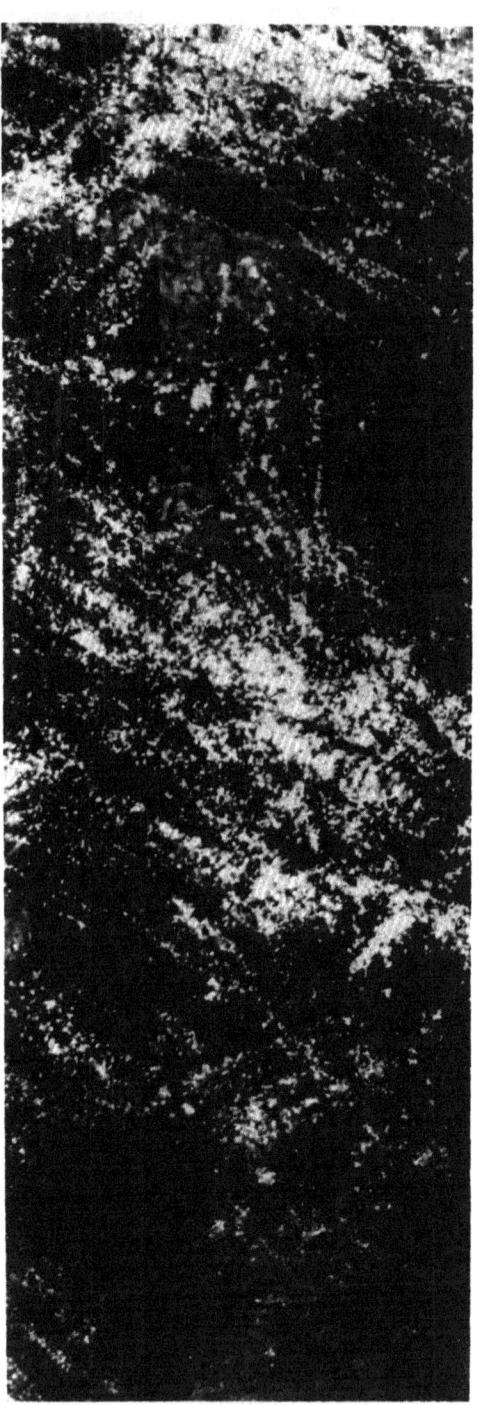

Intensive B-52 bombardment of enemy forces at Khe Sanh is seen in this aerial shot. White dots indicate where bombs fell (white areas on right show cloud cover). The heavy saturation of Hill 881 North (enemy-held) and the sparse pock marks on Hill 881 South (occupied by U.S. Marines) show the remarkable accuracy of the B-52. This montage was pieced together from reconnaissance photos.

beacons seemed too vulnerable to enemy fire, too likely to be masked by the towering hills of northern Quang Tri, and also too confusing since they would needlessly complicate the work of B-52 crews on Skyspot missions.[9]

Discussions continued until February when General Westmoreland, during a meeting attended by General Momyer, expressed dissatisfaction with the employment of B-52's around Khe Sanh. According to General Momyer's account, General Westmoreland directed that General Cushman request strikes within 3 kilometers of the base and told his own staff to examine the feasibility of having B-52's hit targets only 1,000 meters from Marine lines. Admiral Sharp's headquarters reviewed the matter and on 18 February approved, in emergencies, B-52 strikes as close as 1 kilometer to friendly troops.[10]

To the Marines, Con Thien still seemed a doubtful precedent, and General Cushman's headquarters remained wary of close-in B-52 strikes. If there was to be one test rather than a series of strikes that gradually drew closer to Khe Sanh, the general suggested dropping the bombs close to one of the satellite outposts so there would be no "destruction of a vital area if miscalculation occurs." Even if the bombs were dropped near an outpost, the Marine command wanted two evaluation runs, with a single bomb dropped each time, so that an aerial observer could radio any necessary adjustments before the bomber sent the remaining 106 bombs screaming earthward.[11]

A test mission took place on 26 February without benefit of either evaluation runs or supplementary equipment. A single B-52, with a second Stratofortress as its backup, took off from U Tapao carrying 108 500-pound bombs. One Skyspot station checked to make sure the plane's electronic beacon was working properly, directed the bomber to the initial point for its bomb run, and then monitored the run itself in case the second Skyspot ground station, which took over at the initial point, should break down. No equipment failure occurred, however, and the test proved that what had happened accidentally at Con Thien could be repeated successfully at Khe Sanh.[12]

Four close-in missions were flown the following day. As in the test, all bombs fell within the target boxes, and though the detonations shook the earth at Khe Sanh, there was neither injury to the defenders nor damage to bunkers. The spectacle of hundreds of bombs exploding almost simultaneously brought some of the Marines out of their shelters to cheer the B-52's. All the attacks caused secondary explosions or fires, lasting in one instance for 2 or more hours after the raid.[13]

During March, close-in attacks by B-52's became routine. That month the 3d Air Division flew 444 such sorties throughout South Vietnam. In April, with the siege of Khe Sanh broken, the number of close-in B-52 sorties declined to 48.[14]

Results

Assessing the damage done by B-52's was extremely difficult, even though the Strategic Air Command sent additional intelligence officers to South Vietnam and established direct contact between its advance echelon at Tan Son Nhut and the besieged Marine base. The principal tool for collecting data on B-52 strikes was the aerial camera, but various factors hampered photography to the extent that only about 7 percent of all Southeast Asia B-52 strikes could be scored accurately. One factor was visibility. About half the B-52 strikes took place at night, and cloud cover was frequently encountered during the day. Another was the cumulative effect of bombs and shells bursting within a target box; soon

the craters were so numerous that interpreters could not determine which were caused by what weapon.

The most accurate assessments of bomb damage around Khe Sanh were those made by Marine patrols. For example, a 19 March B-52 raid on a frequently attacked target box left a jumble of craters that mocked even the most skilled photo interpreters, but somewhat later a patrol entered the area and found that a group of bunkers numerous enough to have housed an infantry battalion had been totally destroyed.[15]

Records kept by the 3d Air Division indicated that the B-52's had flown 2,548 sorties and dropped 59,542 tons of bombs. Despite the absence of certainty, General Westmoreland's intelligence specialists tried to assess the destruction caused by this heavy bombardment and reduce it to a manageable statistical form. Visual and photo reconnaissance showed that from 15 January through 31 March the bombers had, among other things, destroyed 274 defensive positions (presumably trenches and bunkers) and damaged 67, while also destroying 17 weapon positions and damaging eight others. Bomber crews reported 1,382 secondary explosions and 108 secondary fires. To estimate the number killed by B-52 bombardment was patently impossible.[16]

Indications of the destruction wrought by B-52's among North Vietnamese forces appeared in notebooks and diaries retrieved by Marines and soldiers after they had broken the siege. One such document contained the opinion that the battle for Khe Sanh was fiercer than Dien Bien Phu, a judgment based to a great extent on the unceasing pounding by B-52's, whose bombs could kill even those who had taken refuge in caves or underground shelters. Another notebook disclosed that Stratofortress attacks had caused 300 persons to desert from a North Vietnamese unit of unspecified size.[17]

On the other hand, Pham Van Hong, a North Vietnamese captured in April 1968, told interrogators that his unit had fared much better. After its arrival in Quang Tri province during January of that year, the force received frequent, timely, and accurate warnings of impending B-52 attacks. These alerts came by radio or telephone and usually provided 2 hours' notice, ample time to march out of a threatened area. Where the warnings originated, he did not know, but possibilities included Russian trawlers operating in the western Pacific and the interception and decoding of messages received at or sent from Tan Son Nhut.[18]

Another North Vietnamese outfit reported to have survived B-52 raids with remarkably few casualties was the company that occupied the captured Lang Vei Special Forces camp. Two evening raids, conducted late in March, killed one and wounded six. The prisoner who told this story attributed the few casualties to the strength of the bunkers built there when the site was under American control.[19]

General Westmoreland, who throughout the battle had personally decided what targets the B-52's would hit, was elated by the work of the big bombers. In a speech to the officers and men of the 3d Air Division at Guam on 13 June 1968, the general characterized the Khe Sanh action as "a battle that was won by you and exploited by the 1st Air Cavalry Division of the United States Army and the Marines." He further declared he had chosen the nickname Niagara "because I visualized your bombs falling like water over the famous falls there in northern New York state, and that's exactly what happened." According to General Westmoreland, "the thing that broke their backs was basically the fire of the B-52's." [20]

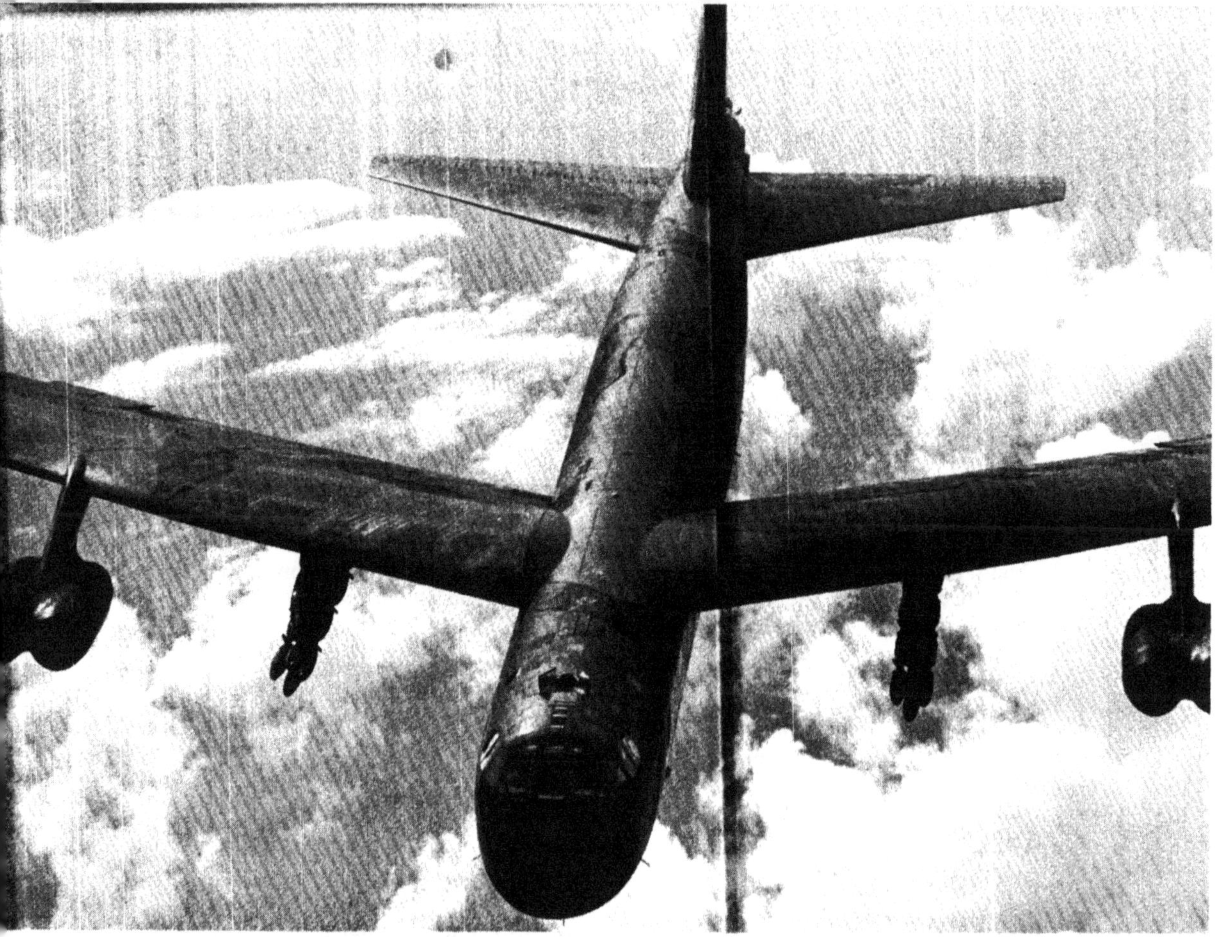

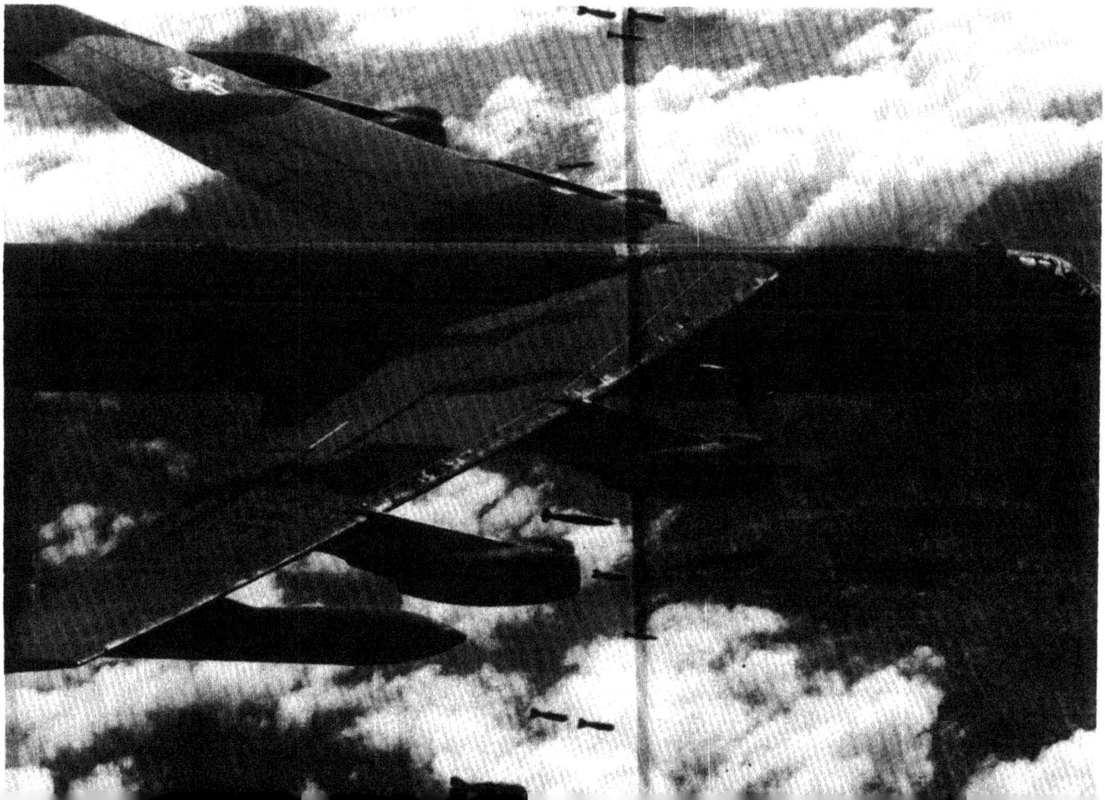

VIII.   BEYOND THE NEXT HILL

"I have been passing my life," the Duke of Wellington once reminisced. "in guessing what I might meet beyond the next hill or around the next corner." Those who directed the defense of Khe Sanh had a distinct advantage over the victor of Waterloo, for in deciding what the enemy had in store for them they could rely more on deduction than on instinct. This was possible because of the variety of means they had at their disposal for gathering data. These methods varied from prisoner interrogation to electronic sensors that enabled the Americans to eavesdrop on the foe.

Intelligence Preparations

Before the struggle for Khe Sanh began, General Westmoreland launched what he called Niagara I, the intelligence preparation for the deluge of high explosives that was Operation Niagara. A Niagara intelligence center was set up at Tan Son Nhut to concentrate on hostile activity around Khe Sanh. Many of the center's photo interpreters and other specialists were normally assigned to Seventh Air Force or U.S. Military Assistance Command, Vietnam, but some were flown to Tan Son Nhut from as far away as the continental United States expressly to assist with the Khe Sanh operation.[1]

Impressive as the work of this center was—its photo specialists, for example, handled twice the weekly amount of film usually processed by Seventh Air Force—it could not provide the up-to-the-minute data needed by American commanders. General Westmoreland realized that the usual sources of intelligence would not be adequate. "While we have available the full resources of Arc Light," he observed, "our ability to preempt or blunt . . . a concerted attack is currently limited by the need for precise intelligence on the location of enemy buildup and staging areas."[2]

The Marines at Khe Sanh had the same problem, though on a lesser scale. They wanted to find out what was happening in the fog and darkness just a few hundred yards away. For instance, a listening post established beyond the perimeter of Lieutenant Colonel Wilkinson's 1st Battalion, 26th Marines, heard dogs barking, estimated the distance to the source of this noise, and called down artillery. The barking stopped, but the defenders had no way of knowing whether hostile troops had actually been present or, if there, how many had been killed or wounded.[3]

An Electronic Battlefield

The likeliest method of improving intelligence coverage seemed to be a system originally designed to ferret out trucks entering South Vietnam by way of Laos and the Ho Chi Minh trail. This surveillance system, whose development had been the responsibility of Army Gen. Alfred D. Starbird's Washington-based Defense Communications Planning Group, involved the use of electronic sensors accurately implanted along known or suspected routes of North Vietnamese infiltration. There were two basic types of sensor: seismic, triggered by shock waves passing through the earth; and acoustic, activated by sound waves that traveled through the air.

These devices broadcast to an orbiting airplane, in this case a specially equipped Lockheed EC-121 which relayed the signal to an infiltration surveillance center at Nakhon Phanom in Thailand. Because of the distinctive shape of one of its antennas, this installation was called Dutch Mill. Here were the computers that compared the incoming signal with previously stored data to determine what had caused the sensor to begin broadcasting.[4]

By way of example, and allowing for some oversimplification, a machine at Dutch Mill might compare the broadcast sound of a truck motor with the same sound recorded and planted in its memory. Since the two matched, the computer would advise the tactical analysis officer who made the query that a truck had activated this particular sensor. As other sensing devices successively reported this same sound, the tactical analysis officers could determine the route the truck was taking and calculate its speed.[5]

In January 1968, few persons were aware how the sensors worked and knew their advantages and limitations. For this reason, Brig. Gen. William P. McBride, the Air Force officer in command at Nakhon Phanom, and several of his subordinates travelled to Dong Ha, South Vietnam, for a conference with Marine leaders, among them General Tompkins, the commander of the Khe Sanh regiment's parent division.

During the discussion, Air Force Col. William L. Walker, Director of Intelligence for Task Force Alpha, as the Dutch Mill contingent was called, told the Marines the surveillance center could help them in two ways. It could interpret sensor data and provide warning of attacks by groups of 100 men or more, and it could in similar fashion improve the effectiveness of unobserved artillery fire at night to harass a weary enemy and impede his movement. Of the two, warning was more important, for at the outset of the struggle elephant grass "grew as high as 20 feet" in the vicinity of the base and, according to Colonel Lownds, enabled men to pass unseen within 50 meters of a defensive outpost.[6]

Prior to Khe Sanh, Task Force Alpha had for some 6 weeks used sensors against truck traffic passing through Laos and had enjoyed a measure of success. An unproven plan existed to use the devices to detect groups moving on foot. Based on this limited experience, Colonel Walker estimated that about 250 sensors would be required to cover the many trails and other avenues of approach over which the North Vietnamese might move. These, he told General Tompkins, could be planted and functioning in a week or 10 days, but that was too slow for the Marines. "If you can cut it to 4 days," the general replied, "I'll consider you've done a good job." Task Force Alpha met this deadline, but not without difficulty.[7]

Planting the Sensors

The major problem in setting out a sensor field was obtaining an accurate location for each and every device. The ideal way to get this accuracy was to provide several teams of men with detailed maps, take them out by helicopter, land them, and have them install the sensors by hand. With the enemy in control of the hinterlands around Khe Sanh, this sort of operation was impossible. Both types had to be planted from the air—the seismic dropped from sufficient height to bury their spiked snouts deep in the ground, and the acoustic eased downward among trees where they could hang undetected and transmit whatever sounds they picked up.[8]

Two kinds of planes were available to drop the sensors. One was the Navy's Lockheed OP-2E, a conventionally powered patrol craft that had been fitted with auxiliary jet engines. The other was the Air Force's Sikorsky CH-3, a turbine-engine helicopter. During sensor drops, both types were shepherded by forward air controllers who could call for flak suppression strikes if ground fire menaced their charges. Because they were very vulnerable to antiaircraft fire, the Lockheeds were later retired in favor of F-4's.[9]

The helicopters had originally been fitted with launchers designed to shoot into the ground a special seismic device called a helosid—contraction for helicopter delivered seismic intrusion detector—thus enabling the craft to hover above the sensor, plot its exact location, and obtain radio verification from Dutch Mill that the device was actually broadcasting. During tests, crews of the CH-3's seldom received this verification, for the shock of smashing into the earth was more than the sensor could endure. The squadron commander continued experimenting, however, but soon gave up entirely on using the helosids. He proposed instead to position a crewman in the door holding an acoustic device which he would toss overboard as the helicopter hovered over the desired location. This method, as effective as it was simple, proved invaluable in meeting General Tompkin's deadline.[10]

Using Sensor Data

Completion of the Khe Sanh sensor field was just a beginning. Successful use of the data it generated would depend on reliable communication and a full understanding of how sensor information should be interpreted to provide targets for artillery and air.

A break in communication oc-

HELOSID (Seismic)

curred early in the fight. On 2 February, a 122-mm rocket plunged through the entrance of a bunker being used by an Army signal detachment. The blast killed four and wounded one, but communication was quickly restored. The tragedy caused the 37th Signal Battalion to insist on blast walls and other protective features in bunkers occupied by its men.[11]

Making intelligent use of the so-called "spotlight reports"—map coordinates radioed from Dutch Mill—was difficult. Despite instructions to the contrary, many officers, Air Force as well as Marine, tended to think of the grid coordinates as a target to be fired upon, rather than as the location of a sensor or string of sensors that had been activated. Fortunately, there was a Marine captain in the Khe Sanh fire support coordination center who was familiar with sensors, having attended a symposium on them before being sent to Vietnam.[12]

He was Capt. Mirza M. Baig, who saw the need to interpret sensor data in light of other intelligence. Aerial photographs, for example, disclosed the supply points, bunkers, trenches, and trails that the enemy used and enabled intelligence specialists to determine a pattern of movement. Once this pattern was understood, Marines in the fire support coordination center could assign a precise meaning to sensor activations. If only a few kept broadcasting for some time, the activity was stationary and could be construction of some sort. If several came on in succession, the enemy was moving; his speed, direction, and route indicated his purpose.[13]

Because the data from Nakhon Phanom frequently dealt with movement—and also because Dutch Mill could not pinpoint all its hurriedly emplaced sensors—the Marines came to employ area bombardment by air and artillery when responding to sensor activations. If the high explosives saturated an area 500 by 1,000 meters, the concentration was called a mini-Arc Light, a less devastating copy of a B-52 strike. If the destruction was confined to a 500-meter square, the term used was micro-Arc Light. The usual time required to plan and execute a mini-Arc Light was 45 minutes, and for a micro-Arc Light only 10 minutes.[14]

Events of 3 to 5 February showed the value of sensor reports on enemy movement. Information sent from Dutch Mill on two consecutive nights convinced Captain Baig that as many as six battalions menaced the Marine outpost on Hill 881S. As the enemy closed in on the hill—or so the captain interpreted the spotlight reports—the sensors fell silent, but the fire support coordination center at Khe Sanh had heard enough to calculate the attacker's speed and likely route. The Leathernecks were thus able to plan a 500- by 600-meter artillery concentration on the mist-shrouded area from which the enemy would have to launch his assault.

The North Vietnamese need not, however, concentrate entirely in the likeliest attack position. They could if they chose send units to outflank the defensive position. To cover this possibility—"to copper-bottom our bet," in Captain Baig's words—the Marines planned additional barrages at the east and west ends of the original target area.

The first shells from Army and Marine artillery began falling at 0230 on the morning of 5 February. More than 500 explosions rocked the approaches to Hill 881S, and the expected attack did not materialize.

As the hostile battalions advanced toward the deadly concentrations planned for them, they passed through an area not monitored by sensors. At this time an estimated two battalions peeled off from the main force and made their way unseen and unheard to the base of Hill 861A. The enemy suddenly materialized out of the fog and stormed the Marine outpost located atop this hill, but the defenders, assisted by air strikes and artillery fire, succeeded in beating him back.[15]

The Khe Sanh sensor field also wrought the destruction of a North Vietnamese antiaircraft unit. Throughout an entire night, a string of sensors near Highway 9 remained active, only to fall silent at first light. Marine artillery lobbed several shells into the area to discourage enemy activity during the following night. Dawn disclosed the

craters left by the nighttime firing, and an alert aerial observer located among these shell holes several freshly dug pits about 10 feet square. After sunset, the signals resumed, and shells once again burst along the highway. Another early morning reconnaissance flight discovered six 37-mm antiaircraft guns, some of them shorn of camouflage by the latest shelling. A mini-Arc Light soon burst upon the area, and the newly dug emplacements were abandoned before the guns had fired a shot.[16]

Gravel Munitions

Task Force Alpha had planned to use a special kind of ordnance in conjunction with the sensors. This was gravel, a tiny explosive mine that could be sown by the thousands from low-flying aircraft. Gravel came in two types, one a mere noisemaker and another powerful enough to wound a man or puncture a truck tire. The designers of the anti-infiltration system believed that gravel would channel enemy movement into areas covered by sensors and would also make enough noise to activate acoustic devices.

In actual practice, however, gravel was little more than a nuisance to the North Vietnamese massing before Khe Sanh. The enemy found that by using oxen pulling logs he could easily clear a gravel minefield, though at some cost in oxen if he was dealing with the casualty-producing kind. The mines, moreover, tended to become inert after a short time.[17]

Gravel unfortunately could not distinguish friend from foe. Those planning the minefields had to avoid impeding patrols or sorties either by troops at Khe Sanh or by a relief column advancing toward the base. Also, pilots whose propeller-driven A-1E Skyraiders were dropping gravel had to be careful of hitting friendly units. This kind of accident happened only once, on 10 February, when gravel fell on the forward slope of a position manned by Colonel Wilkinson's 1st Battalion, 26th Marines.

One Marine suffered wounds serious enough to require his evacuation by air.[18]

Summing Up the Sensor Operation

Despite this misdirected load of gravel munitions and the initial confusion in using sensor data, the Marines were delighted with the work of Task Force Alpha. By Marine estimate, 40 percent of the raw intelligence available to the Khe Sanh fire support coordination center came from the sensors by way of Dutch Mill.

Maj. Jerry E. Hudson, intelligence officer of the 26th Marines, illustrated the importance of sensors by contrasting how artillery performed at night before and after the Marines learned to apply sensor data. "Prior to the coming of sensors," he recalled, "it was command doctrine to shoot numerous harassment and interdiction artillery missions each night . . . usually based on map inspection, suspect areas, and yesterday's intelligence." Once the Marines learned how to put sensor information to work, "the words harassment and interdiction"—again according to Major Hudson—"were removed from the 3d Marine Division vocabulary."[19]

At Khe Sanh, both seismic sensors —other than the too fragile helosids— and the acoustic type demonstrated their worth to air and ground commanders. These devices had so dramatic an impact that the value of other sources of intelligence has sometimes been forgotten. Yet the usefulness of data obtained electronically depended to a large degree on other information. Aerial photography, in particular, enabled the Marines to locate the network of trails and trenches, the bunkers, the supply points and assembly areas upon which the enemy relied. With this sort of intelligence and a knowledge of how the North Vietnamese had conducted previous sieges, Khe Sanh's defenders were able to make effective use of the information sent them from Nakhon Phanom.[20]

A helicopter crewman (l.) prepares to drop a seismic sensor. CH–3's (below) were used to sow sensor fields

IX. THE FIGHT IS WON

March was not a quiet time for the defenders of Khe Sanh, even though the worst was over and by mid-month the enemy was pulling back some of his forces. Intelligence twice indicated the strong possibility of an attack on the base. The first such instance was on 13 and 14 March—the former date being the 14th anniversary of the beginning of the siege of Dien Bien Phu—when a flurry of hostile activity brought a sharp reaction from American artillery and air. On the 14th, B-52 crews reported 59 secondary explosions from their bombs, and tactical aircraft received credit for killing 62 North Vietnamese. Included in this grim total were at least some of the 25 killed by bombs and shells in what seemed to be an assembly area only 2 kilometers southwest of the main base.

A second alarm was sounded on 21-22 March. Once again the attack failed to materialize, despite a hit scored on a Marine ammunition supply point that forced two 105-mm howitzer batteries to suspend firing until the danger from exploding munitions had abated. When an AC-47 gunship appeared over Khe Sanh that evening, hostile activity quickly declined.

According to the Marines, more than 1,000 rounds burst among Khe Sanh's defenses on the 23d. No attack took place, however, possibly because of strikes by B-52's and tactical aviation that detonated an estimated 88 secondary explosions.[1]

Plans and Preparations

Preparations for the relief of Khe Sanh began on 25 January, only 4 days after the first sustained bombardment of the combat base, when General Cushman directed the Army's 1st Cavalry Division (Airmobile) to draft a plan for thrusting westward along Highway 9. The Tet offensive temporarily disrupted planning, but by mid-February III Marine Amphibious Force had resumed work on the problem of reopening the road to Khe Sanh. On 16 February, General Cushman ordered that a Marine regiment take part in the relief. Subsequently, the 1st Marine Division selected its 1st Marines to carry out the assignment in conjunction with Maj. Gen. John Tolson's air cavalry division.

Further delay occurred when General Westmoreland established a provisional corps to direct, subject to General Cushman's guidance, American units in Quang Tri and Thua Thien provinces. Even before General Westmoreland had formally activated this corps, General Cushman assigned to its commander, General Rosson, responsibility for reopening Highway 9 and conducting offensive operations in the vicinity of Khe Sanh.[2]

Discussions involving General Westmoreland, his principal deputy, Gen. Creighton W. Abrams, USA, and Generals Rosson and Cushman resulted in the formulation of a plan of attack. The operation, dubbed Pegasus after the winged steed of classical mythology, would begin about 1 April, the exact date depending on the weather. The 1st

Marines would attack along the highway in conjunction with aerial assaults by General Tolson's airmobile division and an advance by a South Vietnamese task force. The oral agreement was confirmed by a Cushman message that requested General Rosson to continue preparing for a 1 April attack. "Such preparations," the message continued, "should include construction on a C-7A/C-123 strip at Ca Lu and the opening of Route 9 to Ca Lu."[3]

Selection of Ca Lu as a supply base for the relief of Khe Sanh was the most recent in a series of actions undertaken to ensure a steady flow of supplies to Army units in the five northern provinces. When the first Army troops, men of Task Force Oregon which became the Americal Division, entered I Corps, the U.S. Army Support Command at Qui Nhon supervised their logistical support, working through the 80th General Support Group and 34th Supply and Service Battalion, both at Da Nang. Late in February 1968, a U.S. Army Support Command began functioning at Da Nang, taking over the two logistical units already there. A third such unit, the 26th General Support Group from Cam Ranh Bay, moved to Da Nang and became a component of the newly-activated support command.[4]

Logistic support of Operation Pegasus was a cooperative venture coordinated by General Cushman's headquarters and involving the Naval Support Activity at Da Nang as well as the recently organized U.S. Army Support Command. All items not unique to the Marine Corps were provided through the Ca Lu forward support facility, where enough supplies had been stockpiled to see the Pegasus force through 5 days' operation. The Force Logistics Command, which sent both men and cargo handling equipment to Ca Lu, remained responsible for articles used exclusively by Marines.[5]

Highway 9 was the main supply artery for Pegasus. Because of the possibility of interdiction by hostile artillery, an airfield was built at Ca Lu capable of accommodating C-7A's and C-123's. Experience at Khe Sanh had convinced General Cushman that preparations

AC-47 gunships flew night missions over Khe Sanh to suppress enemy shelling

should be made to set up at Ca Lu the kind of radar that would enable Air Force transports to parachute cargo regardless of the weather. A lack of enemy resistance, however, made this precaution unnecessary.[6]

Marine engineers and engineers from the 1st Cavalry Division cooperated with a detachment from Naval Mobile Construction Battalion 5 to complete the Ca Lu airstrip in time for Pegasus. To build the required 2,600-foot runway, the Seabees had to level two hills and gouge away part of a mountainside. Despite the enormity of the job, which began on 16 March, the field was open to C-7A's on 29 March and to the larger C-123's on 7 April. Called Landing Zone Stud by the air cavalry, this field was the principal base for Army helicopters taking part in Pegasus.[7]

The Attack Westward

As the logistic preparations neared completion, both General Tolson's air cavalry and Colonel Lownds' garrison launched operations preliminary to Pegasus itself. Helicopters of the 1st Cavalry Division darted low over the bomb-scarred terrain to locate enemy weapon emplacements and defensive strongpoints. The weather abetted this reconnaissance, for rain seldom continued after dawn, and cloud cover tended to break up by noon.[8]

On the morning of 30 March, the 26th Marines struck a final blow before American forces in northwestern I Corps went over to the offensive. Company B of that regiment's 1st Battalion took advantage of fog and carefully coordinated artillery barrages and air strikes to raid a North Vietnam position. The bursting shells and bombs cleared the way for the advancing Marines but failed to alert the enemy, who occupied an area that had frequently been battered in similar fashion. The assault force erupted from the rising fog and stormed the works with flame throwers, satchel charges, grenades, rifles, and machine guns. The North Vietnamese, caught by surprise, took refuge in their bunkers, but the Marines methodically destroyed these structures, killing an estimated 150 of the enemy. Resistance was largely ineffectual except for the lone mortar round that scored a direct hit on the company command post, killed three, and wounded Capt. Kenneth Pipes, USMC, the company commander.[9]

Maj. Gen. J. J. Tolson III commanded the Army's 1st Cavalry Division (Airmobile)

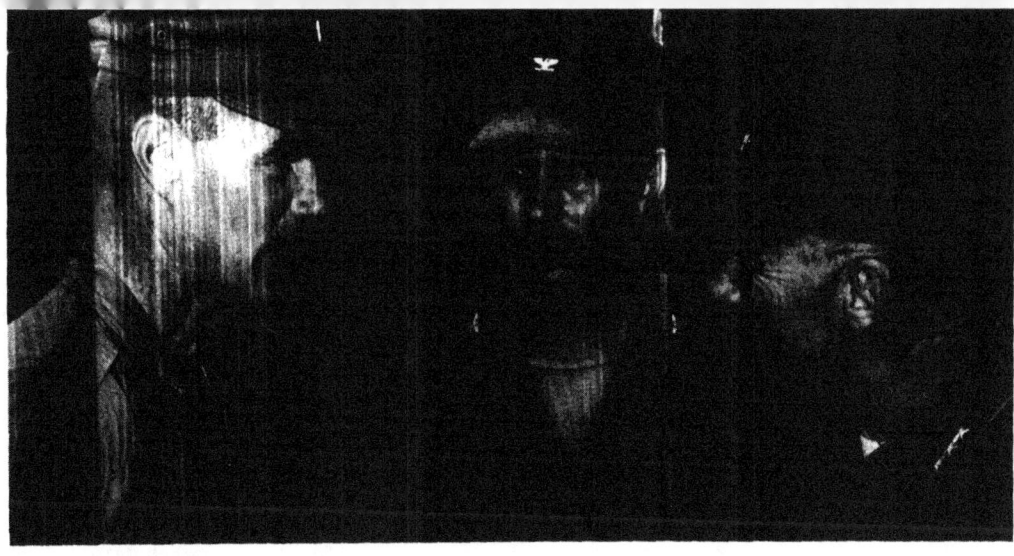

Colonel Lownds (center), commander 26th Marines, Chaplain J. W. McElroy (l.), and Lt. Gen. V. J. Krulak, Commanding General, Fleet Marine Force, Pacific (r.), discuss situation at Khe Sanh

This raid coincided with a diversionary push in the northeastern corner of Quang Tri province. Soldiers and Marines, along with South Vietnamese troops, launched sweeps through the region bounded by Highway 1, the demilitarized zone, the Cua Viet river, and the seacoast. On the following day, operation control of Colonel Lownds' reinforced regiment passed to General Tolson. All was now in readiness for Pegasus.[10]

On 1 April, General Tolson set his troops in motion toward Khe Sanh. Two Marine battalions advanced along Highway 9, screening a group of engineers who repaired the cratered roadway as they moved westward. Acting in concert with this column, air cavalry units seized landing zones selected during the earlier reconnaissance, flew in artillery, and set up fire bases to support the continuing advance.[11]

As the relief force knifed forward, intelligence verified that only the 304th North Vietnamese Division remained in the area. Some of the prisoners taken along Highway 9 were members of the 325C Division, but interrogation revealed that they had remained behind as replacements for casualties suffered by the 304th.[12]

The Khe Sanh Marines also took the offensive on 1 April. Lt. Col. John J. H. Cahill, who had just assumed command of the 1st Battalion, 9th Marines, attacked hostile positions some 2,500 meters south of the Khe Sanh airstrip. The objective was a hill, 471 meters high, that dominated a stretch of Highway 9. A thunderous bombardment killed or demoralized many of the North Vietnamese defenders, and opposition was characterized as light. Unfortunately, enemy mortars scored the same sort of deadly hit that had wounded Captain Pipes a short time before. A shell burst among the command group of Company A, killing two and wounding three. One of the wounded was the new battalion commander, but his injuries were not serious enough to force him to relinquesh command. Later in the day, an enemy counterattack collapsed on the battalion's defenses.[13]

Precisely when the siege ended is open to interpretation. An air cavalry battalion relieved Lieutenant Colonel Cahill's men on the morning of 6 April, and later in the day South Vietnamese troops arrived at Khe Sanh by helicopter to relieve the Ranger battalion that had manned the eastern part of the main perimeter. The official relief took place 2 days later when 2d Battalion, 7th Cavalry, reached the Marine base and the 3d Brigade of General Tolson's division assumed responsibility for its defense.[14]

The relief of Khe Sanh did not mark the end of Operation Pegasus. It continued until 15 April, by which time the Americans and their South Vietnamese allies had regained control of northwestern Quang Tri province. The road to Khe Sanh had been reopened and the site of the Lang Vei Special Forces camp recaptured. The price of these accomplishments was 41 soldiers, 51 Marines, and 33 South Vietnamese killed, 207 soldiers, 459 Marines, and 187 South Vietnamese wounded, and 5 Army men missing in action. No Air Force casualties were attributed to this operation. North Vietnamese deaths during Pegasus were placed at 1,304, with 21 taken prisoner. Equipment left behind by the retreating enemy included 557 rifles, 206 crew-served weapons, 4 trucks, 1 anti-aircraft gun, 1 tank, 1 large artillery piece, and 1 armored personnel carrier.[15]

After the Siege

Once the combat base was securely in American hands, the work of salvage began, as the Air Force mission commander supervised the retrieval of such equipment as ground proximity extraction gear, parachutes, and other salvageable articles used in the supply effort.

Troops of the 1st Cavalry Division (Airmobile) move toward their objective in Operation Pegasus

The siege broken, the Marines were relieved by 1st Cavalry Division troops, shown taking up positions along the trench lines of one of the outposts

Though the siege was broken, danger continued to stalk the Khe Sanh plateau. On 13 April, for instance, an Air Force C-130 swerved off the runway, rolled over some extraction equipment, and in dizzying succession smashed into six recently extracted pallets still loaded with cargo, a truck, and a forklift, before grinding to a stop and bursting into flame. The deadly blaze was just beginning to consume the transport when six members of the Air Force detachment reached the wreckage. They were Lt. Col. Zane G. Brewer, Staff Sergeants Kenneth G. Berg and Joe Hogan, Sergeants J. P. Sink and G. A. Kargis, and A1C S. R. Brown. Working together they rescued five military passengers, none of them hurt in the crash, and one civilian whose injuries proved fatal. The crew came through unscathed and escaped unaided from the plane.

The big Lockheed was a total loss. In an attempt to discover what had caused the accident, propellers number 3 and 4 were salvaged for examination by an investigation team. The props were placed in a cargo sling suspended beneath a Marine helicopter for shipment to Dong Ha, first stop on their journey to Tan Son Nhut. Unfortunately, the load began oscillating wildly shortly after takeoff, and the crew had to cut loose the sling in order to save their aircraft. The jettisoned props could not be recovered because of the likelihood the enemy would use them to bait an ambush.[16]

On 15 April, as the day's second scheduled C-130 was on the ground, the North Vietnamese fired the first of 306 rounds to fall during the day. The pilot of the Hercules immediately taxied into position and took off, carrying with him the American advisers he had brought to Khe Sanh to join the South Vietnamese army unit to which they were assigned. Also on board were the members of the aerial port detachment who had entered the cargo compartment to tie down salvaged articles that were to be loaded inside.[17]

While the handful of airmen at the base gathered up abandoned equipment for shipment eastward by plane, truck, or helicopter, many of the fortifications that had survived the siege were being torn down. The Marines, Lieutenant Colonel Brewer discovered, were planning to leave the base according to a timetable that had the last troops departing on 17 April. Early on the morning of the 15th, before that day's shelling had begun, word arrived that General Westmoreland's headquarters had disapproved the plan.[18]

"We've changed signals," General Cushman told reporters at Da Nang. He explained that only a thousand or so Marines would remain at the base, while the other veterans of the recent battle would form a mobile task force to operate in western Quang Tri. If enemy activity in the area should diminish, he continued, the entire garrison would be withdrawn.[19]

Not until June 1968 were the structures at Khe Sanh at last dismantled. Brig. Gen. Carl W. Hoffman, USMC, who commanded the task force operating in western Quang Tri, confirmed the closing of the base. Emphasis, he declared, had shifted from static defense to a more flexible type of operation. "We have not abandoned our interest in the Khe Sanh plateau," he told the press. "What we have abandoned is the sand bagged island in the middle of it."[20]

X. AFTERMATH OF VICTORY

The battle for Khe Sanh turned out much as President Johnson's military advisers had predicted. The confidence shared by Generals Westmoreland and Wheeler and the service chiefs was thoroughly vindicated. The kind of determined ground assault that had overrun Dien Bien Phu never materialized despite harrowing bombardment and occasional vicious probes of defensive positions.

Compared to the ill-fated French base, Khe Sanh was lavishly supported by artillery and air. More than 150,000 artillery and mortar shells were fired in defense of the Marine base; indeed, the total may have approached 200,000. Operation Niagara lived up to its name, as aircraft ranging in size and complexity from T-28's to B-52's dropped some 100,000 tons of bombs in all sorts of weather, day or night. American cargo planes did what French transports had been unable to do and sustained the 6,000-man garrison with no assistance from any other form of transportation. Estimated weight of supplies delivered by air to Khe Sanh was 12,430 tons, the fruits of 1,124 successful sorties.[1]

Between 20 January and 31 March, the number of Americans killed while manning Khe Sanh's defenses totaled 199. Those wounded during the period numbered 1,600, of whom 845 had to be evacuated for medical treatment. Although only nine North Vietnamese were made prisoner and 41 suspected Viet Cong taken into custody, the "most reasonable estimate" was that the hostile forces massed against Khe Sanh suffered 10,000 casualties—killed and wounded requiring evacuation. Accepting this estimate of 10,000, the number killed and gravely wounded by Khe Sanh's defenders equaled 59 percent of the number of the enemy killed in all of I Corps during the Tet offensive. It was some 3,000 more than the enemy dead in and around the city of Hue, and amounted to 27 percent of the total North Vietnamese and Viet Cong dead throughout all of South Vietnam as a result of the Tet fighting.[2]

The enemy's losses around Khe Sanh cannot, of course, be confirmed since no actual body count was possible. General Westmoreland's Systems Analysis Office prepared four mathematical models from which its technicians concluded that the total enemy killed and seriously wounded numbered between 49 to 65 percent of the force that began the siege—between 9,800 and 13,000 men. The generally cited estimate, 10,000, is half the number of North Vietnamese troops believed committed at the outset of the operation.[3]

President Johnson hailed Khe Sanh as a decisive victory. The Chief Executive, in awarding the Presidential Unit Citation to the 26th Marines, paid tribute to the "most overwhelming, intelligent, and effective use of air power in the history of warfare" and saluted the "endurance—and the artillery—of the Marines at Khe Sanh." According to Mr. Johnson, "by pinning down—and by decimating—two North Vietnamese divisions, the few thousand Marines and their South Vietnamese allies prevented these divisions from entering other major battles such as for Hue and Quang Tri." The fight at Khe Sanh, the President declared, had "vividly demonstrated to the enemy the utter futility of his attempts to win a military victory in the South." [4]

Unfortunately, the successful defense of Khe Sanh was overshadowed by the Tet offensive. Whereas the outcome of Khe Sanh inspired hope and confidence, the Tet fighting generated gloom. The scope and daring of the Tet offensive, rather than the actual military results, jolted American officialdom. According to Admiral Sharp, "They got so damn hysterical back in Washington over the Tet offensive that they sort of went off the deep end and decided to get the war over with even if we weren't going to win it." President Johnson sketched his own picture of dismay in the capital, complaining in a television interview that he had "never seen some of our stalwarts in our operation in Washington dealing with the Southeast Asia theater that were as depressed as they were after Tet.[5]

Why this discouragement at Washington? It apparently was a reaction to the optimism that was rampant just a few months before the enemy deliberately shattered the peace of the Tet holiday. On 21 November, for example, General Westmoreland had told the National Press Club, Washington, D.C., that the enemy was definitely losing the war. He reported that the North Vietnamese and Viet Cong had not won a "major battle" in over a year, that they could employ "large forces" only "at the edges of . . . sanctuaries," and that the Viet Cong guerrillas were suffering diminishing numbers and sagging morale. The speech did not rule out the possibility of counterattack; indeed, General Westmoreland warned that the enemy was trying to prolong the war, mainly to obtain political leverage to force the United States to stop bombing the North, but he described the enemy as "occasionally sallying forth from his sanctuaries and attempting by his countersweep operations to regain control of the population and to rebuild his guerrilla forces." The Tet offensive seemed more than a mere countersweep.[6]

Yet, despite the magnitude of the enemy effort, General Westmoreland's faith in his troops remained unshaken. Nor was this trust misplaced, for they dealt the enemy some staggering blows during the days immediately following Tet. Although aware of the disruption of the South Vietnamese war effort—the closing of training facilities, loss of control over rural areas, and a temporary cessation of recruiting—the American commander looked upon the Tet fighting as an opportunity rather than a setback. He was thinking in terms of bolder action against a battered foe who had lost some 37,000 men killed during the thrust at South Vietnam's cities.[7]

The role of a base such as Khe Sanh had changed between 1965 and 1968. Merely holding it and dispatching lightly armed patrols was no longer sufficient to impede infiltration. Plans did exist, however, to use Khe Sanh as a base from which reconnaissance teams would enter Laos to plant sensors that would report to the infiltration surveillance center at Nakhon Phanom. An offensive launched from Khe Sanh across the border (as done in 1971 by South Vietnamese troops) would have been far more effective than the planned electronic barrier, but such a thrust would have violated the political restrictions then in force.[8]

Khe Sanh appears to have served two major purposes, moral and military, since it provided both a symbol of American determination and an anvil upon which air power could hammer the enemy. In frustrating a North Vietnamese attempt to recreate the triumph of Dien Bien Phu, American forces demonstrated their country's determination and at the same time inflicted the paralyzing casualties that the French had hoped for more than a decade earlier.

Uncertainty clouds the activities and purposes of the enemy. For example, President Johnson publicly linked the Tet offensive, which began on 20-21 January, to North Korea's capture of the intelligence ship *Pueblo* on the 23d. But in doing so, he admitted that he had no positive proof.[9]

Nor was it entirely clear whether the North Vietnamese considered the capture of Khe Sanh an essential part of the Tet offensive. The amount of artillery and number of antiaircraft guns dug in around Khe Sanh were indicative of a major effort, as was the massing of two divisions to deal with a heavily reinforced Marine regiment. On the other hand, the North Vietnamese made no attempt to cut off Khe Sanh's water supply or to tunnel beneath the defensive works. Nor was there any evidence of an extensive network of siege trenches until the third week of February. The enemy, it thus appears, looked upon Khe Sanh as a desirable objective, one whose capture would open an invasion route toward the populous coastal region, but he would have stormed the base only if certain he could do so with acceptable losses. A repeat of the bloody assaults at Dien Bien Phu, which had threatened to demoralize the attacking infantry, was apparently not part of the North Vietnamese plan. But had the American high command been less overwhelming in its support of the Khe Sanh garrison, the enemy might well have tried to storm the base.

Amid these uncertainties looms the Gibraltar-like mass of statistics that deal with aerial and artillery support of Khe Sanh. Seventh Air Force, for example, received credit for 9,691 sorties that dropped a total of 14,223 tons of bombs. The 3d Air Division's B-52's totaled 2,548 sorties and 59,542 tons; the 1st Marine Aircraft Wing launched 7,078 sorties and dropped 17,015 tons; and Navy aviation could point to 5,337 sorties and 7,941 tons dropped. Supporting artillery units also were active, the Marine howitzer and 4.2-inch mortar batteries within the defensive perimeter firing almost 160,000 rounds during the battle.[10]

Unfortunately, weather and other considerations prevented an accurate survey of the damage inflicted upon the enemy. In the case of air attack, the best intelligence specialists could do was to establish a few general categories of targets and try to determine, mainly through photos and visual observation, how air power had fared against each. A typical assessment credited Niagara aircraft with 4,705 secondary explosions, 1,288 enemy killed, 1,061 structures destroyed, 158 damaged, 891 bunkers destroyed, 99 damaged, 253 trucks destroyed, and 52 damaged.[11]

Such a compilation fails to do justice to the effectiveness of American air power in pounding the troops and weapons that threatened Khe Sanh. Statistical uncertainty does not, however, diminish the importance of tactical aircraft and B-52's in expending bombs and rockets to save American and South Vietnamese lives. Rather than cite numbers, one may well accept General Westmoreland's conclusion that the "key to our success at Khe Sanh was firepower, principally aerial firepower."[12]

What was the political effect of the successful defense of Khe Sanh? Minimal, it would seem, for the last of the Niagara bombs had hardly fallen when President Johnson adopted a new course for the United States to follow in seeking peace for Southeast Asia. On 31 March the President announced that he had "ordered our aircraft and our naval vessels to make no attacks on North Vietnam, except in the area north of the demilitarized zone where the enemy buildup directly threatens Allied forward positions and where the movement of their troops and supplies are clearly related to that threat." Mr. Johnson declared that the United States remained ready "to send its representatives to any forum, at any time, to discuss the means of bringing this ugly war to an end," and he invited North Vietnam "to respond positively and favorably to this new step toward peace." After revealing this bold plan, the President stated he would not seek reelection.

Beginning in 1965, increasing numbers of American troops and their growing firepower provided the shield behind which South Vietnam could fashion a workable government. This effort had been successful, for, as President Johnson phrased it, "The South Vietnam of 1965 could not have survived the enemy's Tet offensive of 1968." Emphasis, said the President, was now shifting from protecting the South Vietnamese government to equipping and training its armed forces "to meet the enemy's increased firepower" and "progressively to undertake a larger share of combat operations against the Communist invaders." Soon, it was hoped, the South Vietnamese would be able to fight a Khe Sanh of their own, though perhaps with aid from American aircraft and artillery.[13]

CHRONOLOGY

21 December 1967—Marine forces discover evidence that the enemy is massing around Khe Sanh.

2 January 1968—Five North Vietnamese officers, apparently conducting a reconnaissance, are killed just west of the Khe Sanh combat base.

5 January 1968—Planning begins for Operation Niagara, so named on the following day, the coordinated use of B-52's and tactical aircraft in defense of Khe Sanh.

17 January 1968—A Marine reconnaissance team is ambushed near Hill 881N.

18 January 1968—General Westmoreland advises Admiral Sharp of his desire to place the 1st Marine Aircraft Wing, except for transports and helicopters, under the operational control of General Momyer, his deputy for air. On this same day, General Momyer discusses the Westmoreland proposal with General Cushman, Commanding General III Marine Amphibious Force and senior Marine in South Vietnam.

19 January 1968—A Marine patrol draws fire while searching the site of the 17 January ambush. On the following day, a more powerful Marine force returns and attacks the entrenched enemy.

20 January 1968—A lieutenant in the North Vietnamese army surrenders to the Marines and warns them of an impending attack on Khe Sanh. The Marine unit in action on the slopes of Hill 881N is ordered to break contact and fall back to the outpost on Hill 881S.

21 January 1968—North Vietnamese infantry fail to overrun the Marine outpost on Hill 861. The main base at Khe Sanh comes under fire from enemy artillery, and the shelling causes the destruction of 98 percent of the munitions stored in the main ammunition dump.

22 January 1968—Representatives of the Seventh Air Force and III Marine Amphibious Force confer at Da Nang and establish rules for the control and coordination of air support at Khe Sanh. General Westmoreland, however, continues thinking in terms of a single manager for aviation.

23 January 1968—North Korean naval units seize the intelligence ship USS *Pueblo*.

25 January 1968—Planning begins for the relief of Khe Sanh.

29 January 1968—Because of the threat to Khe Sanh, the Saigon headquarters cancels the Tet cease fire in I Corps. The truce, however, goes into effect throughout the rest of South Vietnam.

30-31 January 1968—The Tet offensive begins. The enemy makes his greatest gains at Hue, in I Corps, where he seizes the ancient walled city that served as imperial capital.

5 February 1968—An ammunition-laden C-130 piloted by Lt. Col. Howard Dallman is set ablaze by hostile shells after landing at Khe Sanh. The crew extinguishes the fire and flies the damaged transport to Da Nang.

7 February 1968—A hostile force aided by tanks overwhelms the Lang Vei Special Forces camp.

The last of 26 B-52's dispatched in response to the *Pueblo* incident arrive in the western Pacific. Fifteen of the planes are at Kadena AB, Okinawa, and the remainder at Andersen AFB, Guam.

11 February 1968—An Air Force C-130 flown by Capt. Edwin Jenks is crippled by shell fragments after landing at Khe Sanh. A mechanic from Da Nang arrives to make emergency repairs that enable one plane to take off about noon on the 13th and reach Da Nang where ground crewmen count 242 holes in the aircraft.

12 February 1968—The JCS advise Admiral Sharp's command that Okinawa-based B-52's may fly combat missions to Southeast Asia.

An order by General Momyer goes into effect forbidding Air Force C-130's to land at Khe Sanh. The ban is lifted for the last 4 days of February, then reimposed throughout March.

13 February 1968—Ground radar directs the first successful foul weather delivery of parachute cargo to the Khe Sanh garrison.

16 February 1968—The low altitude parachute extraction system is used for the first time during the siege.

23 February 1968—An estimated 1,300 shells batter Khe Sanh. An ammunition dump catches fire, and 1,500 90-mm and 106-mm rounds are destroyed.

24 February 1968—South Vietnamese troops raise their flag above the palace grounds in Hue's walled city. Mopping up lasts until 2 March.

26 February 1968—B-52's fly a test mission during which one plane drops 108 500-pound bombs on a target box 1,000 meters from friendly positions. Such close-in strikes are common throughout the remainder of the battle.

2 March 1968—Admiral Sharp approves a revised version of General Westmoreland's plan to appoint General Momyer as single manager for air.

6 March 1968—An Air Force C-123K is shot down near Khe Sanh; 48 perish.

10 March 1968—Emergency requests for air support are processed for the first time by the newly approved single manager system.

12 March 1968—Senator Eugene J. McCarthy, an opponent of President Johnson's Vietnam policy, wins 40 percent of the Democratic vote in the New Hampshire primary. The write-in vote for the President, whose name is not on the ballot, totals 49 percent, but the results are interpreted as a defeat for Mr. Johnson.

15 March 1968—American intelligence verifies the withdrawal of part of the North Vietnamese force around Khe Sanh.

21 March 1968—Air strikes planned in advance to support specific ground operations come under single manager procedures.

29 March 1968—The new airstrip at Ca Lu is opened to C-7A's and helicopters that are supporting the impending attack toward Khe Sanh.

30 March 1968—The ground proximity extraction system is used for the first time at Khe Sanh.

31 March 1968—President Johnson announces the end of aerial and naval bombardment of North Vietnam "except in the area north of the demilitarized zone where the continuing enemy buildup directly threatens allied forward positions and where the movement of their troops and supplies are clearly related to that threat." The President calls upon North Vietnam to respond by agreeing to negotiate an end to the hostilities. Mr. Johnson also removes himself from the 1968 Presidential race.

1 April 1968—Operation Pegasus, the advance to Khe Sanh, gets underway.

6 April 1968—South Vietnamese troops arrive by helicopter to relieve a South Vietnamese Ranger unit that has manned a segment of the Khe Sanh perimeter since 27 January.

8 April 1968—The 2d Battalion, 7th Cavalry, 1st Cavalry Division, arrives at Khe Sanh, and the division's 3d Brigade assumes responsibility for the security of the base.

13 May 1968—Delegations from the United States and North Vietnam hold their first formal session at Paris.

20 May 1968—The Chairman, Joint Chiefs of Staff, advises Admiral Sharp and General Westmoreland that Paul Nitze, Deputy Secretary of Defense, has endorsed the decision to select a single manager for tactical air. Mr. Nitze warns, however, that this arrangement should not be cited as a precedent for centralized control, since it has been set up to meet a specific situation.

23 June 1968—The Khe Sanh combat base is dismantled and abandoned.

NOTES

Chapter I

The Signs of War Advance

1. Commander in Chief, Pacific, and Commander, U.S. Military Assistance Command, Vietnam, *Report on the War in Vietnam* (Washington, 1968), pp 131-32 (hereafter cited as *Report on the War*); Gen William C. Westmoreland, "Progress Report on the War in Vietnam," *Department of State Bulletin*, 11 Dec 67, pp 785-88.

2. U.S. Military Assistance Command, Vietnam, "Year-End Review of Vietnam," 1 Jan 68.

3. HQ, USMACV, J-5, Strategic/Tactical Study, "Khe Sanh Viewed from the Dien Bien Phu Perspective," Mar 68.

4. Capt Moyers B. Shore II, *The Battle For Khe Sanh* (Washington, 1969), pp 6-7 (hereafter cited as Shore, *Khe Sanh*); *Report on the War*, pp 91, 123; atch to ltr, Gen William W. Momyer, USAF, to Maj Gen Robert N. Ginsburgh, USAF, no subj, 23 May 72 (hereafter cited as Momyer Comments); ltr, Vice Adm Edwin B. Hooper, USN (Ret) to Brig Gen Brian S. Gunderson, USAF, Chief of Air Force History, no subj, 26 Sep 72 (hereafter cited as Hooper Ltr).

5. TSgt Bruce W. Pollica and TSgt Joe R. Rickey, *834th Air Division Tactical Airlift Support for Khe Sanh, 21 Jan-8 Apr 68*, pp 6-8 (hereafter cited as Pollica and Rickey); Momyer Comments.

6. Pollica and Rickey, pp 7-8; Annual Ops Rprt, U.S. Naval Construction Bn Maintenance Unit 301, 26 Jan-25 Apr 68; Hooper Ltr.

7. HQ, USMACV, J-5 Study, "Khe Sanh Viewed from the Dien Bien Phu Perspective," cited above.

8. Pollica and Rickey, pp 8-9.

9. The section on principal commands and commanders is based in part on Lt Col Robert M. Burch, USAF, *Command and Control, 1966-1968* (HQ PACAF, Project CHECO, 1 Aug 69), pp 4-7, 24-25, 29-31.

10. *Report on the War*, p 101.

11. *Ibid.*, p 142.

12. 7AF Op Order 100-68, 15 Dec 67.

13. USAF Biography of Maj Gen Burl W. McLaughlin, 15 Feb 70; Maj David R. Mets, *Tactical Airlift Operations* (HQ PACAF, Project CHECO, 30 Jun 69), p 2; intvw, author with Maj Gen Robert N. Ginsburgh, USAF, 27 Mar 72; Col Ray L. Bowers, USAF, Comments on draft chapter, 17 apr 72.

14. *Report on the War*, pp 126, 163; 7AF Op Order 100-68, 15 Dec 67.

15. Shore, *Khe Sanh*, pp 3, 23, 26; USMC Biographies of Lt Gen Robert E. Cushman, Jr., May 69; Maj Gen Rathvon McC. Tompkins, Jul 71, Col David Lownds, Jan 68.

16. John T. McAlister, *Vietnam: The Origins of Revolution* (Center for Research in Social Systems, American University, 1968), p 69; *Armed Forces Journal*, Sep 71, p 26.

17. Statement by Maj Gen Rathvon McC. Tompkins, USMC, 19 Nov 70, in Hearings before Electronic Battlefield Subcmte, Senate Preparedness Investigating Subcmte, Cmte on the Armed Services, 91st Cong., 2d Sess, *Investigation into the Electronic Battlefield Program*, pp 81-82 (hereafter cited as Senate Hearings, *Electronic Battlefield Program*).

18. HQ USMACV, J-5 Study, "Khe Sanh Viewed from the Dien Bien Phu Perspective."

19. General Tompkins Statement, 19 Nov 70, in Senate Hearings, *Electronic Battlefield Program*, pp 81-82.

20. Extracts from DIA Intelligence Bulletin, 5 Feb 68, p A-12.

21. General Tompkins Statement, 19 Nov 70, in Senate Hearings, *Electronic Battlefield Program* p 82; msg. COMUSMACV to AIG 7051, *et al*,

subj: J-2 DISUM 23-26 (220001-222400 Jan 68), (260215Z Jan 68), in Warren A. Trest, *Khe Sanh (Operation Niagara), 22 Jan- 31 Mar 68* (HQ PACAF, Project CHECO, 13 Sep 68), Exhibit 74 (hereafter cited as Trest, *Khe Sanh (Operation Niagara)*.

22. Military Assistance Command, Combat Operations Center Fact Sheet, subj: Chronology of Operation Niagara, 19 Apr 68; Brig Gen Edwin H. Simmons, USMC, "Marine Corps Operations in Vietnam, 1968," *U.S. Naval Institute Proceedings,* May 1970, p 296.

23. Fleet Marine Force, Pacific, *Operations of Marine Forces in Vietnam,* Sep 67, p 9.

24. *Report on the War,* p 163.

25. Simmons, "Marine Corps Operations in Vietnam, 1968," p 297; Shore, *Khe Sanh,* pp 26-27.

26. FMFPAC, *Operations of Marine Forces in Vietnam,* Jan 68, p 10.

27. Simmons, "Marine Corps Operations in Vietnam, 1968," p 297.

28. Unless otherwise noted, this section is based on a 2-part interview, conducted by Col John E. Van Duyn, USAF, and Maj Richard B. Clement, USAF, with Maj Gen Robert N. Ginsburgh, USAF, 26 May and 3 Jun 71. For another account of how President Johnson and his advisers reacted to Khe Sanh, see Henry Graff, *The Tuesday Cabinet: Deliberation and Decision on Peace and War Under Lyndon B. Johnson* (Englewood Cliffs, N.J.: Prentice Hall, 1970).

29. Addresses by Gen Earle G. Wheeler, USA, Chairman, Joint Chiefs of Staff, Washington, D.C., 7 July 64 to 2 Jul 70, pt II, p 204.

30. Intvw, Maj Richard B. Clement, USAF, and Jacob Van Staaveren, with Gen Maxwell D. Taylor, USA, 11 Jan 72.

31. Don Oberdorfer, *Tet!* (Garden City, N.Y.: Doubleday and Co., 1971), p 110.

32. Intvw, author with Gen Ginsburgh, 27 Mar 72.

Chapter II

The Precedent of Dien Bien Phu

1. Unless otherwise noted, this chapter is based on Bernard B. Fall, *Hell in a Very Small Place: The Siege of Dien Bien Phu* (New York: J. B. Lippincott Co., 1967).

2. HQ USMACV, J-5 Study, "Khe Sanh as Viewed from the Dien Bien Phu Perspective," cited above.

3. *Ibid.*

4. *Ibid.*

5. *Ibid.*; MACV Study, "Comparisons Between the Battle of Dien Bien Phu and the Analagous Khe Sanh Situation," Mar 68; intvw, author with Gen Ginsburgh, 27 Mar 72.

6. *Report on the War,* pp 162-63; atch to ltr, Westmoreland to Gen Leonard F. Chapman, Jr., USMC, no subj, 29 Mar 69.

7. Atch to memo, Special Assistant for Counterinsurgency and Special Activities, JCS, for Dir/Joint Staff, subj: Questions Concerning Vietnam, 12 Feb 68.

8. Sir Robert Thompson, *No Exit from Vietnam* (New York: David McKay, Inc., 1970), pp 134-35.

9. "Address on U.S. Policy in Vietnam Delivered Before a Joint Session of the Tennessee State Legislature," 15 Mar 67, in *Public Papers of the Presidents of the United States, Lyndon B. Johnson, 1967* (Washington, 1968), I, Item 116, pp 348-354.

Chapter III

Encirclement

1. Msg, COMUSMACV to CINCPAC, subj: Command Status Rprt, 160230Z Jan 68.

2. Shore, *Khe Sanh,* pp 33-39.

3. *Ibid.,* pp 39-41.

4. III MAF Command Chronology, Jan 68, p III:30; PACOM Command Center 0730 Briefing Notes, 22 Jan 68, pt I, p IV:2; rprt, U.S. Naval Construction Battalions, Pacific, Ops and Civic Action, Jan 68, p 5; Hooper Ltr.

5. PACOM Command Center 0730 Briefing Notes, 22 Jan 68, pt I; Op Niagara BDA, 24 Jan 68.

6. 1st Bn, 9th Marines Command Chronology, Jan 68, Pt II; HMM-164 Command Chronology, Jan 68, pt II, p 5.

7. Pollica and Rickey, p 5; Lt Col Edmund B. Crandall, USAF, *et al,* USAF Tactical Airlift Center, *Tactical Airlift in*

SEA, 1 Jan 65-31 Mar 68, p II:60.

8. Command Chronology, 3d Mar Div, FMF, Jan 68; PACOM Command Center 0730 Briefing Notes, 23 Jan 68, pp IV:2-3.

9. Shore, *Khe Sanh,* pp 48-51.

10. Msg, Intrigue 6 to Beach Boy 6, subj: 26th Marines SITREP (241300H), (241325H Jan 68); FMFPAC, *Operations of Marine Forces in Vietnam,* Feb 68, p 26.

11. PACOM Command Center 0730 Briefing Notes, 25 Jan 68; msg, 26th Marines to CG, 3d Mar Div, subj: Op Scotland SITREP no 347 (261201-261800H Jan 68), (261200Z Jan 68).

12. PACOM Command Center 0730 Briefing Notes, 24 Jan 68, p IV:8; msg, CG, III MAF to COMUSMACV, subj: Daily SITREP no 25 (250001H to 252400H Jan 68), (260111Z Jan 68); Trest, *Khe Sanh (Operation Niagara),* pp 14-15.

13. Khe Sanh Analysis, n d, extracted from MACV Study, in Hist, 3d Air Div, Jan-Jun 68, Exhibit 187.

14. Simmons, "Marine Corps Operations in Vietnam, 1968," pp 298-99; *Report on the War,* pp 158-59; Momyer Comments.

15. Simmons, "Marine Corps Operations in Vietnam, 1968," p 299.

16. *Ibid.,* pp 299-301.

17. Ginsburgh intvw, 26 May 71, p 12.

18. Douglas Pike, *Viet Cong: The Organization and Techniques of the National Liberation Front of South Vietnam* (Cambridge, Mass.: MIT Press, 1966), p. 77.

19. Robert Shaplen, *The Road from War, 1965-1970* (New York: Harper and Row, 1970), pp 212-14, 282.

20. Hist. USMACV, 1968, vol I, p. 131.

21. Thompson, *No Exit from Vietnam,* pp 69-70; *Armed Forces Journal,* 26 Feb 68, p 8; atch to ltr, Westmoreland to Gen Leonard F. Chapman, Jr., USMC, 29 Mar 69.

22. 26th Marines Command Chronology, Feb 68, pt II, pp 9-10; Tompkins Statement, 19 Nov 70, containing ltr from Maj Mirza Baig, USMC, in Senate Hearings, *Electronic Battlefield Program,* pp 84-85.

23. Chronology, 315th Air Div, Jan-Jun 68, in Hist, 315th Air Div, Jan-June 68; *Air Force Times,* 3 Apr 68.

24. The account of the action at Lang Vei is based upon Maj John A. Cash, USA, "The Battle of Lang Vei," in *Seven Firefighters in Vietnam* (Washington, 1970), pp 109-138, supplemented by the sources indicated.

25. Msg. COMUSMACV to CG, III MAF, and CO, 5th Special Forces Group, subj: Lang Vei Special Forces Camp, 140801Z Jan 68.

26. Intvw, Warren Trest with Capt Gerald L. Harrington, USAF, 19 Feb 68, in Trest, *Khe Sanh (Operation Niagara),* Exhibit 34.

27. *Ibid.*

28. Shore, *Khe Sanh,* pp 67-68.

29. Intvw, Warren Trest with Capt Charles Rushforth, USAF, 19 Feb 68, in Trest, *Khe Sanh (Operation Niagara),* Exhibit 44.

30. Msg, CO, Company C, 5th SFGA, Da Nang, to CO, 5th SFGA, Nha Trang, 080745Z Feb 68; Shore, *Khe Sanh,* p 69.

31. PACOM Command Center 0730 Briefing Notes, 10 Feb 68, pt I; Shore, *Khe Sanh,* pp 70-71.

32. PACOM Command Center 0730 Briefing Notes, 10 Feb 68, pt I; Shore, *Khe Sanh,* p 76.

33. Pollica and Rickey, p 86.

34. *Ibid.,* pp 12-13; Capt Ken Kashiwahara, USAF, "Lifeline to Khe Sanh," *The Airman,* Jul 68, p 7; Col William R. Smith, USAF, Comments on draft chapter, 14 Apr 72.

35. MR, Col Ray L. Bowers, USAF, 6 Nov 70, subj: General Momyer Presentation to Airlift Symposium at Pope AFB, N.C., 3 Nov 70; Maj Gen Burl W. McLaughlin, USAF, "Khe Sanh: Keeping an Outpost Alive, An Appraisal," *Air University Review,* Nov-Dec 68, p 59.

36. III MAF Command Chronology, p III:18; 1st Bn, 26th Marines, Command Chronology, Feb 6, p III:7; Shore, *Khe Sanh,* pp 55-56, 62, 63, 122-24; PACOM Command Center 0730 Briefing Notes, 24 Feb 68, pp IV:2-3.

37. FMFPAC, *Operations of Marine Forces in Vietnam,* Jul 67, p 10.

38. Msg, 2d Mar Div COC to III MAF COC, subj: 26th Marine SITREP (292000H Feb 68), (292000Z Feb 68); PACOM Command Center 0730 Briefing Notes, 2 Mar 68, p IV:2.

39. Lt Col John F. Masters, Jr., USAF, Mission Commander's Rprt, 22 Feb-3 Mar 68, in Pollica and Rickey, Exhibit 124.
40. *Life*, 23 Feb 68.
41. *Washington Post*, 22 Mar 68.
42. Oliver E. Clubb, Jr., "Khe Sanh—A Goat Tied to a Stake," *New Republic*, 6 Apr 68.
43. James Burnham, "Khe Sanh: Whose Mistake?", *National Review*, 12 Mar 68.
44. *Philadelphia Inquirer*, 3 Mar 68.

Chapter IV

An Aerial Highway

1. Maj Gen Burl W. McLaughlin, End of Tour Rprt, Nov 67-Jun 69, pp I:2-5; Fall, *Hell in a Very Small Place*, pp 2-3; George K. Tanham, *Communist Revolutionary Warfare: The Viet Minh in Indochina* (New York: Praeger, 1961), p 105; intvw, author with Gen Ginsburgh, 27 Mar 72; Col Ray L. Bowers, USAF, Comments on draft chapter, 17 Apr 72.
2. McLaughlin, End of Tour Rprt, p I:5.
3. *Ibid.*, p I:21; Pollica and Rickey, p 41; McLaughlin, "Khe Sanh: Keeping an Outpost Alive," p 68; Fall, *Hell in a Very Small Place*, pp 7-9.
4. Col Ray L. Bowers, USAF, Comments on draft chapter, 22 Dec 71.
5. *Ibid.*
6. Pollica and Rickey, pp 11-12; Shore, *Khe Sanh*, pp 74, 78, 103.
7. Pollica and Rickey, pp 11-12.
8. MR, Col Ray L. Bowers, USAF, subj: Speed Offloading of Transport Aircraft, 5 Nov 71; Col William R. Smith, USAF, Comments on draft chapter, 14 Apr 72.
9. Lt Col William R. Smith, USAF, Mission Commander's Rprt, 7-23 Feb 68, in Pollica and Rickey, Exhibit 25; Col William R. Smith, USAF, Comments on draft chapter, 14 Apr 72.
10. McLaughlin, "Khe Sanh: Keeping an Outpost Alive," pp 65-66, 68.
11. Pollica and Rickey, pp 11-12; Trest, *Khe Sanh (Operation Niagara)*, pp 126-28.
12. McLaughlin, "Khe Sanh: Keeping an Outpost Alive," pp 64-65; Shore, *Khe Sanh*, pp 74-76.
13. PACOM Command Center 0730 Briefing Notes, 1 Mar 68, pt I; msg, 7AF to CINCPACAF *et al*, subj: Special Rprt on Air Ops, 080730Z Mar 68, in Pollica and Rickey, Exhibit 20.
14. Pollica and Rickey, p 50.
15. MR, Rear Adm. S.D. Cramer, USN, Dep Dir for Ops (NMCC), subj: Aircraft Combat Loss and Enemy Mortar Attack on US Army Base Camp, 6 Mar 68. Pollica and Rickey, p 15, say 49 died, but Shore on p 80 accepts 48.
16. Pollica and Rickey, p 19; McLaughlin, "Khe Sanh: Keeping an Outpost Alive," p 61.
17. Pollica and Rickey, pp 9-11.
18. *Ibid.*, pp 26-27; McLaughlin, End of Tour Rprt, p I:18.
19. Pollica and Rickey, pp 27-29.
20. McLaughlin, "Khe Sanh: Keeping an Outpost Alive," pp 60-61; memo, Lt Col Paul W. Arcari, USAF, to Office of Air Force History, subj: Historical Study, "The Fight for Khe Sanh," 6 Apr 72.
21. Pollica and Rickey, pp 21-22.
22. Hist, 315th Air Div, PACAF, Jan-Jun 69, p 71.
23. McLaughlin, "Khe Sanh: Keeping an Outpost Alive," pp 60-63.
24. Shore, *Khe Sanh*, pp 63-64.
25. Lt Col William R. Smith, USAF, Mission Commander's Rprt, 7-23 Feb 68, in Pollica and Rickey, Exhibit 25.
26. Pollica and Rickey, p 50.
27. Msgs, 834th Air Div to Dets 1 and 2, 834th Air Div, subj: Resupply of Khe Sanh, 8 Mar 68, in Pollica and Rickey, Exhibit 50; III MAF COC to MACV COC, subj: Opn Scotland SITREP no 491 (021201-021800H Mar 68), (022233Z Mar 68).
28. Ltr, 834th Air Div (ALCE) to 834th Air Div (ALCC), subj: Khe Sanh Airland and Airdrop Ops (Da Nang), 12 Mar 68, in Pollica and Rickey, Exhibit 96; Lt Col Donald M. Davis, USAF, Mission Commander's Rprt, 16-30 Mar 68, in Pollica and Rickey, Exhibit 42.
29. Ltr, Maj Kenneth D. Stahl, USAF, to Dir/Ops, 834th Air Div, subj: Tactical Airlift Support for Khe Sanh, 21 Jan-8 Apr 48, n d, in Pollica and Rickey, Exhibit 2.
30. Pollica and Rickey, pp 34-35.
31. Ltr, 834th Air Div (ALCE) to 834 Air Div (ALCC), subj: Khe Sanh Airland/Airdrop (Da Nang), 9 Mar 68, in Pollica and Rickey, Exhibit 94.

32 Pollica and Rickey, pp 34, 36-37; Col William R. Smith, USAF, Comments on draft chapter, 14 Apr 72; memo, Lt Col Paul W. Arcari, USAF, to Office of Air Force History, subj: Historical Study, "The Fight for Khe Sanh," 6 Apr 72.

33. Pollica and Rickey, p 35.

34. *Ibid.*, pp 39-40.

35. Msg, TAC to 315th Air Div, subj: GPES, 152158 Mar 68, in Pollica and Rickey, Exhibit 68.

36. Msg, CG, USARV, Long Binh, to 834th Air Div, 191805 Mar 68.

37. Pollica and Rickey, pp 37, 39-40.

38. Shore, *Khe Sanh*, p 78; Col Ray L. Bowers, Comments on draft chapter, 16 Jan 73.

39. Pollica and Rickey, p 37.

40. *Ibid.*, pp 42-43.

41. *Ibid.*, p 44, app IV; Lt Col William R. Smith, USAF, Mission Commander's Rprt, 7-23 Feb 68, and Lt Col Donald M. Davis, USAF, Mission Commander's Rprt, 16-30 Mar 68, in Pollica and Rickey, Exhibits 25 and 42.

42. Lt Col Donald M. Davis, USAF, Mission Commander's Rprt, 16-30 Mar 68, in Pollica and Rickey, Exhibit 42; McLaughlin, "Khe Sanh; Keeping an Outpost Alive," p 65.

43. Lt Col Lewis H. Dunagan, USAF, Mission Commander's Rprt, 2-17 Mar 68, in Pollica and Rickey, Exhibit 41.

44. Pollica and Rickey, pp 44-45.

45. Lt Col Donald M. Davis, USAF, Mission Commander's Rprt, 16-30 Mar 68, in Pollica and Rickey, Exhibit 42.

46. Encl to ltr, Brig Gen E. H. Simmons, USMC (Ret) to Brig Gen Brian S. Gunderson, USAF, no subj, 29 Sep 72.

47. Lt Col Donald M. Davis, USAF, Mission Commander's Rprt, 16-30 Mar 68, in Pollica and Rickey, Exhibit 42.

48. Pollica and Rickey, pp 44-45.

49. Lt Col John F. Masters, Jr., Mission Commander's Rprt, 22 Feb-3 Mar 68, in Pollica and Rickey, Exhibit 124.

50. Shore, *Khe Sanh*, pp 81-82.

51. *Ibid.*, p 82; Command Chronology, 3d Mar Div, Feb 68.

52. Shore, *Khe Sanh*, pp 83, 85-86.

53. *Ibid.*, p 90; 3d Bn, 26th Marines After Action Rprt, 15 Apr 68, in 3d Bn, 26th Marines Command Chronology.

54. Ltr, Maj Kenneth D. Stahl, USAF, to DOC 834th Air Div, subj: Tactical Airlift Support for Khe Sanh, 21 Jan-8 Apr 68, n d, in Pollica and Rickey, Exhibit 2.

55. Pollica and Rickey, pp 15, 86; Rprt, Hq 834th Air Div, Tactical Airlift Support for Khe Sanh, 21 Jan-8 Apr 68, 15 Apr 68, in Pollica and Rickey, App II; Col Ray L. Bowers, Comments on draft chapter, 16 Jan 73.

56. Pollica and Rickey, pp 15, 86.

57. Shore, *Khe Sanh*, pp 76, 86.

Chapter V

Tactical Teamwork

1. Hist, 31st TFW, Jan-Mar 68, vol I, p. 22.

2. Hist, 355th TFS, atch to Hist, 37th TFW, Jan-Mar 68, p 27.

3. Hist, 56th ACW, Jan-Mar 68, p 49.

4. Msg, COMUSMACV to NMCC, subj: Special Telecon, 211000Z Mar 68.

5. Col Paul C. Watson, USAF, End of Tour Rprt, 17 Jan 68-2 Jan 69, p 28.

6. *Report on the War*, p 44.

7. "Khe Sanh Draws U.S. Air Forces," *Aviation Week and Space Technology*, 19 Feb 68, p 17.

8. U.S. Seventh Fleet, Monthly Historical Summary, Feb 68, pp 1, 15; Mar 68, p 1.

9. Hist, CINCPAC, 1967, vol II, p 620.

10. Msg, *USS Ticonderoga* to CTE 70.2.1.1, subj: Strike Press Release, 101436Z Feb 68.

11. Msg, COMUSMACV to Comdr 7AF, et al, subj: Air Strikes, Khe Sanh Area, 290415Z Feb 68.

12. Msg, CTE 70.2.1.1 to CTE 77 no subj, 010815Z Feb 68.

13. *Ibid.*

14. Msg, *USS Enterprise* to CTE 70.2.1.1, subj: Press Release, 061910Z Mar 68.

15. Msgs, CTG 77.4 to AIG 918, subj: TG 77.4 Op Rprt, 061738Z Feb 68; CTG 77.6 to AIG 918, subj: TG 77.4 Op Rprt, 271322Z Mar 68.

16. 7AF Revisions to Trest, *Khe Sanh (Operation Niagara)*.

17. Msg, 7AF TAC to 834th Air Div, et al, subj: Escort of Airlift in Support of Khe Sanh, 061245Z Mar 68, in Pollica and Rickey, Exhibit 12; Lt Col Lewis H. Dunagan, USAF, Mission Commander's Rprt, 2-17 Mar 68, in Pollica and Rickey, Exhibit 41; memo, Lt Col Paul W. Arcari,

USAF, to Office of Air Force History, subj: Historical Study, "The Fight for Khe Sanh," 6 Apr 72.

18. Msg, 366 TFW to 7AF, subj: VMC Aerial Delivery Tactics for Khe Sanh, 200930Z Apr 68, in Hist, 366th TFW, Apr-Jun 68, Document 7.

19. 7AF Revisions to Trest, *Khe Sanh (Operation Niagara)*.

20. *Ibid*.

21. Memo, CJCS for President, subj: Situation in the Khe Sanh Area, 8 Feb 68; ltr, Col Paul C. Watson, USAF, to Brig Gen Jones E. Bolt, USAF, 26 Feb 68, w/atch, in Hist, 366th TFW, Jan-Mar 68, Document 26.

22. Shore, *Khe Sanh*, pp 93-94.

23. Hist, Khe Sanh Forward Operating Base, 20th TASS, atch to Hist, 504th TASG, Jan-Mar 68.

24. Intvw, Warren Trest with Capt Charles Rushforth, 19 Feb 68, in Trest, *Khe Sanh (Operation Niagara)*, Exhibit 44.

25. Intvw, Warren Trest with Capt Joseph P. Johnson, USAF, 19 Feb 68, in Trest, *Khe Sanh (Operation Niagara)*, Exhibit 33.

26. *Ibid*.

27. Hist, 557th TFS, atch to Hist, 12th TFW, Jan-Mar 68.

28. Intwv, Warren Trest with Capt Charles Rushforth, 19 Feb 68, in Trest, *Khe Sanh (Operation Niagara)*, Exhibit 44.

29. Intvw, Warren Trest with Maj Milton G. Hartenbower, 19 Feb 68, in Trest, *Khe Sanh (Operation Niagara)*, Exhibit 32.

30. Maj Richard A. Durkee, USAF, *Combat Skyspot* (HQ PACAF, Project CHECO, 9 Aug 67), pp 1-3.

31. Ltr, w/atchs, Col Paul C. Watson, USAF, to Brig Gen Jones E. Bolt, USAF, 26 Feb 68, in Hist, 366th TFW, Jan-Mar 68, Document 26.

Chapter VI

Appointment of a Single Manager for Air

1. Momyer Comments.
2. Lt Col Robert M. Burch, USAF, *Single Manager for Air in SVN* (HQ PACAF, Project CHECO, 18 Mar 69), p 5 (hereafter cited as Burch, *Single Manager*, Mar 69).

3. Trest, *Khe Sanh (Operation Niagara)*, pp 6-7.

4. Capt Russell W. Mank, USAF, *TACC Fragging Procedures* (HQ PACAF, Project CHECO, 15 Aug 69), pp 5-6 (hereafter cited as Mank, *TACC Fragging Procedures*).

5. Burch, *Single Manager*, Mar 69, p 3.

6. *Ibid*.; Lt Gen Keith B. McCutcheon, USMC, "Marine Aviation in Vietnam, 1962-1970," *U.S. Naval Institute Proceedings*, May 71, p 137.

7. Burch, *Single Manager*, Mar 69, p 3; Warren A. Trest, *Single Manager for Air in SVN* (HQ PACAF, Project CHECO, 1 Jul 68), pp 2-3 (hereafter cited as Trest, *Single Manager*, Jul 68).

8. Maj Robert M. Burch, USAF, *The ABCC in SEA* (HQ PACAF, Project CHECO, 15 Jan 69), pp 3-4.

9. Trest, *Khe Sanh (Operation Niagara)*, p 10.

10. Shore, *Khe Sanh*, pp 94-95.

11. Ltr, Maj Gen Norman J. Anderson, USMC, to Editor, *Armed Forces Journal*, Oct 71, p 20.

12. Memo, Brig Gen Jones E. Bolt, USAF, for Gen Momyer, subj: Trip Report, 24 Jan 68, in Trest, *Khe Sanh (Operation Niagara)*, Exhibit 15; Momyer Comments.

13. Trest, *Khe Sanh (Operation Niagara)*, pp 82-83; Momyer Comments; Capt Kenneth Alnwick, USAF, *Direct Air Support in I Corps, Jul 65-Jun 69* (HQ PACAF, Project CHECO, 31 Aug 69), p 19 (hereafter cited as Alnwick, *Direct Air Support in I Corps*).

14. Trest, *Single Manager*, Jul 68, pp 27-28.

15. Hist, USMACV, 1968, vol I, pp 436-37.

16. Trest, *Single Manager*, Jul 68, p 25.

17. FMFPAC, *Operations of Marine Forces in Vietnam*, Mar 68.

18. Intvw, Robert W. Kritt with Adm U. S. Grant Sharp, USN, 19 Feb 71.

19. Mank, *TACC Fragging Procedures*, pp 4-5; Alnwick, *Direct Air Support in I Corps*, p 19; Maj Miles D. Waldron, USA, and Spec 5 Richard W. Beavers, *The Critical Year 1968: The XXIV Corps Team*.

20. Trest, *Single Manager,* Jul 68, p 1.
21. *Ibid.,* pp 21-24.
22. McCutcheon, "Marine Aviation in Vietnam, 1962-1970," p 137.
23. Trest, *Single Manager,* Jul 68, pp 32-35.
24. Mank, *TACC Fragging Procedures,* pp 5-6.
25. Trest, *Single Manager,* Jul 68, p 35; Trest, *Khe Sanh (Operation Niagara),* pp 112-14.
26. Ltr, Gen William W. Momyer, USAF, to COMUSMACV, subj: Single Management of Strike and Reconnaissance Forces, 15 May 68.
27. McCutcheon, "Marine Aviation in Vietnam, 1962-1968," pp 136-37.
28. Hist, USMACV, 1968, vol I, pp 439-440.
29. McCutcheon, "Marine Aviation in Vietnam, 1962-1968," p 137.
30. *Ibid.*

Chapter VII

The Thing That Broke Their Back

1. Maj James B. Pralle, USAF, *Arc Light, June 67-Dec 68* (HQ PACAF, Project CHECO, 15 Aug 69), pp 25-26 (hereafter cited as Pralle, *Arc Light*).
2. *Ibid.,* p 28; Hist, 3d Air Div, Jan-Jun 68, vol I, pp 179-180.
3. 7AF Revisions to Trest, *Khe Sanh (Operation Niagara).*
4. Msg, 3d Air Div to 4133 BW (Prov), *et al,* subj: Bugle Note, 13 Feb 68, in Hist, 3d Air Div, Jul-Dec 68, Exhibit 105.
5. Charles H. Hildreth, *et al, Air Force Response to the Pueblo Crisis* (USAF Hist Div Liaison Office, Jan 69), pp 41-45.
6. Hist, 3d Air Div, Jan-Jun 68, vol I, pp 126-28; msg, 3d Air Div to SAC, subj: Bugle Note, 161052Z Feb 68; msg, 3d Air Div to SAC, subj: Revision to Bugle Note Schedule, 220712Z Feb 68, in Hist, 3d Air Div, Jan-Jun 68, Exhibits 108 and 109.
7. Msgs, 7AF to 3d Air Div, subj: Arc Light Mission Papa 7, 171400Z Nov 67; 7AF to SAC, 3d Air Div, and SAC ADVON, 200800Z Nov 67, in Hist, 3d Air Div, Jul-Dec 67, Exhibits 191 and 192.
8. Hist, 3d Air Div, Jan-Jun 68, vol I, pp 151-53.
9. Msg, 3d Air Div to SAC, subj: B-52 Bomb Delivery with Beacon Backup, 130640Z Feb 68, in Hist, 3d Air Div, Jan-Jun 68, Exhibit 150.
10. MR, Gen William W. Momyer, USAF, subj: Meeting at MACV, 8 Feb 68; Pralle, *Arc Light,* p 29.
11. Msg, 7AF to SAC, subj: Special Arc Light Strikes, 201000Z Feb 68, in Hist, 3d Air Div, Jan-Jun 68, Exhibit 151.
12. Hist, 3d Air Div, Jan-Jun 68, vol I, p 154; msg, CINCSAC CP to SAC ADVON, *et al,* subj: Special Arc Light Strikes, 251714Z Feb 68, in Hist, 3d Air Div, Jan-Jun 68, Exhibit 152.
13. Msgs, Dep COMUSMACV for Air to SAC and 3d Air Div, subj: Assessment of Close-in Arc Lights, 280750Z Feb 68; 3d Air Div to Subordinate Units, subj: Arc Light Mission Yankee 37, 290645Z Feb 68, in Hist, 3d Air Div, Jan-Jun 68, Exhibits 154 and 156.
14. Hist, 3d Air Div, Jan-Jun 68, vol I, pp 137-38.
15. *Ibid.,* p 182; msg, SAC to CINCPAC (retransmitted by CINCPAC AdminO to COMUSMACV, *et al,*), subj: Close-in Arc Light Strikes, 041958 Apr 68, in Hist, 3d Air Div, Jan-Jun 68, Exhibit 158; Robert M. Kipp, "The Search for B-52 Effectiveness in the Vietnam War," *Aerospace Commentary,* Winter 70, p 53.
16. Dir/Ops, HQ USAF, *Trends, Indicators, and Analyses,* Jul 68, p II:2; msg. COMUSMACV to JCS, *et al,* subj: Effect of B-52 Strikes on Forces in the Khe Sanh Area, 201206Z Apr 68, in Trest, *Khe Sanh (Operation Niagara),* Exhibit 8.
17. Summary of Captured Documents, subj: Khe Sanh, 22 Apr 68.
18. Combined Military Interrogation Center, Interrogation Rprt, US 894-68, 14 Apr 68, in Trest, *Khe Sanh (Operation Niagara),* Exhibit 26.
19. Combined Military Interrogation Center, Interrogation Rprt, US 1071-68, 1 May 68, in Trest, *Khe Sanh (Operation Niagara),* Exhibit 21.
20. Westmoreland Speech to 3d Air Div, Guam, 13 Jun 68, in Hist, 3d Air Div, Jan-Jun 68, Exhibit 180.

Chapter VIII

Beyond the Next Hill

1. 7AF Revisions to Trest, *Khe Sanh (Operation Niagara)*.
2. 7AF Weekly Air Intelligence Summary, 11 May 68; rprt, Evaluation of an Anti-Infiltration System, 15 Oct 68.
3. Msg, CG, III MAF to COMUSMACV, subj; Daily SITREP no 24 (240001H to 242400H, Jan 68), (250111Z Jan 68).
4. Hist, Task Force Alpha, 1 Oct 67-30 Apr 68, p 3; intvw, author with Col William L. Walker, USAF, 8 Jun 71.
5. Walker intvw.
6. Rprt, Evaluation of an Anti-infiltration System, 15 Oct 68, p 34; Hist, Task Force Alpha, 1 Oct 67-30 Apr 68, p 49; Response by Col David E. Lownds, 19 Nov 70, in Senate Hearings, *Electronic Battlefield Program*, p 90.
7. Walker intvw.
8. *Ibid.*
9. Hist, Task Force Alpha, 1 Oct 67-30 Apr 68, p 50.
10. Walker intvw.
11. Operational Rprt, 37th Signal Bn for period ending 30 Apr 68.
12. Rprt, MACV Six-month Summary of Muscle Shoals, 31 May 68; Statement by Maj Jerry E. Hudson, USMC, 19 Nov 70, in Senate Hearings, *Electronic Battlefield Program*, p 88; Ernest Bivans, Dep Special Assistant to CofS, MACV, *Muscle Shoals and the Siege of Khe Sanh*, 1 May 68.
13. Bivans, *Muscle Shoals and the Siege of Khe Sanh*.
14. *Ibid.*; Shore, *Khe Sanh*, pp 110-11.
15. Statement by General Tompkins, 19 Nov 70, in Senate Hearings, *Electronic Battlefield Program* containing ltr from Maj Mirza M. Baig, USMC, pp 84-85.
16. Bivans, *Muscle Shoals and the Siege of Khe Sanh*.
17. *Ibid.*; Walker intvw.
18. Msg, COMUSMACV to CINCPAC, subj: Khe Sanh Situation, 040449Z Jan 68; 26th Marines Command Chronology, Feb 68, p III:15.
19. Hist, Task Force Alpha, 1 Oct 67-30 Apr 68, p 57; Statement by Maj Jerry E. Hudson, USMC, 19 Nov 70, in Senate Hearings, *Electronic Battlefield Program*, p 88.
20. Bivans, *Muscle Shoals and the Siege of Khe Sanh*; Hist, Task Force Alpha, 1 Oct 67-30 Apr 68, p 54.

Chapter IX

The Fight is Won

1. Shore, *Khe Sanh*, p 127; PACOM Command Center 0730 Briefing Notes, 17 Mar 68, p IV:2; and 23 Mar, pt IV; Op Niagara BDA Rprt, 14 Mar 68, 23 Mar 68; Trest, *Khe Sanh (Operation Niagara)*, pp 88-89, 95.
2. 31st Military History Detachment, HQ Provisional Corps, Vietnam, Study 3-68, Operation Pegasus, p 2; Waldron and Beavers, *The Critical Year 1968*, pp 16, 20-22.
3. 31st Military History Detachment Study 3-68, p 6; msg, III MAF to CG, Prov Corps, Vietnam, 110846 Mar 69.
4. Hist, Army Assumption of Common Service Support Mission from the Navy in I Corps.
5. 31st Military History Detachment Study 3-68, p 23; Rprt of Pegasus Administrative Matters.
6. 31st Military History Detachment Study 3-68, pp 22-23.
7. Shore, *Khe Sanh*, p 133; Hist, Naval Construction Bn 5, 1967-1968 Deployment.
8. Lt Col John R. Galvin, USA, "The Relief of Khe Sanh," *Military Review*, Jan 70, pp 126-27.
9. Shore, *Khe Sanh*, pp 128-30; 26th Marine Command Chronology, Mar 68, pt II.
10. Shore, *Khe Sanh*, pp 130, 134.
11. Galvin, "The Relief of Khe Sanh," pp 89-90.
12. Intelligence Portion of After Action Rprt, Op Pegasus, 19 May 68.
13. Shore, *Khe Sanh*, pp 135-36.
14. *Ibid.*, p 137; Galvin, "The Relief of Khe Sanh," p 92.
15. Intelligence Portion of After Action Rprt, Op Pegasus, 19 May 68.
16. Lt Col Zane G. Brewer, USAF, Mission Commander's Rprt, 12-26 Apr 68, in Pollica and Rickey, Exhibit 133; Col Zane G. Brewer, USAF, Comments on draft chapter, 13 Apr 72.

17. Pollica and Rickey, p 46.
18. Lt Col Zane G. Brewer, USAF, Mission Commander's Rprt, 12-26 Apr 68, in Pollica and Rickey, Exhibit 133.
19. *Baltimore Sun,* 16 Apr 68.
20. *Washington Post,* 15 Jul 68.

Chapter X

Aftermath of Victory

1. Shore, *Khe Sanh,* p 145; Trest, *Khe Sanh (Operation Niagara),* pp 90, 125-29.
2. JCS Fact Sheet on Khe Sanh, 26 Apr 68; Hist, USMACV, 1968, vol II, pp 887, 889, 906.
3. Hist, MACV, 1968, vol I, pp 423-24.
4. "Remarks Upon Presenting the Presidential Unit Citation to the 26th Marines (Reinforced), 3d Marine Division (Reinforced)," 23 May 68, in *Public Papers of the Presidents of the United States, Lyndon B. Johnson, 1968* (Washington, 1970), I, Item 267, pp 632-34. The Citation also was awarded other elements on the ground at Khe Sanh, including the following Air Force units: Det, (Operating Location AJ), 15th Aerial Port Squadron; Det, 366th Transport Squadron, 366th Combat Support Group; Det "A", 834th Air Division.
5. Intvw, Robert Kritt with Adm U. S. Grant Sharp, USN, 19 Feb 71; Transcript of CBS News Special, *LBJ: The Decision to Halt the Bombing,* 6 Feb 70, p 12.
6. Gen William C. Westmoreland, USA, "Progress Report on the War in Vietnam," *Department of State Bulletin,* 11 Dec 67, p 786; Hist, USMACV, 1968, vol. II, p 906.
7. John B. Henry, "February 1968," *Foreign Policy,* Fall 71, pp 15-18.
8. Msg, COMUSMACV to CINCPAC, et al, subj: Dye Marker, 040011Z Sep. 67; msg, COMUSMACV to DCG, USARV, et al, subj: Prairie Fire/Nickle Steel/Muscle Shoals/Daniel Boone Ops, 270825Z Dec 67.
9. "The President's News Conference of 2 Feb 68," in *Public Papers of the Presidents of the United States, Lyndon B. Johnson, 1968* (Washington, 1970), I, Item 51, p 159.
10. Dir/Ops, HQ USAF, *Trends, Indicators, and Analyses,* Jul 68, p II:2; Shore, *Khe Sanh,* pp 106-107; 1st MAW Command Chronology, Mar 68, p II:2.
11. Hist, MACV, 1968, vol I, p 423.
12. *Report on the War,* p 171.
13. "The President's Address to the Nation Announcing Steps to Limit the War in Vietnam and Reporting His Decision Not to Seek Reelection," in *Public Papers of the Presidents of the United States, Lyndon B. Johnson, 1968* (Washington, 1970), I, Item 170, pp 469-476.

GLOSSARY OF TERMS AND ABBREVIATIONS

A-1   A piston-powered attack plane, the single-engine Douglas A-1 was designed to serve on board aircraft carriers. Its ruggedness, fuel capacity, and the weight of ordnance it carried made it a deadly Air Force weapon during the battle for Khe Sanh.

A-4   This single-seat, single-engine, turbojet attack plane was designed by Douglas as an extremely maneuverable carrier aircraft. During Khe Sanh operations Marine and Navy pilots flew these Sky Hawks, some of which were built after the McDonnell-Douglas corporate merger.

A-6   Grumman's A-6 Intruder, a twin-jet attack plane, was designed to fly beneath enemy radar and drop its bombs despite weather or darkness. Fitted out with elaborate electronic gear, the Intruder was flown by Marine and Navy airmen against targets at Khe Sanh.

AB   Air Base

ABCCC   Airborne Battlefield Command and Control Center

AC-47   A Douglas C-47 modified to serve as a gunship, its principal weapons are 7.62-mm revolving barrel guns that fire downward from the side of the fuselage.

ACW   Air Commando Wing

AD   Air Division

Adm   Admiral

AdminO   Administrative Officer

ADVON   Advance Echelon

AF   Air Force

AFB   Air Force Base

AIG   Address Indicator Group

ALCC   Airlift Control Center

ALCE   Airlift Control Element

alft   airlift

Arc Light   The nickname used in connection with B-52 operations in Southeast Asia; for example, Arc Light strikes.

ARVN   Army of the Republic of Vietnam

atch   Attachment

B-52   A huge, 8-engine heavy bomber, the Boeing Stratofortress carried as many as 108 500-lb bombs per plane in support of the Marines at Khe Sanh.

B-57   This American-built, twin-jet tactical bomber is a version of the British Canberra. The Martin Company built the original B-57's, some of which were extensively modified for reconnaissance missions.

BDA   bomb damage assessment

bn   battalion

Brig Gen   Brigadier General

BW   Bombardment Wing

C-7   Built by deHavilland for the U.S. Army, these twin-engine, piston powered transports were reassigned to the Air Force and used to supply outlying bases in South Vietnam.

C-47   A twin-engine aircraft based on the Douglas DC-3, which revolutionized air travel in the late 1930's. The C-47 was the U.S. Army Air Forces' standard transport during World War II.

C-123   Built by Fairchild, this twin-engine, high-wing monoplane features a ramp at the rear of the fuselage to facilitate cargo handling. The C-123K has two pod-mounted turbojets in addition to its piston engines.

C-130   This 4-engine, high-wing, turboprop transport was built by Lockheed and served with distinction at Khe Sanh. A ramp provides easy access to the Hercules' cargo compartment.

Capt   Captain

CG   Commanding General

CH-3   This twin-turbine, single rotor helicopter, built by Sikorsky, was employed to implant electronic sensors around Khe Sanh.

CH-46 A twin-turbine, tandem rotor helicopter, the Boeing CH-46 was used extensively by Marine aviators to resupply Khe Sanh's hilltop outposts.

CHECO A *Contemporary Historical Evaluation of Combat Operations*, Project CHECO supported Air Force planning and study requirements.

CINCPAC Commander in Chief, Pacific

CINCPACAF Commander in Chief, Pacific Air Forces

CINCSAC Commander in Chief, Strategic Air Command

CM Chairman's memorandum

cmbt combat

cmdo commando

co company

COC Combat Operations Center

Col Colonel

COMUSMACV Commander, U.S. Military Assistance Command, Vietnam

Container Delivery System A method of parachuting cargo in which loads are lashed to pallets and covered with a canvas "container."

CP Command Post

CRC Control and Reporting Center

CTE Commander, Task Element

CTG Commander, Task Group

CTOC Corps Tactical Operations Center

DASC Direct Air Support Center

D/Cdr Deputy Commander

DCG Deputy Commanding General

Demilitarized Zone The buffer established at the 17th parallel between North and South Vietnam.

dep deputy

Dep CofS Deputy Chief of Staff

dept department

det detachment

DIA Defense Intelligence Agency

dir director

DISUM Daily Intelligence Summary

div division

Drop Zone The area designated for the landing of parachuted cargo or troops.

DTOC Division Tactical Operation Center.

Dutch Mill Nickname for the surveillance center at Nakhon Phanom, Thailand, which forwarded to Khe Sanh's defenders data obtained from sensors planted around the base.

EC-121 A 4-engine Lockheed Super Constellation modified to carry electronic gear, this aircraft served to link the Khe Sanh sensor network to the surveillance center at Nakhon Phanom, Thailand.

F-4 This twin-jet aircraft was originally designed by McDonnell (now McDonnell Douglas) as a carrier plane. It was used by Air Force, Navy, and Marine squadrons during Operation Niagara. A low wing, 2-place fighter-bomber, whose recent versions carry cannon as well as air-to-air missiles, the F-4 also carries a great variety of munitions for attacking ground targets.

F8F The last prop driven fighter selected by the U.S. Navy, this single-place, single-engine Grumman aircraft saw service during the siege of Dien Bien Phu.

F-100 The North American F-100, a single-engine, turbojet fighter-bomber, saw extensive service in South Vietnam.

Flying Boxcar This twin-engine, twin-boom Fairchild transport served in limited numbers during the siege of Dien Bien Phu.

FMF Fleet Marine Force

FMFPAC Fleet Marine Force, Pacific.

FSC Fire Support Coordinator

FSCC Fire Support Coordination Center.

ftr fighter

Gen General

gp group
GPES Ground Proximity Extraction System.
Gravel A type of munition resembling a pebble and used in conjunction with sensor fields. One variety of gravel was a noisemaker, designed solely to trigger sensors, but a second was powerful enough to cause casualties as well.
Ground Proximity Extraction System A method of cargo extraction in which a hook trailing from a swiftly rolling aircraft engages a cable stretched across the runway.
Gun, 175-mm An Army weapon mounted on a tracked chassis and able to fire a 147-pound shell almost 33,000 meters. The maximum rate of fire is one round every 2 minutes.
hist history

HMM Marine Medium Helicopter Squadron.
Howitzer, 105-mm The standard Marine light artillery piece, it has a maximum range of about 11,000 meters and a maximum rate of fire of four rounds per minute.
HQ Headquarters

inc incorporated
intvw interview

JCS Joint Chiefs of Staff

KC-130 A tanker variant of the Lockheed C-130, used during the Khe Sanh operation exclusively by Marines.

LAPES Low Altitude Parachute Extraction System.
Light Assault Weapon, M-72 This 1-shot rocket launcher comes loaded with an antitank round. Once fired, the weapon is discarded.
Lt Lieutenant
Lt Col Lieutenant Colonel
Lt Gen Lieutenant General
Lt(jg.) Lieutenant (junior grade)
ltr letter

MAC Military Airlift Command
MACV Military Assistance Command, Vietnam.
MAF Marine Amphibious Force
Maj Major
Maj Gen Major General
Mar Div Marine Division
MAS Marine Airlift Squadron
MAW Marine Aircraft Wing
memo memorandum
Micro-Arc Light A combined air and artillery strike delivered against a target block measure 500 by 500 meters.
Mini-Arc Light A combined air and artillery strike delivered against a target block measuring 500 by 1,000 meters.
Morane 500 This single-engine, high-wing reconnaissance and liaison plane was the French version of Germany's wartime Fieseler *Storch*.
Mortar, 60-mm A smooth-bore, muzzle-loaded weapon used by both the Americans and North Vietnamese, it has an effective range of about 2,000 meters.
Mortar, 81-mm A Marine weapon resembling the 60-mm type, it propels a larger shell for an effective range up to 3,650 meters.
Mortar, 82-mm An intermediate mortar used by the North Vietnamese, with an effective range of about 3,000 meters.
Mortar, 120-mm The largest and longest range North Vietnamese mortar used at Khe Sanh. It can be fired by dropping a finned shell down the tube so that a cartridge in the base strikes a firing pin. Unlike most other mortars, it has a trigger that can release the firing pin after the round is seated.
Mortar, 4.2-inch The largest of Marine mortars at Khe Sanh, it has a rifled bore and can fire with effect some 4,000 meters. The shell has in its base a soft metal that expands into the rifling when the propellant explodes.
msg message

n d   no date

Niagara   Nickname for aerial operations in defense of Khe Sanh. Intelligence preparations were referred to as Niagara I; strike operations as Niagara II.

NMCC   National Military Command Center.

no   number

O-1   A 2-seat, high-wing monoplane built by Cessna for liaison and observation duties, the O-1 is a single-engine light aircraft.

O-2A   This replacement for the O-1 is a twin-engine, twin-boom Cessna monoplane. Engines are mounted fore and aft of the 2-place cabin, with the booms serving to support the tail surfaces.

ofc   office

Ontos   This Marine weapon consists of six 106-mm recoilless rifles mounted coaxially on a tracked chassis.

OP-2E   A 4-engine patrol plane built by Lockheed for the Navy.

Operational Control   The control exercised by a commander or other constituted authority over persons or units that gives him the power to compose forces according to his own judgment, to assign tasks, to designate objectives, and to give directions through subordinate commanders for the conduct of operations.

op   operation

org   organization

OSAF   Office of the Secretary of the Air Force.

OSD   Office of the Secretary of Defense.

p   page

PACAF   Pacific Air Forces

PACOM   Pacific Command

pallet   A platform of wood, steel, or wood and metal, to which cargo is secured for ease of handling.

Pegasus   Nickname for the operation to reopen Highway 9 to Khe Sanh and drive the enemy from the region.

Privateer   Consolidated Aircraft built this long-range reconnaisance bomber, which was based on the B-24 Liberator. The 4-engine shoulder-wing monoplane served the French in Indochina.

prov   provisional

pt   part

Pueblo   A cargo ship converted to gather intelligence along hostile coasts, this U.S. Navy vessel was seized by North Korea in January 1968.

Radar, MSQ-77, Combat Skyspot   A van-mounted Air Force radar used to direct aerial bombardment missions, it was especially successful with B-52's.

Radar, TPQ-10   Besides controlling air strikes at Khe Sanh, this Marine radar also served to guide transports to release points from which to parachute cargo onto the drop zone.

R Adm   Rear Admiral

recce   reconnaissance

Recoilless Rifle, 57-mm   The smallest of U.S. recoilless weapons, it was employed at the Lang Vei Special Forces Camp. Adjustable openings in the breech permit the escape of gas generated by the explosion of a specially encased propellant, thus keeping the weapon in equilibrium.

Recoilless Rifle, 106-mm   A breech-loaded weapon similar to the 57-mm type, it fired a special lightweight ammunition that was considered effective against tanks.

regt   regiment

Rifle, M-16   This U.S. infantry weapon weighs only 7.6 pounds, uses a 5.62-mm cartridge, and is capable of semi-automatic or fully automatic operation.

Rocket, 107-mm   Lighter and less powerful than the 122-mm type, this enemy weapon was used at Khe Sanh.

Rocket, 122-mm   This North Vietnamese weapon, much used against Khe Sanh, makes up in mobility, ease of operation, and range for its lack of accuracy.

rprt   report
RTB   Royal Thai Air Force Base; Royal Thai Base.
RW   Reconnaissance Wing

SAC   Strategic Air Command
SEA   Southeast Asia
Seabees   Members of U.S. Naval Construction Battalions. The nickname dates from World War II.
Sensor, Acoustic   An electronic device designed to pickup and transmit sounds made by movement of enemy troops or vehicles.
Sensor, Seismic   An electronic device designed to pickup and transmit earth tremors caused by enemy movements.
SFG   Special Forces Group
SITREP   Situation Report
spec   specialist
Speed Offloading   A procedure for unloading cargo from taxiing C-123's or C-130's so that the plane can take off with the least delay.
spt   support
subj   subject
Super Gaggle   Nickname for the highly successful Marine technique for delivering supplies by helicopter to Khe Sanh's outposts.
SVN   South Vietnam

T-28   A converted trainer built by North American, the T-28D is a single-engine, 2-place attack plane capable of carrying a variety of ordnance on counterinsurgency missions.
TA-4   A 2-seat model of the A-4 intended as a trainer.
TAC   Tactical Air Command
TACAN   Tactical Air Navigation
TACC   Tactical Air Control Center
TACP   Tactical Air Control Party
Tactical Air Navigation   An aerial navigation system that employs ground radio transmitters and airborne distance measuring equipment to determine an aircraft's distance and bearing from a transmitting station.
TADC   Tactical Air Direction Center.
Tank, M-48   The Marines used this 50.7-ton armored vehicle, which mounted a 90-mm gun and two machane guns.
Tank, PT-76   A lightly armored, Russian-built amphibious vehicle weighing 15.4 tons and mounting a 76-mm gun.
TAS   Tactical Airlift Squadron
TASE   Tactical Airlift Support Element.
TASG   Tactical Air Support Group
Task Force Alpha   The Air Force unit responsible for the Nakhon Phanom, Thailand, infiltration surveillance center.
TASS   Tactical Air Support Squadron.
TAW   Tactical Airlift Wing
Tet   The lunar New Year, a time of celebration throughout South Vietnam.
TFS   Tactical Fighter Squadron
TFW   Tactical Fighter Wing
TG   Task Group
Transponder   An electronic device that responds with its own signal when triggered by radar waves.
TRS   Tactical Reconnaissance Squadron.
TRW   Tactical Reconnaissance Wing.
TSgt   technical sergeant
TUOC   Tactical Unit Operations Center.
UH-1   This single-turbine, single-rotor helicopter, built by Bell, was used as a gunship by the Marines at Khe Sanh.
USA   U.S. Army
USAF   U.S. Air Force
USARV   U.S. Army, Vietnam
USMC   U.S. Marine Corps
USN   U.S. Navy
VMC   visual meteorological conditions.
vol   volume
Wg   Wing

BIBLIOGRAPHY

Air Force Unit Histories

TSgt Bruce W. Pollica and TSgt Joe R. Rickey. *834th Air Division Tactical Airlift Support for Khe Sanh, 21 Jan-8 Apr 68.*

Recurring Histories.
   3d Air Division.
   315th Air Division.
   Task Force Alpha.
   56th Air Commando Wing.
   12th Tactical Fighter Wing.
   31st Tactical Fighter Wing.
   37th Tactical Fighter Wing.
   366th Tactical Fighter Wing.
   504th Tactical Air Support Wing.

Supporting Mission Commanders' Reports

Lt Col Zane G. Brewer, 12-26 Apr 68.
Lt Col Donald M. Davis, 16-30 Mar 68.
Lt Col Lewis H. Dunagan, 2-17 Mar 68.
Lt Col John F. Masters, Jr., 22 Feb-3 Mar 68.
Lt Col William R. Smith, 7-23 Feb 68.

Project CHECO Reports

Capt Kenneth J. Alnwick. *Direct Air Support in I Corps, Jul 65-Aug 69*, 31 Aug 69.

Lt Col Robert M. Burch. *Single Manager for Air in SVN*, 18 Mar 69.

_____. *The ABCCC in SEA*, 15 Jan 69.

Maj Richard A. Durkee. *Combat Skyspot*, 9 Aug 67.

Capt Russell W. Mank. *TACC Fragging Procedures*, 15 Aug 69.

Maj James B. Pralle. *Arc Light, Jun 67-Dec 68*, 15 Aug 69.

Warren A. Trest. *Single Manager for Air in SVN*, 1 Jul 68.

_____. *Khe Sanh (Operation Niagara), 22 Jan-31 Mar 68*, 13 Sep 68.

Other Air Force Documents

Lt Col Edmund B. Crandall, et al. *Tactical Airlift in SEA, 1 Jan 65-31 Mar 68.*

Charles H. Hildreth, et al. *Air Force Response to the Pueblo Crisis*. USAF Historical Division Liaison Office, Jan 69.

Maj Gen Burl W. McLaughlin, Vietnam End of Tour Report, Nov 67-Jun 69.

Directorate of Operations, Hq USAF. *Trends, Indicators, and Analyses*, Jul 68.

Pacific Air Forces. Pacific Command Center 0730 Briefing Notes, 22 Jan-31 Mar 68.

Seventh Air Force. Operations Order 100-68, 15 Dec 67.

_____. Revisions to Trest, *Khe Sanh (Operation Niagara)*.

_____. Weekly Intelligence Summary.

Lt Col Norman G. Smith. Vietnam End of Tour Report, Nov 67-Jun 69.

Col Paul C. Watson. Vietnam End of Tour Report, 17 Jan 68-2 Jan 69.

Military Assistance Command, Vietnam, Documents

Ernest Bivans, Deputy Assistant to Chief of Staff. *Muscle Shoals and the Siege of Khe Sanh*, 1 May 68.

Combat Operations Center Fact Sheet. Chronology of Operation Niagara, 19 Apr 68.

Combined Military Interrogation Center. Interrogation Reports US 894-68, 14 Apr 68, and US 1071-68, 1 May 68.

J-5 Strategic/Tactical Study. Khe Sanh Viewed from the Dien Bien Phu Perspective, Mar 68.

Hq USMACV, History, 1968.

Operation Niagara Bomb Damage Assessment Reports, 22 Jan-31 Mar 68.

Report. Evaluation of an Anti-infiltration System, 15 Oct 68.

Study. Comparison between the Battle

of Dien Bien Phu and the Analogous Khe Sanh Situation, Mar 68.
Summary of Captured Documents, subj: Khe Sanh, 22 Apr 68.
Year-end Review of Vietnam, 1 Jan 68.

Marine Corps Documents

Fleet Marine Force, Pacific. *Operations of Marine Forces in Vietnam.*
Command Chronologies.
    III Marine Amphibious Force.
    1st Marine Aircraft Wing.
    3d Marine Division.
    26th Marines.
    1st Battalion, 9th Marines.
    3d Battalion, 26th Marines.
    Marine Air Support Squadron 3.
    Marine Medium Helicopter Squadron 164.
    Marine Medium Helicopter Squadron 362.

Army Documents

After Action Report. Operation Pegasus, 19 May 68.
History, Army Assumption of Common Service Support Mission from Navy in I Corps, 1968.
Report of Pegasus Administrative Matters.
31st Military History Detachment, Hq Provisional Corps, Vietnam. Study 3-68, *Operation Pegasus.*
37th Signal Battalion. Operational Report for period ending 30 Apr 68.
Maj Miles D. Waldron and Spec 5 Richard W. Beavers. *The Critical Year 1968: The XXIV Corps Team.*

Navy Documents

U.S. Naval Construction Battalion Maintenance Unit 301. Operations Report, 26 Jan-25 Apr 68.
U.S. Naval Construction Battalions, Pacific. Operations and Civic Action, Jan 68.
U.S. Fleet. Monthly Historical Summary.

JCS and OSD Documents

Attachment to Memo, Special Assistant for Counterinsurgency and Special Activities, JCS, for Director, Joint Staff, 12 Feb 68, subj: Questions Concerning Vietnam.
Extracts from DIA Intelligence Bulletin, 5 Feb. 68.
JCS Fact Sheet on Khe Sanh, 26 Apr 68.
Memo, CJCS for President, subj: Situation in the Khe Sanh Area, 8 Feb 68.

Interviews

Interviews, Col John E. Van Duyn, USAF, and Maj Richard B. Clement, USAF with Maj Gen Robert N. Ginsburgh, USAF, 26 May 71 and 3 Jun 71; author with Gen Ginsburgh, 27 Mar 72.
Interview, Warren Trest with Capt Gerald L. Harrington, USAF, 19 Feb 68.
Interview, Warren Trest with Maj Milton G. Hartenbower, USAF, 19 Feb 68.
Interview, Warren Trest with Capt Joseph P. Johnson, USAF, 19 Feb 68.
Transcript of CBS News Special. LBJ: The Decision to Halt the Bombing, 6 Feb 70.
Interview, Warren Trest with Capt Charles Rushforth, USAF, 19 Feb 68.
Interview, Robert W. Kritt with Adm U. S. G. Sharp, USN, 19 Feb 71.
Interview, Maj Richard B. Clement, USAF, and Jacob Van Staaveren with Gen Maxwell D. Taylor, USA, 11 Jan 72.
Interview, author with Col William L. Walker, USAF, 8 Jun 71.

Congressional Publications

Hearings before the Electronic Battlefield Subcommittee of the Preparedness Investigating Subcommittee of the Senate Committee on the Armed Services, 91st Congress, 2d Session *Investigation into the Electronic Battlefield Program.*
Wheeler Report to the President on Tet.

Congressional Record, 92d Congress, 1st Session, 8 Jul 71.

Books

CINCPAC and COMUSMACV. *Report on the War in Vietnam*. Washington: Government Printing Office, n.d.

Bernard B. Fall, *Hell in a Very Small Place: The Siege of Dien Bien Phu*. New York: J. B. Lippincott, 1967.

Henry Graff, *The Tuesday Cabinet: Deliberation and Decision on Peace and War under Lyndon B. Johnson*. Englewood Cliffs, New Jersey: Prentice Hall, 1970.

Vice Adm Edwin B. Hooper, USN. *Mobility, Support, Endurance: A Story of Naval Operational Logistics in the Vietnam War, 1965-1968*. Washington: Naval Historical Division, Department of the Navy, 1972.

Marvin Kalb and Elie Abel, *Roots of Involvement: The U.S. in Asia, 1784-1971*. New York: W. W. Norton, 1971.

John T. McAlister, *Vietnam: The Origins of Revolution*. Washington: Center for Research in Social Systems, American University, 1968.

Don Oberdorfer. *Tet!* Garden City, New York: Doubleday, 1971.

Douglas Pike. *Viet Cong: The Organization and Techniques of the National Liberation Front of South Vietnam*. Cambridge, Massachusetts: MIT Press, 1966.

Robert Shaplen. *The Road from War, 1965-1970*. New York: Harper and Row, 1970.

Capt Moyers S. Shore, II, USMC. *The Battle for Khe Sanh*. Washington: Hq USMC, 1969.

George K. Tanham, *Communist Revolutionary Warfare: The Viet Minh in Indo-China*. New York: Frederick Praeger, 1961.

Public Papers of the Presidents of the United States, Lyndon B. Johnson, 1967. Washington: Government Printing Office, 1968.

_____, *Lyndon B. Johnson, 1968*. Washington: Government Printing Office, 1970.

Sir Robert Thompson, *No Exit from Vietnam*. New York: David McKay, 1970.

Articles

James Burnham, "Khe Sanh: Whose Mistake?", *National Review* (12 Mar 68).

Maj John A. Cash, USA, "The Battle of Lang Vei," *Seven Fire Fights in Vietnam*. Washington: Office of Chief of Military History, 1970.

Clark M. Clifford. "A Vietnam Reappraisal: The Personal History of One Man's View and How It Evolved." *Foreign Affairs* (Jul 69).

Oliver E. Clubb, Jr., "Khe Sanh—A Goat Tied to a Stake." *New Republic* (6 Apr 68).

Lt Col John R. Galvin, USA, "The Relief of Khe Sanh." *Military Review* (Jan 70).

John B. Henry, "February 1968." *Foreign Policy* (Fall 71).

Capt Ken Kashiwahara, USAF, "Lifeline to Khe Sanh," *The Airman* (Jul 68).

Robert M. Kipp. "The Search for B-52 Effectiveness in the Vietnam War," *Aerospace Commentary* (Winter 70).

Lt Gen Keith B. McCutcheon, USMC, "Marine Aviation in Vietnam, 1962-1970." *U.S. Naval Institute Proceedings* (May 71).

Maj Gen Burl W. McLaughlin, USAF, "Khe Sanh: Keeping an Outpost Alive, An Appraisal," *Air University Review* (Nov-Dec 68).

Brig Gen Edwin H. Simmons, USMC, "Marine Corps Operations in Vietnam, 1968," *U.S. Naval Institute Proceedings* (May 70).

Gen William C. Westmoreland, USA, "Progress Report on the War in Vietnam," *Department of State Bulletin* (11 Dec 67).

INDEX

Abrams, Creighton W., 96
Aerial photography
    See reconnaissance activities
Aerial port group, 42, 55-56
    See also Cargo handling
Aerial port mobility team
    See aerial port group
Airborne battlefield command and control center, 63, 64, 72, 74
Aircraft
    See Aircraft types, Bombing operations, Fighter operations
Aircraft carriers, 60, 79, 80
    See also U.S. Navy
Aircraft types
    A-1: 34, 35, 60, 94
    A-4: 56-67, 62
    A-6: 20, 60, 61
    A-37: 78
    AC-47: 96
    B-24: 19
    B-52: 12, 13, 21, 25, 26, 41, 64, 67, 68, 82, 83, 84, 86, 87, 88, 89, 93, 96, 103
    C-7: 8, 12, 20, 38, 42, 58, 97, 98
    C-47: 20, 42
    C-82 (Packet): 20
    C-119 (Flying Boxcar): 19
    C-123: 9, 12, 20, 25, 26, 36, 37, 42, 43, 44, 45, 54, 58, 97, 98
    C-130: 8, 9, 12, 20, 23, 31, 35, 36, 37, 38, 39, 42, 43, 44, 45, 46, 47, 51, 52, 53, 54, 58, 72, 73, 101, 102
    EC-121: 91
    F-4: 60, 61, 64, 67, 92
    F-8F: 19
    F-100: 60
    KC 130: 35, 59
    KC 135: 13
    Morane 500: 19
    MiG: 64
    O-1: 64, 66, 67

    O-2: 65
    OP2E: 92
Air Divisions (USAF)
    3d: 12, 82, 83, 86, 88, 105
    315th: 12, 42
    834th: 12, 25, 42, 51, 52, 53
Air drops
    See Airlift; Low-altitude parachute extraction system; Parachute supply drops
Airlift
    of supplies to Khe Sanh, 25-26, 35, 42-59, 60
    of Troops, 23, 25
    See also helicopter; Aircraft; Parachute supply drops
Air supply
    See Airlift
Air traffic control, 43
Alderman, Harry L., 15
Allen, Richard H., 34
Allies, 3, 28
    See also South Vietnam, Korea
Anderson AFB, Guam, 12, 82, 88
Anderson, Norman J., 73, 80
Arc Light, 82, 90, 93, 94
    See also Bombing operations
Arleth, George, 50
Artillery,
    See Khe Sanh
A Shau Valley, 21, 66, 67
Ashley, Eugene, 34

Bach Mai Airfield, 42
Baig, Mirza M., 93
Ban Houaysan, 26, 32, 34
Beach, Dwight E., 10, 11
Behnke, Roland F., 31
Berg, Kenneth G., 101
Bien Hoa, 28
Black Panther Company, 28
Bolsheviks, 30

127

Bombing operations, 13, 15, 25, 26, 28, 41, 74
    at Dien Bien Phu, 18
    at Khe Sanh, 62, 64, 73, 82, 89, 93, 99, 103, 105
    at Lang Vei, 33-34
    objectives outlined, 22
    sortie statistics, 88
    in Vietnam, 21-22
    See also Fighter operations; Khe Sanh
Bowditch, Thomas A., 25
Brault, Charles F., 31
Brett, Robert B., 38
Brewer, Zane G., 101, 102
Brown, S. R., 101
Buckley, William F., 40
Bugle Note, 82, 83
Bunker, Ellsworth, 11
Burnham, James, 40-41

Cahill, John H., 99, 100
Ca Lu, 97
Cambodia, 3
Cam Lo, 4
Camp Carroll, 4, 15, 20, 65, 82
Cam Ranh Bay, 42, 97
Can Tho, 29
Cargo extraction system, 51-53, 63
    See also Airlift; Cargo handling; Low-Altitude Parachute Extraction System; Parachute supply drops
Cargo handling, 42, 44-45, 54-56
    See also Speed offloading
Chapman, Leonard F., 9, 10
Chaternuck, Mary Lee, 16
Chu Lai, 57
Civilian Irregular Defense Group, 34
    Lang Vei, 4
    Rao Quan and Highway 9: 5
Close air support
    See Bombing operations, Fighter operations; Khe Sanh
Clubb, Oliver E. Jr., 40
Combat control team, 54, 55
Combat Skyspot, 66, 67, 82, 86
Communism
    suffers from Tet failure, 31
    theories in Tet Offensive, 30
    threat to South Vietnam, 3

Con Thien, 15, 38, 62, 82, 83, 84, 86
Corps
    I: 4, 13, 21, 28, 31, 42, 68, 74, 77, 78, 79, 97, 98, 103
    II: 79
Cua Viet River, 4, 99
Cushman, Robert E. Jr., 8, 13, 25, 28, 34, 68, 69, 72, 74, 77, 78, 79, 84, 86, 96, 97, 102

Dabney, William H., 23
Dallman, Howard M., 31, 32
Dalton, Windall K., 60
Da Nang, 21, 33
    Air Base, 23, 28, 32, 35, 36, 42, 54, 56, 60, 68, 69, 77, 78, 79, 97, 102
Davis, Donald M., 54, 55
Defense Communications Planning Group, 90
Defoliation operations, 42
Demilitarized zone, 28, 38, 62, 64, 106
Dien Bien Phu, 13, 18-22, 31, 38, 41, 42, 96, 103, 105
Direct air support center
    Da Nang 75, 79, 80
    Khe Sanh, 73
Divisions (NVN)
    2d: 28
    304th: 14, 99
    325C: 14, 99
    320th: 14
Division (SVN)
    1st: 28, 29
Divisions (US)
    1st Marine: 13, 28, 69, 96
    3d Marine: 13, 95
    1st Cavalry, 76, 88, 96, 97, 98, 101
    101st Airborne, 76
    Americal, 97
Dong Ha, 56, 57, 82, 91, 101
Drugan, Peter F., 50
Dutch Mill, 91, 92, 93, 95

Eggert, Lowell F., 62
Electronic sensors, 41
    barrier, 104
Elephants
    used in pack trains, 26
Ervin, Lawrence R., 50

Evacuation
    casualties, 56, 58
    refugees, 26, 27, 34

Fifth Air Force, 69
5th Special Forces Group, 32
Fighter-bombers
    See Fighter operations
Fighter operations
    counterinsurgency, 60
    direction of air strikes, 33, 43, 50, 66, 79, 80, 81
    enemy, 64
    escort for transports, 43, 46, 60, 63
    in ground support, 23, 25, 33, 34, 60-67, 68
    napalm, 23, 26, 33, 34, 65
    naval, 11, 12, 25, 34, 56-57, 60-62, 80-81, 105
    sorties flown, 105
    USMC, 20, 25, 56-57, 60, 105
        Aircraft types;
        Khe Sanh;
    See also U.S. Air Force; U.S. Marine Corps; U.S. Navy
Force Logistics Command, 97
Forward air control, 33, 34, 46, 62, 64, 66, 67, 80
    for naval aircraft, 79
    procedures, 65
    in sensor drops, 92
France
    Troops in Vietnam 8, 13
    defeat at Dien Bien Phu, 18-22, 42
    compared with U.S. attempts in Khe Sanh, 103-106

Geneva Agreement (1954), 22
Giap, Vo Nguyen, 13, 18-22, 40, 41
Ginsburgh, Robert N., 16, 17, 29
Gio Linh, 38
Great Britain, 31
Green Berets, 5, 32, 33
    See also U.S. Army
Green, Wade H., 31
Ground Proximity Extraction System, 20, 52, 53, 58
    See also Cargo extraction system; Cargo handling; Low-Altitude Parachute Extraction System; Parachute supply drops

Haiphong, 61
Hanoi
    defense of, 61
    government in, 13, 21, 30, 31
    under French, 18, 42
Harrington, Gerald L., 33
Hartenbower, Milton, 65, 66
Heath, Francis, Jr., 15
Helicopters, 34, 35, 46, 80
    attacks on, 25, 57, 59, 62
    command, 28
    evacuation by, 34, 56, 57, 58
    gunships, 56, 57
    in sensor drops, 92
    supply movement by, 25, 62, 101
    troop movement by, 23, 25, 32-33, 58-58, 98, 100
Helicopter types
    CH-46: 57
    UH-1: 57
    CH-3: 92
Hennelly, John A., 15, 73
Highway 1: 4, 99
Highway 9: 4, 5, 21, 25, 31, 32, 34, 59, 66, 93, 96, 97, 99
Hill 558: 5, 56
Hill 861: 5, 8, 23, 56
Hill 861A: 5, 31, 93
Hill 881N: 5, 8, 23, 84
Hill 881S: 5, 8, 23, 26, 31, 56, 57, 62, 84, 93
Hill 950: 5, 26, 57
Hill 1015: 5
Ho Chi Minh, 22
Ho Chi Minh Trail, 90
Hoffman, Carl W., 102
Hogan, Joe, 101
Hoi An, 28
Howder, John, 50
Hudson, Jerry E., 95
Hue, 21, 28-29, 30, 31, 54, 103, 104
Hyland, John J., 10, 11, 12

Intelligence, 4, 5, 13, 14, 15, 16, 17, 21, 31, 41, 63, 78, 86, 88, 90-95, 96, 104
    capture of *Pueblo*, 39, 83, 105
    See also Reconnaissance

Japan,
    aircraft operating from, 12
Jenks, Edwin, 35-36

Johnson, Gerald O., 32
Johnson, Harold K., 9, 10
Johnson, Joel, 34
Johnson, Lyndon B., 3n, 9, 16, 17, 22, 31, 103-106
Joint Chiefs of Staff, 9, 10, 16, 17, 83, 103
    See also Wheeler

Kadena Air Base, Okinawa, 12, 83
Kargis, G. A., 101
Keskinen, Richard, 65
Kham Duc, 80
Khe Sanh
    aerial supply for, 8, 17, 20, 31, 42-59, 62, 63, 105
    airfield, 7, 8, 9, 21, 25, 26, 36, 38, 43, 44, 45
    American advisers at, 102
    artillery support for, 15, 38, 31, 32, 92-96, 103, 105
    assessment of, 88, 103-106
    B-52 support for, 82, 83, 84, 86, 88, 91, 92, 103
    casualties, 31, 35, 36, 38, 46, 51, 56, 58, 59, 90, 99, 100, 103
    combat base, 4, 5, 9, 21, 31, 65, 92, 93, 95, 100
    combat operations center, 13, 23
    compared with Dien Bien Phu, 18-22, 31, 38-41, 42, 88, 103-106
    control tower, 54, 73, 81, 84, 98
    coordination of air power at, 68-81, 82-84, 86
    dismantling of structures at, 102
    direct air support center, 73, 78
    enemy antiaircraft at 20, 35-36, 42-43, 57, 62-64, 93, 94
    enemy buildup near, 7, 8, 13, 14, 16, 21, 28, 94
    enemy casualties at, 25, 35, 90
    enemy objectives at, 16, 21, 31, 96, 105
    enemy positions near, 9, 25, 38, 62, 88, 89, 93, 94, 95, 98, 99, 105
    enemy prisoners taken at, 14, 89
    enemy weapons at, 5, 14, 20, 25, 26, 28, 33, 56, 58, 62-64, 94, 96, 100, 105
    emplacements, 8-9, 23, 31, 38, 56, 103
    French at, 8, 105
    infiltration, 5, 13, 26, 34, 39, 40, 62, 104
    North Vietnamese command at, 13
    Press reaction to, 38-41
    reinforcement of, 8, 15, 17, 23, 24, 31, 34, 42, 45, 46
    relief of, 96, 97, 99, 100
    rocket attacks on, 23, 31, 32, 35-36, 38, 43, 45, 46, 50, 56, 98, 99, 102
    salvage at, 100, 101
    sensors near, 90-95
    siege broken, 100-102
    a symbol, 21, 104
    terrain model of, 17
    threat recedes at, 41, 98
    USMC offensive at, 96-102, 104
    U.S. troops arrive at, 5, 15
    U.S. weapons at, 15-16, 20-22, 26, 31, 32, 33
    village, 26
    water supply for 105
    weather restrictions at, 9, 20, 36, 38, 43, 46, 47, 50, 57, 60, 63, 98, 105
    White House interest in, 16-17, 103-106
    See also
    Aircraft; Airlift; Bombing operations; Fighter operations; Intelligence; Parachute supply drops; Tet offensive
Komer, Robert W., 11
Korean War
    air operations in, 69
Krulak, Victor H., 99

Landing Zone Stud, 98
Lang Vei, 4, 5, 8, 38, 32, 33, 34-35, 65, 66, 88, 100
Lanigan, John P., 8, 14
Laos, 3, 4, 5, 66
    Army troops, 34
    binder, 26, 32, 80
    reconnaissance into, 104
    supply dumps in, 21
    targets in, 62, 82
    truck traffic through, 90, 91
Life, 39
Low Altitude Parachute Extraction System, 8, 36, 45, 51, 52, 53, 58

See also Airlift: Parachute supply drops
Lownds, David E., 13, 15, 25, 26, 32, 34, 54, 56, 65, 91, 98, 99
Luang, Prabang, 18

McBride, William P., 9
McCafferty, Art, 16
McConnell, John P., 9, 10
McCutcheon, B., 69, 81
McElroy, J. W., 99
McLaughlin, Burl W., 12, 25, 42, 46, 51, 52, 53
McNamara, Robert S., 9
Mahaffy, Robert, 36
Malaya pacification, 31
Marble Mountain, 28
Marshall, S. L. A., 41
Martin, Clifford, 60
Masters, John F., Jr., 56
Mitchell, John F., 25, 34
Momyer, William W., 11, 12, 13, 36, 45, 62, 68, 69, 72, 74, 77, 78, 80, 86
Montagnards, 32
Moorer, Thomas H., 9, 10
Myrtle Beach, S.C., 60

Nakhom Phanom, Thailand, 60, 91, 93, 95, 104
Napalm strikes, 23, 26, 33, 34, 65
  See also Fighter operations
National Review, 40
Naval Mobile Construction Battalion 5: 98
Naval Support Activity, 97
New Republic, 40
New York Times, 41
Nha Trang Airfield, 20, 42
Nitze, Paul, 80
North Korea, 83
North Vietnam
  air strikes against, 3n, 10, 11, 12, 22, 61, 62, 82, 96, 106
  artillery, 14, 24-25, 28, 93, 102
  attacks on Khe Sanh, 23, 24-25, 26, 31, 32, 35, 38, 43, 45, 46, 50, 56, 98, 99, 102
  casualties, 25, 26, 29, 35, 89, 104
  command at Khe Sanh, 13
  defection from, 14, 23
  fighter opposition, 64
  impressment of refugees by, 66
  infiltration routes through 90, 91
  military buildup at Khe Sanh, 3, 4, 5, 13, 14, 23, 28, 104
  positions at Khe Sanh, 9, 25, 38, 62, 88, 89, 93, 94, 95, 98, 99, 105
  prisoners, 23, 89, 103
  supply dumps in Laos, 21, 26, 32
  Tet offensive by, 28-31, 104, 105
  See also Khe Sanh, Viet Cong, Viet Minh

Okinawa, 53
  aircraft operating from, 12
Operation Neutralize, 15, 62, 82
Operation Niagara, 15, 73, 74, 80, 82, 90, 103, 105
Operation Pegasus, 96, 97, 98, 99, 100
Orris, William S., 62

Pacific Air Force, 10
Pacification campaign, 11
Pacific Command, 9, 76
Pacific Fleet, 10
Padley, John J., 8, 15
Parachute supply drops, 19, 20, 36, 38, 45, 46-51, 54, 63
  accuracy of, 50, 51
  French, 42
  ground-radar aerial delivery system, 47, 98
  retrieving, 50, 54-55
  using container delivery method, 47
  volume in, 58
  See also Airlift: Low Altitude Parachute Extraction System
Pattee, John, 60
Pegasus
  See Operation Pegasus
Perfume River, 29
Peters, Charles R., 60
Philippine Island
  aircraft operating from, 12
Phu Bai, 54
Pham Van Hong, 88
Pipes, Kenneth, 98, 99
Pleiku, 18

131

Pope Air Force Base, N.C., 47
Press reacting to U.S. policy, 38-41
Prophett, Abner, 60
Provisional Corps, Vietnam, 77

Quang Nam, 4
Quang Ngai, 4
Quang Tin, 4
Quang Tri
    City, 8, 57, 104
    Province, 4, 9, 15, 31, 68, 77, 82, 86, 88, 96, 99, 100, 102
    River, 4, 5
Qui Nhan, 97

Radar, 30, 43, 47, 51, 72, 84, 98
    bomb scoring, 67
    Combined Skyspot (USQ-77), 66, 67, 82, 86
    TPQ-10: 43, 50, 66
Radio, 50, 54, 88
    relay station, 13
Rao Quan River, 5, 26, 38
Reconnaissance activities
    aerial, 15, 60, 66, 78, 79, 82, 86, 88, 90, 93, 94, 95, 98, 99
    ground, 23, 28, 38, 41, 88, 94, 104
Refugees, 26, 27, 34, 66
Regiments (ARVN)
    3d: 28
Regiments (US)
    1st Marines, 96-97
    3d Marines, 8, 14
    9th Marines, 25, 26, 34, 50, 51, 99
    13th Marines, 15, 73
    26th Marines, 8, 15, 23, 33, 90, 94, 95, 98, 99, 103
    7th Cavalry, 100
Roberts, Gene, 41
Robinson, Joe C., 60
Rock Pile, 4, 15, 20, 65
Rosson, William B., 77, 78, 80, 96, 97
Rostow, Walt W., 16, 17, 29
Rushforth, Charles, 66
Ryan, John D., 10, 12, 13

Saigon, 10, 28, 30, 78
Schlesinger, Arthur, Jr., 39-41
Seabees
    See U.S. Navy

Secretary of Defense, 9, 79
Seno, 18
Sensors, 90-95
Seventh Air Force, 11, 12, 13, 62, 72, 74, 77, 78, 80, 90, 105
    See also U.S. Air Force
Shaplen, Robert, 30
Sharp, U.S. Grant, 9, 10, 12, 61, 69, 76, 78, 79, 83, 86, 104
Single Manager for air, 68-81
Sink, J. P., 101
Smith, William R., 36, 52
Southeast Asia, 12, 22, 83, 86, 104, 105
South Korea
    troops in Vietnam, 77
South Vietnam, 40, 42
    air to, 3, 10, 31, 106
    air operations in, 11, 22, 26, 60-62, 74, 78, 80, 82, 86
    armed forces of, 3, 10, 12, 26, 28-29, 32, 38, 78, 97, 100, 102
    casualties of, 104
    economy of, 3
    enemy casualties in, 100
    firepower against enemy forces, 22
    infiltration routes in, 5, 18, 21, 90
    morale in, 3, 31, 104
    pacification program in, 11
    task force at Khe Sanh, 97, 99, 103-104
    Tet offensive in, 28-31
Speed offloading, 44, 45, 46
    See also cargo handling
Spivey, Ronald C., 50
Squadrons (numbered)
    164th Marine Medium Helicopter, 25
    779th Tactical Airlift, 50
    355th Tactical Fighter, 60
Starbird, Alfred D., 90
Strategic Air Command, 13, 67, 86
Super Gaggle, 56, 57, 59
Surface-to-air missiles, 64

Tachikawa, Japan, 42
Tactical Air Navigation (TACAN), 50
Taiwan
    aircraft operating from, 12
Tan Son Nhut Air Base, 11, 28, 42, 68, 74, 78, 79, 80, 86, 88, 90, 101
Task Force Alpha, 91, 94, 95

Task Force Oregon, 97
Task Force 77: 11, 12, 61, 62
    See also U.S. Navy
Taylor, Maxwell D., 17
Tet Offensive, 28-31, 39, 42, 65, 96, 104, 106
    casualties in, 103
    compared with World War II and Korea, 30
    linked with Pueblo, 105
    use of enemy tanks in, 33
Texas, 67
Thailand, 60
    USAF aircraft in, 11, 12
III Marine Amphibious Force, 8, 13, 32, 69, 74, 77, 78, 79, 80, 81, 84, 96
    See also U.S. Marines
3d Shore Party Battalion, 55
Thompson, Sir Robert, 31
Thua Thien, 4, 31, 68, 77, 96
Tolson, John, 96, 97, 98, 99, 100
Tompkins, Rathvon M., 13, 34, 91, 92
Tuy Hoa, 18, 42

United States
    policy in Asia, 39-41, 104-106
    reaction to Tet offensive, 104
U.S. Air Force, 40
    air strikes on North Vietnam, 11
    cargo handling, 54-56
    centralized control of combat aviation, 68-81
    command at Khe Sanh, 10, 11, 12, 36, 52, 68-81
    evacuation by, 31, 56, 58
    fighter strikes, 25, 33, 34, 60-67, 68
    gunship operations, 96
    operations from Guam, 12, 83, 88
    operations from Okinawa, 12, 53
    operations from Philippines, 12
    operations from Taiwan, 12
    operations from Thailand, 11, 12, 83, 86
    sensor operations, 91-95
    sorties flown, 89, 103, 105
    supplies to Khe Sanh, 12, 42-59
    See also Aircraft; Aircraft types; Air Divisions; Bombing operations; Momyer; Parachute supply drops; Reconnaissance Seventh Air Force
U.S. Army, 52
    buildup in I Corps, 13, 79
    Command at Khe Sanh, 9, 10, 96-100
    engineers, 7, 8
    Green Berets, 5, 7, 8, 32, 33, 34
    Helicopters, 98
    logistic specialists, 53
    relief at Khe Sanh, 96-102
    Troops in Tet offensive, 28, 29
    weapons at Khe Sanh, 15-16, 26
    26th General Support Group, 97
    37th Signal Battalion, 92
    34th Supply & Service Battalion, 97
    80th General Support Group, 97
U.S. Army Forces, Pacific, 10
U.S. Army Support Command, 97
U.S. Department of State
    diplomatic mission in Saigon, 10-11, 17
    role in war, 11
U.S. Marine Corps
    air-ground coordination, 33, 34, 46, 60, 62, 64, 66, 67, 68-81, 82-84, 86-89, 92-93
    assist at Hue, 29
    buildup at Khe Sanh, 5, 7, 8, 14
    cargo handling, 54-56, 60
    casualty statistics, 100
    cited for service at Khe Sanh, 103
    command at Khe Sanh, 7, 9, 10, 13, 15, 25, 26, 32, 34, 54, 56, 65, 91, 98, 99
    emplacements at Khe Sanh, 7-9, 23-24, 31, 32, 38, 56, 89, 103
    engineers, 98
    intelligence near Khe Sanh, 90-95
    logistics, 20, 25, 31, 35, 42-59, 60
    offensive at Khe Sanh, 96-102
    relieved at Khe Sanh, 96-102
    repel Khe Sanh attacks, 14, 31, 32, 38
    weapons at Khe Sanh, 15, 26, 31, 96, 105
    write enemy at Lang Vei, 32-35
    See also Bombing operations; Divisions; Fighter operations, Helicopters, Khe Sanh, Regiments, Wings

U.S. Military Assistance Command, Vietnam (COMUSMACV), 3, 4, 9, 11, 29, 81, 90
   Systems Analysis Office, 103
U.S. Navy
   aircraft carrier operations, 11, 20, 25, 34, 35, 56-57, 60-64, 80, 81, 94
   command, 9, 10, 12, 61, 69, 78, 80, 81, 83, 86, 104
   engineers (Seabees), 7, 8, 51, 54, 98
USS *Coral Sea*, 35
USS Pueblo, 39, 60, 83, 105
U Tapao Air Base, Thailand, 12, 83, 86

Viet Cong, 3, 10, 28, 29, 30, 31, 66, 103, 104

Viet Minh, 13, 18-22
Vietnamization, 3

Walker, William L., 91
Walt, Lewis H., 8, 41
Washington Post, 39
Wells, Selmon W., 12, 83, 84
Westmoreland, William C., 3, 9, 10, 11, 12, 13, 14, 17, 21, 22, 31, 32, 62, 68, 69, 71, 74, 77, 80, 81, 86, 88, 90, 96, 102, 103-105
Wheeler, Earle G., 9, 12, 17, 103
Wilkinson, James B., 15, 90, 94
Willoughby, Frank C., 32, 33, 34
Wings
   1st Marine Aircraft, 13, 62, 68, 73, 74, 78, 80, 105

Xe Pone River, 32

www.ingramcontent.com/pod-product-compliance
Lightning Source LLC
Chambersburg PA
CBHW080512110426
42742CB00017B/3090